ABOUT THE AUTHOR

Bob Jackson, born in Carlisle in 1941 and the eldest of three brothers, spent his life at sea in the Merchant Navy, trading round the world's major, and minor, ports. He is now retired at lives in Carlisle with his wife and their dogs.

Cover design by www.cannymarshall.com

Worse Things Happen

Bob Jackson

CHAPTERS

PREFACE

This volume covers the second half of my life at sea serving as master on a variety of ships with several companies. The first volume entitled *"I think I'll go to sea"* details my service working up through the ranks.

The original intention of these memoirs was to provide my children with some sort of record of my life and experiences at sea as when my father died I suddenly realised how little I knew about his life especially in his younger days. Once I'd started writing I could see that this is a way of life that no longer exists so I had the first book published and to my amazement was it really well received.

Writing this, I have referred to my journals, and as I read through them I came to realise that I only noted down the day-to-day problems, and sometimes their solutions, and the disasters I encountered. I never tended to write down that, "It was a good day," and the only reference I can find in the twenty volumes, which noted things were good, was when I wrote, "Brilliant day," after a lovely day wandering round Venice with my wife, Diane, and on that occasion I wasn't even on board the ship.

I apologise in advance for the repetitiveness and the boring bits but that was life at sea: weeks of boredom interspersed with days of mad hectic activity then back to the boredom. In retrospect, there seems to have been far too much consumption of cold cans of beer and other alcoholic beverages. Nowadays it does appear a bit excessive but it was more acceptable then and, after all, it was my reward at the end of a day for a job well done.

Now, completely retired and living in Carlisle, I look back and obviously wish I'd done some things differently but all in all I enjoyed my career at sea though I wouldn't want to be starting again now.

CHAPTER ONE

The Start

When I was growing up as a kid in Carlisle I'd often heard the phrase, "Worse things happen at sea," when people were discussing a disaster of some sort. I never thought about it much but with over 40 years at sea under my belt I've a feeling they knew what they were talking about.

My career at sea began when I enrolled on the Pre-Sea Cadet Course at South Shields Marine and Technical College when I was 16 in 1957. I must admit to having no aspirations of eventually being a shipmaster and all I wanted to do was go to sea, see the world, drink a lot of beer and meet some nice girls, though not necessarily in that order. I supposed I'd take things from there. There were 28 of us on the course and I think when we started most had the same idea as me.

About halfway through I remember our tutor, Captain Proudlock, trying to drum into us the concept of the celestial sphere and the intricacies of spherical trigonometry, without much success. In exasperation he said, "I am now looking at 28 potential captains of our illustrious Merchant Navy and you can't even work out where you are. God help us." I glanced round at my classmates and saw a determination in most of their faces and felt that one day most of us would get our Master's Foreign Going Certificates and command a vessel. It turned out I was right.

I also remember us trying to tap up some sixth form girls from the school along the road from our digs and when they asked what we did we said we were training to be ship's captains but it didn't get us anywhere – I don't think they were too impressed.

Anyhow, exactly 20 years since I started the course I had worked

1

my way up through the ranks of 3rd, 2nd and 1st mate and gained all my certificates and qualifications without too much hassle and I was now about to take command of my first ship.

It felt like a bit of an anti-climax really. I was confident I could do the job, as in my progression through the ranks I had sailed with some real no-hopers as master and figured that if they could muddle through so could I. I had also been privileged to sail with some brilliant skippers and seen how things should be done properly.

My first years at sea were spent as an apprentice with Port Line running to Australasia and back carrying general and refrigerated cargo. I have to say that these were the best days of my life, serving in a top company in well-maintained ships with quality crews.

After I completed my apprenticeship I obtained my 2nd mate's certificate without too much difficulty and decided that I'd like to see the rest of the world rather than trade back and forth to Australia and New Zealand. I don't know whether this was a good decision or not as wages and conditions were really good in Port Line but promotion was really slow and in the end the company ceased to exist in the 1970s when containerships took over the trade. Anyhow…

There were two main ways of getting a job. The first was to apply in writing direct to the company of choice but this was slow, as often they would take ages to reply. The other was to sign on with the Merchant Navy Establishment, which was a government agency organised to crew ships. My nearest Establishment was on the quayside in Newcastle upon Tyne so I had to travel over by train from Carlisle to see what they had to offer. They had notice boards up with the ships' names and what ranks they were requiring and where the ship was trading and how long it expected to be away. It was quite exciting going in and checking the boards and deciding where in the world I would go this time. The downside was that the ships were nearly always downmarket and the wages pretty basic.

So I progressed up through the ranks serving on a variety of ships varying from 1,150 tons to 106,000 tons and gaining lots of experience in different cargoes and also learning to cope with all the problems sea life could throw up.

I eventually ended up in Kuwait Shipping Company in 1975 serving as 1st mate. It was, as the name suggests, an Arab owned company but they manned their vessels with mainly British officers and Indian, Pakistani or Sierra Leonean crews. They were a new outfit and determined to be considered a top company so they advertised above average conditions and pay. Promotion prospects were brilliant, as they seemed to buy a new ship every month. After two years with them I could see things were starting to happen and I finally got the call to say they would like me to command one of their vessels.

I had to travel down by train from my home in Cumbria to the UK office in Liverpool for a day to be introduced to the various managers and superintendents. I was given a very brief pep talk by the fleet manager about how the company expected its masters to behave then I was given an overview of how the accounts worked and given samples of all the forms I was expected to fill in. The fleet manager also took me for a very pleasant lunch. I quite enjoyed the day and was surprised by how many people I'd met previously or been in contact with. It was good to put faces to names. I was impressed by how well the office seemed to run so was quite looking forward to doing my bit at the sharp end. At four o'clock they decided I'd been overloaded with information and let me go clutching a huge folder of specimen forms.

As I was down in Liverpool I decided to visit Goldbergs, the naval outfitters, as I would need new braid for my uniform jacket and also a couple of sets of new epaulettes. I was surprised by how expensive they were but the salesman explained that because of the extra stripe there was a lot more gold braid. He also tried to sell me a new captain's cap, which had gold braid along the peak. I tried a couple on and had to admit that I thought I looked rather dashing with all the gold shining on the peak. When the salesman told me it was nearly £90 I decided I looked dashing enough and would make do with my old cap, which I hardly ever wore anyway. I ended up buying a couple more white shirts, though, so I felt I'd spent quite enough money. I then wandered up to Lime Street Station and caught the train north to Carlisle.

I had a further two weeks at home waiting to be assigned a ship. I spent a few evenings going through the company forms and began to realise there was a lot more to commanding a ship than I thought. I dug out some textbooks on shipmaster's business and put them beside my case ready to pack.

CHAPTER TWO

Captain at last – my first command

m.v. Al Gurainiah
11th August 1977 – 25th November 1977

Eventually I got instructions to join the *Al Gurainiah* in Valencia. She had loaded round the continent for the Arabian Gulf and had nearly completed her load. I flew out from Heathrow on the afternoon of the 10th August arriving late evening but the ship was stuck out at anchor awaiting a berth so I was put up in a hotel for a night. I joined early the following morning just after she had tied up. I was relieving Colin Jones, who I'd met before when doing a job as supercargo. He was really pleased to see me. He had been expecting to take the ship out to the Gulf and was over the moon to get off two weeks early.

The handover went very smoothly with the biggest task being counting the money on board which was into the thousands of pounds and dollars and agreeing the accounts. Colin had made copious notes on everything even detailing the messages I had to send once we'd sailed. The agent had organised Colin's flight home for early afternoon so he left just after ten o'clock and I found myself in command of a ship for the first time. I had quite an advantage in that I'd sailed as 1st mate on two sister ships to the *Al Gurainiah* so I knew backwards how they worked and I'd also had the opportunity to manoeuvre them in and out of port. There was no time to relax, though, as there was a constant stream of crew and shore personnel knocking at the door all needing answers to questions, which I had to answer as there was nobody else to ask. This seemed to go on all day

4

until they stopped loading for the day at eight o'clock in the evening. It then went quiet so I was able to close the cabin door and relax with the obligatory cold beer. I read through Colin's notes again and although there were quite a few problems on board nothing seemed insurmountable so I turned in for an early night and had a surprisingly good night's sleep.

The loading went pretty smoothly and we were ready to sail two days later. Just as we were about to sail, the accommodation alleyways began to fill with thick black smoke and the fire alarms went off. There was an initial panic with everyone running round like headless chickens trying to locate the source. It turned out to be a large pan of chips on fire in the galley. Luckily we managed to put it out quite quickly. There wasn't much damage apart from over-cooked chips.

We sailed for Genoa mid afternoon and I was a bit concerned as it was blowing a full gale from the south. We managed to turn round inside the harbour without any problems and the pilot asked me if he could get off inside the breakwaters as it was really rough outside. I turned to ask the captain and suddenly realised that it was me! I let the pilot off and then had to con the ship out through the entrance, which I thought I managed pretty well. We set course for Genoa and I nipped down to my cabin to organise all the radio messages. It was really important that all the messages were sent and with the correct information as the ship would be delayed at considerable expense if anything was wrong or omitted. I went through all the information I'd got from the office and the notes left by Colin and eventually got them all sent off.

The gale eased off as we crossed the Northern Mediterranean and it was very pleasant by the time we arrived in Genoa early on Monday morning. It turned out it was a national holiday so we had an unexpected break and I was taken ashore by the agent for a very nice lunch, which lasted until three o'clock. I opted to walk back to the ship afterwards and wandered back through a marina with some pretty luxurious yachts tied up alongside. I found a little café and sat for a while with a beer and enjoyed watching all the comings and goings.

It took two days to load the cargo of marble slabs and ceramics and then we were on our way to the Suez Canal and the Arabian Gulf. We had quite a few discharge ports and three of them –

Muttrah (Oman), Basrah (Iraq) and Khorramshar (Iran) – I'd never been to before so needed to do a bit of research before we got there. We transited the Suez Canal without any problems and I managed to send off all the radio messages without too much hassle. I was starting to settle in the job. When I had been 1st mate I always thought the captain, or Old Man as he was known, had very little to do and just swanned about earning all sorts of money. I couldn't believe how many people came knocking at my door with questions and it was me that had to come up with the right answers or advice. The seven days through the Red Sea and Gulf of Aden flew past and we berthed in Muttrah at the end of August.

We had quite a few problems with the cargo discharge as a lot of containers and cases for Kuwait had been loaded on top of the Muttrah cargo and had to be unloaded first. The Harbour Authority insisted I signed a letter saying the Kuwait Shipping Company were responsible for all the extra costs which were into the thousands of pounds but I had to sign it otherwise they wouldn't unload the cargo. I started to feel I was earning my pay. Everything went smoothly in the end and we sailed two days later all the way up to Kuwait at the top of the Arabian Gulf where we anchored off the port and discharged containers onto a barge. This only took a couple of hours and then we sailed two hours down the coast to the oil port of Mina Al Ahmadi.

We had a great deal of equipment for the oil refinery and the discharge went very slowly as we had to be careful it wasn't damaged. It was mostly made from polished steel and looked really futuristic with pipes and valves sticking out in all directions. We managed to discharge it in good condition though later while cleaning the holds when the ship was empty we found three large pieces of pipe and several valves so I bet they'd had an interesting time putting it all together after we left. We could easily have just dropped them over the side and no one would be any the wiser but being somewhat naïve I sent a radio message with all the details to the company. It stirred up a whole hornets nest as it was too late to land them in the Gulf and the company ended up flying them at their expense from Antwerp when we got back there.

Our next port for discharge was Dammam in Saudi Arabia but there was a huge backlog of ships waiting to discharge there so we were sent to anchor off Shuwayk Port in Kuwait to wait until our turn came up. I was hoping for a few quiet days at anchor but it was not to be. Colin had warned me when I joined that there were some troublemakers among the engine room crew and there had been the odd grumble since I joined. The crew had been on board for ten months and wanted to be relieved so were coming up with all sorts of reasons why they should be paid off. As soon as we anchored off Kuwait they demanded to see the Pakistani Consul to air their grievances. They refused to even discuss their problems with me so I had contact head office and explain the situation.

The next day a large delegation consisting of consular officials, company superintendents, union representatives and the company crew manager boarded us by launch. They all repaired to my cabin and started to consume my beer. We had lunch for an hour and then returned to my cabin for more beer. Eventually they went down to interview the crew and came back half an hour later saying it was a storm in a teacup and everything was sorted. They then left with me feeling rather inadequate that I couldn't have sorted it myself. An hour after they'd left the chief engineer came and told me that all the engine crew were now on strike and refusing to do any work at all. I had to go down and tell them that they wouldn't be paid if they didn't work but they still refused. Next morning I contacted the company and let them know the situation and was told to stop paying the strikers until they resumed work and they would soon settle down. This went on for three days with the engineers having to do all the extra work involved. It was also causing a fair bit of unrest amongst the other crew. I decided enough was enough so called the company and told them I was sacking all those involved and required immediate replacements. I expected to have problems with this decision but all I got was a short message saying replacements were being organised and to repatriate the sacked crew as soon as possible. I managed to get them off the ship the next morning and their reliefs arrived the following day.

Everything settled down after that and the next day we sailed down to Dammam to discharge. When we got there the whole approach to the port was clogged with anchored ships waiting to unload. I managed to find a space quite close to the port entrance and we anchored to wait our turn. Talking on the radio to other ships in the anchorage it looked like we could be there for a month, which wasn't good as the Saudi customs boarded straight away and locked up all the booze. At least it was giving my liver a chance to recuperate.

Much to our surprise after two days at anchor a tug arrived alongside with a barge and a gang of stevedores and we started to discharge out at anchor. It only took them three days to unload the Dammam cargo, which was mainly constructional steelwork and tiles from Italy. We sailed back up to Kuwait where we had to anchor again for another two days before going into Shuwayk port. Most of our cargo was for Kuwait so we spent a week there and the discharge went pretty smoothly.

Having got the crew sorted out I was now starting to have problems with the officers. I had to have words with quite a few of them about excessive drinking and made myself pretty unpopular when I threatened to close the bar and stop them drinking altogether but it worked and they seemed to steady up. I was also having serious problems with the 1st mate, John, who was bone idle. There were problems with the cargo stowage, too, which could have been averted with a modicum of supervision by him. I was tearing a strip off him one morning when one of the superintendents walked in. The next day there was a message from head office saying a relief mate was joining in the next port and word got round that I had sacked him, which I hadn't, but people started to take a lot more notice when I gave instructions.

We sailed from Shuwayk on the 25th September for Basrah in Iraq. I wasn't looking forward to this at all as I'd heard plenty of horror stories about the passage up the Shatt al Arab River. Basrah was about 60 miles inland but was still affected by tides, which could cause problems if we had to anchor anywhere. The river was only just wider than the length of the ship so it was very easy to damage the rudder or propeller when turning round. We had to anchor overnight a mile downriver from Basrah until our berth was available which meant we had to swing to the tide twice and I have to admit to being pretty nervous. It went off all right in the end though we were so close to the side that the Arab boys on shore were throwing bags of dates to the crew on board in exchange for cigarettes.

We berthed the following morning and it turned into a chaotic nightmare. The customs officers declared that some cargo we were carrying (octanol) was dangerous and refused to let us start

8

discharge. I understood it was a type of alcohol used in making perfumes but the officials refused to be convinced and it cost six bottles of whisky and several hundred cigarettes before it was resolved. The agent failed to appear with our papers so this cost some more cigarettes to the port officials before they would allow the stevedores on board. Miraculously the agent appeared as soon as the cigarettes had been dispensed. I also had to work with a very bolshie mate who was being very disruptive because he thought I had sacked him.

The chief engineer asked if we could get permission to immobilise the main engine for some essential repairs. This required several bottles of whisky and more cigarettes to obtain and then it was cancelled after an hour because we had to leave the berth and move to buoys in the middle of the river to finish discharge. I was rapidly losing the plot. Once on the buoys life quietened down a bit and we continued the discharge into barges. It took a week to unload as there were hardly ever any empty barges available but it looked even worse on the quayside with huge piles of cargo waiting to be moved. We received a message saying a new mate was waiting to join in the next port, which was Khorramshar. John, the present 1st mate, suddenly realised that I had to report on his performance when he left so he suddenly turned super efficient to impress me. At least it made my life a bit easier but he always seemed to be in my cabin either asking questions or telling me unimportant information. I was glad when we eventually sailed from Basrah down the river to Khorramshar, which was half way down the Shatt al Arab River but on the east bank in Iran.

Again it was chaotic here with all the jetties occupied and huge piles of construction materials everywhere. We had to anchor in the middle of the river and discharge into barges. At least the river was a bit wider here but we still seemed to get very close to the bank when we swung round on each change of tide. The agent boarded shortly after we anchored and told us that the new 1st mate was in the local hospital with food poisoning and wouldn't be able to join. John decided he couldn't keep up the super efficiency any longer and reverted to idle mode, which actually suited me.

It took two days to discharge the cargo for Iran. There wasn't all that much but we had major problems with two hydraulic cranes so could only work one hatch at a time which doubled the discharge time. At last on the 10th October we finally completed discharge and got our orders to proceed towards the Suez Canal where we would receive our next orders. It was a relief to get to sea and settle down to a routine. It was quite a pleasant passage with nice warm days and light winds. The weather was always an important factor at sea. Just three or four days of good weather would lift morale and I always enjoyed going up to the bridge first thing in the morning with a mug of tea and watching the sunrise. We arrived at Port Tewfik at the southern end of the Canal mid October. The new 1st mate joined and seemed pretty switched on – at least he couldn't be worse than the last one. We passed through the Canal the next day without incident and set off westwards towards Gibraltar.

The ship was in a pretty poor state with lots of problems in the engineroom with leaking oil coolers and unreliable generators. On deck was just as bad – two of our nine cranes were completely out of action and a third with major faults. As we sailed from Suez the radar blew up and was unrepairable and the autopilot, which had been giving problems for months, also gave up the ghost so we had to have seamen steering all the time. This meant fewer people available for maintenance so I was pleased when we received orders a day after leaving Suez to proceed to Tilbury to drydock. At least we should get everything sorted out there.

The passage through the Mediterranean was pretty pleasant but once we turned north after Gibraltar we seemed to have strong winds and heavy seas all the way back until we entered the Thames. The drydock was at the far end of the Royal Albert Dock ten miles up river from Tilbury. The last time I had been there was when I was an apprentice 20 years previously when every berth would be occupied with cranes swinging to and fro with all sorts of cargo hanging from their hooks. It was really depressing to see all the empty berths and the whole place in a sad state of disrepair. Now there were only two ships tied up in the entire dock, which could cater for at least 30, and both of these seemed to be lying idle. The containerisation of cargoes had been the downfall of these docks coupled with the unwillingness of the dockers to accept new working practices. The dock pilot and I reminisced about this as we progressed up the dock shepherded by a couple of tugs. Once we were in the drydock it seemed no lessons had been learnt because the shore labour promptly went on strike for better conditions. We lay there for a day waiting for the dispute to be resolved and then Kuwait Shipping decided they had had enough and we got orders to head to Antwerp where there was a drydock available. We left early afternoon on the 1st November and tied up in a shipyard in Antwerp early the next morning and started repairs straight away.

It was a really miserable time as the weather was terrible with snow and sleet and a cold easterly wind. The Pakistani crew decided to go sick en masse so in the end I sent for a doctor to come and check them all over. It turned out that two of them had infectious TB so they had to be hospitalised and everyone else had to go up to the hospital to be X-rayed. The 1st mate found a good job for the crew painting in the holds, which was dry and relatively warm, so they all returned to work. The ship was crawling with technicians sorting out all our problems and overhauling the deck machinery and cranes. It was quite difficult getting the ship hull painted, though, as it never seemed to stop raining. They ended up painting all night just before we sailed. It seemed a different ship to the one we'd brought in; all nicely painted and things actually worked when we switched them on.

We sailed out into a north westerly storm force ten and the pilot had to get off before we got to Flushing at the entrance to the River Schelte. I had to navigate out through hundreds of ships anchored waiting for the weather to improve. I thought about anchoring, too, but couldn't find anywhere safe so kept on going. We had a real battering on our way up the North Sea to Bremen. We had to stay in shipping lanes so were unable to alter course and ease the rolling. There was quite a bit of damage caused by some drums of hydraulic oil we had lashed on deck, breaking adrift and smashing round.

The Bremen pilots wouldn't come outside the port because of the heavy seas so I had to take the ship in myself and pick up a pilot inside the port. It went really well and I was pleased with myself but I'd been to Bremen quite a few times and knew the place well. At least it impressed the crew. It was nice to be safely tied up in port though. However, we were promptly boarded by the river police complaining we were leaking oil into the river. It was from the broken oil drums so we got the crew mopping up and spraying the area with chemicals and with the aid of a couple of bottles of whisky it was all sorted.

We started loading the next morning but it was pretty slow as it was pouring with rain and blowing really hard. It took them three days to load mainly steel girders and some machinery and then we shifted up the coast to Hamburg arriving there mid November.

We loaded for two days but it took another twelve hours lashing everything down before we dare sail. The weather forecast was atrocious so we made sure everything was doubly secure before we sailed. Again the pilot only took us halfway down the River Elbe and I had to navigate out past Helgoland. I was getting quite blasé about it by this time. Again we had a terrible passage down the North Sea but the wind eased and veered as we passed Dover so we had a reasonable trip down the Channel. Once we got to the Lizard we again encountered storm force ten winds from the north so we bounced our way up to Liverpool and berthed in the Langton Dock at one o'clock in the morning.

I didn't expect to see any shore officials until breakfast time so was surprised when I was invaded by agents, customs, a company superintendent, two police officers and a security guard bringing me £7,000 in cash. It appeared they had been told the ship would berth about eight o'clock so had adjourned to the pub to wait for us. They invaded my fridge for more beer whilst I counted the cash and signed the receipt for the money. The police were there as a crew member waiting to join the ship had been arrested for shoplifting so they had to hand him over to my custody. I duly signed for him and they departed after downing another couple of beers. I then dealt with the customs and the agents getting all the papers signed and they left about three in the morning leaving only Joe Ross, the marine superintendent. He was flying out to Kuwait that afternoon and wanted to see how I'd managed on my first voyage before he left. It seemed the company were pleased with my efforts so far and we ended up yarning and knocking back a few beers until four o'clock in the morning. I then managed to get to bed slightly the worse for wear. I was woken by my steward at seven and when I wandered through into my office I was shocked to find all the cash still lying on my desk. It had been there in full view of everyone with the door wide open. I quickly locked it in the safe and reflected that it wouldn't have been the best end to my first trip if it had been stolen.

After breakfast I opened all the mail and was delighted to find that I was to be relieved two days later by John Towill. I then had a mad panic to get all the paperwork sorted out and everything ready

12

for the handover. John joined two days later and it turned out he also came from Carlisle. It was his first trip with the company so I stayed on until late afternoon to explain how things worked. I then got a taxi up to Lime Street and caught the train to Penrith where Diane met me at the station.

It had only been three and a half months but I'd managed my first trip as master without any serious mishaps and, thinking back, I'd actually enjoyed the responsibility. When I'd heard I was being relieved before doing the usual five month trip I was a little concerned but it turned out that the company had an excess of captains so it worked out well. It also meant I was going to get Christmas at home with the family which was a real bonus.

CHAPTER THREE

Second trip – getting the hang of things

m.v. Ibn Khallikan
19th January 1978 – 15th May 1978

I had a really good leave if a busy one. Diane had moved into our new house in Newton Reigny beside Penrith while I was away on my first trip as skipper so there was an endless list of things to do to get the house as we wanted it. I seemed to put up a new shelf every day. There was a bit of land attached to the house and I had all sorts of grand ideas about growing vegetables and keeping livestock but I only had time to organise a dozen bantams into a henhouse before I got the inevitable phone call from Liverpool. I was to join the *Ibn Khallikan* in Immingham where she was loading for the Arabian Gulf.

Immingham was a real pain of a place to get to so I decided to catch a train to Hull then take a taxi over the Humber Bridge, which seemed by far the easiest way. I caught a train first thing cross-country to Hull. I'd naturally assumed the Humber Bridge would be open as they had started building it years before but as we arrived in Hull I glanced out of the window and was somewhat disconcerted to see that the Humber Bridge consisted of two towers with a wire stretching between them and was months if not years from completion. I did a quick rethink and caught the ferry over the river and then a tram to Immingham arriving a lot later than I had intended. Captain Tennant, who I was relieving, wasn't best pleased, as he'd been hoping to leave first thing. It was a very quick handover, which mainly involved counting the cash on board which was nearly £10,000, and he was gone.

Actually it was a very easy ship to take over. The *Ibn Khallikan* was only six months old and doing her second voyage. She was one of the new type of vessels called K Class and built in Korea by Kuwait Shipping to their own design and I was impressed with the cargo handling and versatility of the ship. The design was very utilitarian with no frills and was completely different from the streamlined Port Line ships I'd first gone to sea in. It was her last loading port and it was nearly all constructional steel and railway lines with a few hundred tons of general and chemicals on top. The officers were a mixed bunch but the ship looked well run. It had the makings of a good trip.

The loading went really slowly mainly due to continuous rain and sleet. It took ten days to get the 4,000 tons of steel on board and lashed and we sailed at the end of January and headed off towards the Suez Canal and hopefully some warmer and drier weather. It turned out to be a really miserable trip all the way to Suez and having all the weight of steel in the bottom of the holds caused us to roll pretty violently at times. Once we got through the Suez Canal, though, we were into the good weather and could enjoy life a bit more.

This ship was a complete contrast to my first command, the *Al Gurainiah*. Whereas the *Al Gurainiah* was getting on a bit, with things breaking down all the time, everything on here was brand new and any teething problems had been ironed out before I joined. The other difference was the personnel on board. On the whole, the officers on the *Al Gurainiah* had been a good bunch and easy to work with and it had been the Pakistani crew who gave me constant problems. Here the crew were Indian and a complete contrast to the Pakistanis. They were efficient, worked hard and always seemed polite and cheerful. The officers on the other hand were a real pain. I had a cracking 1st mate in the form of Pete Walley who with the 3rd and 4th engineers were the only people I seemed to have any rapport with.

The main problem was the variety of nationalities and this coupled with the fact that everyone seemed to hate each other had the makings of a personnel nightmare. The 2nd mate was an Indian who had a very high opinion of himself, which wasn't shared by anyone else. We also had an extra 2nd mate, who was Egyptian, and although he had just joined the company thought he was the senior because he was an Arab as it was an Arab owned company. We also had four Arab cadets: a Palestinian who hated everything British and had been one of Arafat's bodyguards, a Kuwaiti and two Saudi Arabians. Apart from disliking the other officers they loathed each other and refused to even speak to one another. On top of this the purser was a bone idle alcoholic who refused to get up in the morning and never completed any paperwork correctly. The picture was completed by the chief and 2nd engineers who, although they were competent engineers, disliked the deck department and seemed to go out of their way to cause problems.

I was looking forward to a nice peaceful passage in lovely weather after Suez but it was not to be. There was a constant stream of people knocking at my door complaining about everything from the food, inadequate air conditioning, drinking parties and some people's personal hygiene to anti-Islamic sentiments. I began to dread the sound of approaching feet and the knock on my office door. By the time we arrived in Juaymah in the Arabian Gulf I felt I was starting to get the hang of sorting things out though there always seemed something simmering waiting to explode.

We had 200 tons of drilling equipment for Aramco, which was one of the big American oil companies. They employed Filipino surveyors to check the cargo for any damage and they competed with each other to see who could find the most damage. Needless to say it developed into a huge argument as to whether the damage was caused by the ship or their stevedores discharging it. Our only satisfaction came when a complex piece of piping and valves fell over on the barge and was badly damaged. We were only in port for 16 hours but I was really glad to sail.

Our next port was Dammam in Saudi Arabia where we arrived early in the morning. The discharge went really well. The cargo operations were run by a bunch of Liverpool dockers and they certainly knew the job. They had nearly 1,000 tons of steel and chemicals discharged with the minimum of fuss and we sailed at four o'clock the following morning.

Our next port was Mina in Kuwait to discharge only about 50 tons of steel pipes and valves. Mina was just a pier sticking out into the sea for loading the oil tankers and not designed for unloading cargo but things went surprisingly smoothly and we managed to discharge in eight hours and then we shifted along the coast to berth in Shuwayk the main commercial port for Kuwait. The majority of our cargo was for here (approximately 5,000 tons) so we reckoned on a week to unload which left only about 600 tons for Dubai and the remaining 1,000 for Bandar Shapour in Iran.

I wasn't looking forward to the week in Shuwayk as the company had their head office there and we would be inundated by the Europeans from the office looking for free meals and beer (not necessarily in that order). On top of that we were changing the entire Indian crew so all their wages had to be worked out and there would be numerous arguments about overtime payments and the amounts of various bonuses. I was told the crew would be relieved in two days so I went down to see the purser only to find him still in bed at ten o'clock in the morning. I had a bit of a rant and left him to get up. When I went down a couple of hours later to sort out the crew paperwork he was legless and completely out of the game. While I was in the middle of my second rant of the morning the fleet manager came on board and witnessed the whole incident. He said he was very impressed by my rant and thought the purser would sort himself out, though I was doubtful. I confiscated the purser's keys to the bond and banned him from the bar but all this resulted in was him stumbling drunkenly into my cabin complaining that he was being victimised. When I'd ejected him I went and collected all the paperwork relating to the crew pay off as it was obvious he wasn't going to do it.

Things went from bad to worse as the paperwork was a disaster and as the crew had been on board for a year I had to go back and check every entry. Luckily Pete, the 1st mate, gave me a hand and we eventually had it sorted by one in the morning. When Pete went off to bed he stumbled over the purser who had passed out in the alleyway so he had found another source of alcohol somewhere.

The following morning the Indian crew packed their bags and got ready to leave but at eleven o'clock there was a message that the reliefs were stuck in Bombay and now wouldn't be joining until Dubai five days later. The crew merely shrugged their shoulders and unpacked their gear and resumed work but for me it meant that all the wages calculations had to be redone to account for the extra days so all our work had been for nothing. I was seriously thinking of joining the purser in his alcoholic haze.

I was sitting in my cabin consoling myself with a cold beer when the 3rd mate burst in to say his cabin had been broken into and demanding the police be called. This was duly done and four very smart Kuwaiti police officers arrived very promptly and inspected his cabin. They then went onto the quay and arrested four random Pakistani labourers and proudly pronounced the case solved. I felt very sorry for the labourers but it seemed that was how the system worked.

The rest of the time in Shuwayk was a nightmare with the purser stumbling round pissed as a rat. The 3rd mate was bitten on the arm by some sort of spider so we had to organise him up to hospital where they put his arm in a plaster cast, which even to me didn't seem the right thing. His arm swelled up and he was in agony so we had to cut the plaster off and send him back to the hospital but they returned him hours later with a supply of painkillers. Luckily the swelling subsided after a couple of days but I was quite worried. The next afternoon I had a visit from Jake Scallan who was skipper on the ship astern of us. I thought it was a social visit but he'd come to complain that our purser had taken up residence in their bar and was becoming a real nuisance. I sent a couple of our officers over to retrieve him but I gather he just moved to another ship. The only good thing was that the fleet manager had witnessed the purser's antics and had promised to get him relieved as soon as possible.

The day before we sailed I had a visit from the agency manager accompanied by a couple of Kuwaiti customs officials. It didn't bode well but it turned out not too bad. It appeared that the customs had a large collection of bottles of alcohol that they had confiscated from inbound passengers at the airport. They wanted to dispose of them at sea so our ship had been chosen. I wasn't too keen as it seemed obvious to me a scam was going on somewhere. They reluctantly admitted that it wasn't completely above board and they wouldn't actually be bringing the bottles and they just wanted my signature on a form to say I would receive the booze and dump it overboard outside Kuwaiti waters. Needless to say I didn't want any part of it but in the end a compromise was reached where I would receive 40 cases on board with no mention of the contents and dump them after we sailed. Next day a truck turned up with the 40 cases and we stored them in a spare cabin and sealed the door. We finished discharge in the evening and sailed for Dubai. I was really pleased to get away from Shuwayk and all the hassle.

As soon as we cleared the port I got Pete, the 1st mate, and some of the crew up and we dumped the cases over the side. It was obvious that the cases had anything but bottles in them but four of them were different so we opened them to find 30 odd bottles of the finest malt whisky and champagne. We decided it would be a dreadful waste to dump them and agreed to keep them as a reward for our efforts. The trouble was that I don't like whisky and when I left the ship two months later I'd only managed to consume two bottles of the champagne and I found that most disappointing.

On the passage to Dubai the purser sobered up and actually performed his duties pretty well but I'd had enough and insisted he was relieved before we left the Gulf.

We arrived in Dubai early in the morning and for once everything went smoothly. We changed the Indian crew without any problems, got the 3rd mate to hospital again and he came back with new medication and swelling of his arm reduced considerably. I was even able to get ashore for a meal with Fred Roberts, the cargo superintendent. We sailed after two days all the way back up the Gulf to Bandar Shapour in Iran to discharge the last 800 tons of cargo. On the way there we got our orders for the next voyage, which was to pick up empty containers in Dammam and Dubai for the Far East and load a cargo back to the Arabian Gulf. This would be my first trip in command out to the Far East and I was quite looking forward to the experience.

Discharge went slowly in Bandar Shapour mainly because they were short of transport to take the cargo away. The whole port seemed very disorganised which surprised me as the Iranians always came across as pretty efficient. It took a week to complete the discharge and we sailed mid March down to Dammam. It was a mad panic on board to clean the holds to enable the empty containers to be loaded but somehow it was done and we berthed early in the morning on the following day.

Again loading here under the supervision of the Liverpool dockers was really quick. I was beginning to worry that I'd be stuck with the purser all the way to the Far East and back as there was no sign of a relief for him and he was reverting to his old habits of lying in bed until late morning. He resolved the situation for me, though, by going ashore to the see the doctor. He returned with a sick note stating he should be repatriated immediately due to stress and depression. When I went down to his cabin three hours later to check through his paperwork I found he had paid himself off and already left for the airport. I sent a quick telex off to the company to advise them of the situation and resigned myself to having to do the purser's job as well as mine until we reached Japan. At least it would be better than chasing him up every day and I was already doing most of the paperwork.

We were loaded with 200 empty containers and ready to sail when the port was engulfed by a huge sandstorm. It was really impressive with visibility down to a few feet and the radar was no help, as it couldn't penetrate the sand. I was getting a bit worried about navigating my way out when the port suspended all operations for the night so I was able to relax and have a quiet night. When I got up the following morning it was lovely and clear with a brilliant blue sky but everything was covered in a layer of fine brown dust. We sailed at breakfast time and once we got going at full speed the wind blew all the sand off though it seemed to be in our food for days after. We berthed in Dubai the following morning and loaded a further 80 containers. It surprised me how much space they took up and we had to lash quite a few on deck. To my surprise a new purser joined mid morning so I happily handed all the paperwork over to him. I was now looking forward to a peaceful two weeks at sea.

It was not to be. The weather was fantastic with blue skies and calm seas but from the time I opened my office door in the morning until last thing at night there was a constant stream of people knocking at the door with complaints and problems so I began to suspect some sort of conspiracy to drive me mad. It wasn't the life I had envisaged at all. I had hoped to spend my days making decisions about the general running of the ship and now and again conning her in and out of port and the remaining time drinking cold beers and watching the sunset. No way.

Today's big problem was that the purser had not provided an alternative to pork for the Arab officers for the evening meal. He should have known better so I tore a strip off him, which resulted in him resigning and demanding to be repatriated on arrival in Japan. Eventually it was sorted but I was starting to lose the will to live and was more than pleased when we arrived in Kobe to unload the empty containers at the end of March. This only took a few hours and then we moved into the Inland Sea to a small port called Aioi to undergo our annual drydocking.

As the ship was just over a year old it was merely a formality and it presented an opportunity to paint the ship's side. This only took three days and once we undocked we sailed to Busan in Korea to commence loading. We had to wait at anchor for three days as our cargo wasn't available but once it appeared they had it on board very quickly and we sailed to Keelung in Taiwan. We then nipped round several ports in quick succession namely Kaohsiung (Taiwan), Hong Kong, Singapore and Port Klang in Malaysia. It was a very diverse cargo ranging from hundreds of cartons of clothing and footwear to crates of washing machines and electronic goods topped off with bulldozers, forklift trucks and pickup trucks. It must have been worth millions of pounds.

We sailed from Port Klang at the beginning of May and headed off for our first discharge port, which was Muttrah in Oman. The sea passage was a lot pleasanter than the outward run as I think most people had run out of things to complain about. I actually enjoyed this leg of the trip and we had a couple of barbecues on deck, which everyone seemed to enjoy.

We berthed in Muttrah a week later and started discharge unloading the bulldozers. I was a bit disconcerted to get a brief telex from the company to say that my wife, Diane, had been hospitalised and I would be relieved on arrival in Dubai. I was in a bit of a panic as I didn't know whether she'd been in an accident and what had happened to the kids. Unable to get any further information from the company I cadged a lift up to the agent's office and phoned home. It appeared Diane had been taken in to hospital the previous day with severe abdominal pains and was still awaiting a diagnosis. My parents in law were staying at the house and looking after the kids (and dogs and chickens). I walked back to the ship through the port. It was a fascinating walk alongside the dhow harbour where they were all loading and discharging cargoes from India. It was like going back hundreds of years and I could have stayed and watched for ages but obviously I was thinking about the situation at home.

Luckily discharge went quickly and we sailed early the following morning. I was running around like a headless chicken trying to get the accounts right and my handover notes completed. We berthed in Dubai after breakfast on the 15th May and my relief Jack Waldock joined shortly afterwards. His arrival was greeted with consternation by several of the officers as he was known for his no-nonsense attitude and had already sailed with them before. I began to think I must have been a soft touch and vowed to toughen up for the next voyage. Jack was happy with all the paperwork and the handover went really quickly. Two hours later I was on my way to the airport and a flight home.

CHAPTER FOUR

Surely nothing else can break?

m.v. Al Sabahiah
19th July 1978 – 17th January 1979

I had a great flight home from Dubai with Singapore Airlines. I think they were trying to get themselves a good name, as there seemed an unending supply of booze and good food dispensed by beautiful hostesses in sarongs. We landed at Heathrow late in the evening and luckily I managed to get a berth on the sleeper train to Carlisle. Charles, my father in law, picked me up at the station and drove me home. Diane was still in hospital and had been diagnosed with colitis and they were going to keep her in for a few days more. I got in to see her in the afternoon and couldn't believe how much weight she'd lost. She seemed pretty cheerful though and she reckoned she was on the mend. I then returned home to take over the house and two kids, two dogs and a few hens. Thankfully there was plenty of food in and I soon got my head round things. Diane came home two days later but was still pretty poorly so I had to carry on with the housekeeping. I reckoned it was easier at sea. Diane had been harassing me for years to buy an automatic washing machine which I reckoned was a total extravagance but after two weeks of housekeeping duties I came round to her way of thinking and bought a top of the range model.

After a month everything was back to normal and I had another month messing around in the garden and generally enjoying life. I got instructions to join the *Al Sabahiah* in New York on the 19th July so I was back to one of the company's older vessels again. She had just started loading a general cargo back to the Gulf. It was a night flight and we touched down in Newark early in the morning. Luckily the ship was berthed in Newark so it was a five minute taxi ride down to the ship getting there in time for breakfast. It didn't look a promising start as breakfast was delayed because there wasn't enough power to supply the galley ranges. Only one of the three generators was operational and that was blowing out black smoke and making funny noises. Captain Hobkirk handed over in double quick time and shot off to catch a plane.

I had a wander round to see what I'd joined. It wasn't good. There was insufficient power to supply the ship's cranes so they had hired in shore cranes and loading was going very slowly. The officers seemed a really good bunch – in fact the 2nd engineer was my friend, John Bannister, who I'd gone to school with and had been instrumental in me going to sea in the first place. After a good look round and a chat with the 1st mate and the chief engineer it was obvious that the ship was falling apart. Not only were there major difficulties with the generators but the main engine had been giving numerous problems and all the machinery on deck seemed to be broken or in the process of failing.

My first command had been problems with the crew, the second had been the officers and now it looked like on my third trip my main occupation would be keeping the ship together and trying to keep up morale. I felt more comfortable with this as I was beginning to realise that personnel relations wasn't my strongest point.

The loading went pretty smoothly though very slowly. We had been assigned a cargo superintendent, or supercargo, to organise the load and liaise with the agents and stevedores. Although he was a great bloke he was useless at his job and his main aim was to hire the biggest Cadillac he could find in every port and book himself into the best hotel in town. He must have cost a fortune in expenses claims. His plans for stowing the cargo were a disaster and we had to sit down and redo the whole thing which luckily didn't delay the loading much.

We sailed early morning three days later having stayed in overnight to try to progress the generator repairs. We dropped the pilot close to the Ambrose Lightship and I rang the telegraph to full ahead. Instead of the roar of the engine picking up speed there was an ominous silence – the generator had failed again. I had a nervous

24

time for three hours while we drifted around quite close to the Ambrose Lightship but eventually the generator came to life amid dense clouds of black smoke and we got the main engine started again and limped off southwards. This was to be the pattern for the rest of our load around the US coast. We staggered on to Baltimore, Newport News and New Orleans having to use shore cranes at great expense. I had a feeling the company wouldn't be making much money out of this voyage.

We arrived in New Orleans on the 30th July and berthed close to the centre of town and all the famous places such as Bourbon Street and Canal Street. By this time the engineers had managed to get two of the three generators running so we started to load using the ship's cranes. This lasted just over an hour before one of the generators died again. They couldn't organise any shore cranes so loading was abandoned for the day. There was nothing else to do so most of us wandered ashore to sample the delights. When I'd visited the port 20 years ago as an apprentice it had been an amazing place with fantastic jazz bars and nightclubs with reasonable prices but now it was all very tacky and commercialised and exorbitant prices for drink. We kept ending up in gay bars where the booze was cheap.

Loading resumed the following morning using shore cranes and we managed to load the remainder of the cargo without mishap. When I had first joined New Orleans was to be the final port but the company found some more cargo in Houston and Mobile so off we went to pick it up. There wasn't much but it was various sorts of pipework for the Gulf refineries and a real pain to stow and lash.

When we got to Mobile I was told we had to go to Gulfport to load some special cargo. I had no idea what special cargo meant but soon found out it was 50 tons of Semtex high explosive in five containers and one container of eight tons of detonators. The containers were to be loaded on deck using our own cranes, which didn't bode well. The company was over the moon as it paid very high freight but we weren't too thrilled. We first had to be inspected by the coastguard to make sure we complied with all the regulations regarding the carriage of explosives, which of course we failed miserably so there was a mad panic to try to rectify things.

We sailed from Mobile along the coast to Gulfport and tied up to a jetty in the back of beyond just in case we blew up. I was dreading the coastguard inspection and it looked even worse when three very efficient young coastguard officers boarded just after we berthed. Things didn't begin well when the generators started throwing clouds of sparks from the funnel. I needn't have worried, though, as our port manager arrived shortly afterwards with his niece and her friend in tow. They were really attractive girls and dressed to kill. A party started in the 1st mate's cabin even though it was only ten in the morning and the coastguard took no further interest in the inspection. The loading went smoothly though I tried to insist we loaded the detonators first in case they dropped them and set off the rest of the stuff but the stevedore reckoned it wouldn't make any difference as the detonators would have taken out the ship and the jetty without the Semtex. We waved goodbye to the coastguard officers and sailed in the afternoon and I have to admit that if they had breathalysed the deck officers and me on sailing we would have failed miserably. We sailed without mishap, though, and set off across the Atlantic towards Suez.

We had a very slow passage going most of the time at reduced speed because of high engine temperatures. The engine broke down every other day mainly because of leaking fuel pipes but at one stage we stopped for nearly two days while the engineers renewed the bearings on one of turbo blowers. Halfway across the Atlantic I figured out that we had been stopped more we had been travelling. On top of this the engine was using a huge amount of lubricating oil and we were beginning to think we would have to stop at Gibraltar to pick some up. We were also drastically short of fresh water and had to go on water rationing. Luckily we had taken on large stocks of Coors beer in the States so we struggled on. Morale was surprisingly high though the engineers were just about worn out.

We arrived at Port Said, the northern end of the Suez Canal, early morning on the 1st September and most unusually entered straight away. Normally we would tie up for a few hours, which enabled us to take on stores and fresh water, but we steamed straight through. I found out later that it was because of the explosives and the Egyptians didn't want us around longer than necessary. This meant we had to manage another week, until we got to Dubai, on restricted water, which didn't go down well. The engineers managed to cure a major oil leak on the main engine so at least we didn't have to worry about lubricating oil. Then the generators started playing up again. We didn't have enough power for the galley so made do with cold lunches and barbecues at night, which I have to admit weren't too great a hardship.

The 2nd mate, Pete Luker, was into gadgets and had bought himself a navigational calculator. You just entered the altitude of the sun or star and the time and it gave you a position. I was slightly jealous but there was no point in me having one as I left all the position calculating to the mates. The mates also used to work out the eta's and average speed etc. Pete seemed pretty switched on so I very rarely checked his figures. When we turned the corner at Oman and started to head up towards the Arabian Gulf I sent off our eta's to everyone and was sitting on deck with a can of cold beer looking at the spectacular Omani coastline when I realised there was something wrong with his calculations and we should get to Dubai a lot sooner than he had worked out. I went up and checked his figures and found he had added an extra 150 miles for some reason. There was a mad panic to send off new messages with our correct arrival time, which was eleven hours sooner. Surprisingly nobody on shore seemed bothered or asked how we'd suddenly made up all this time.

We arrived in Dubai early September and I expected there to be problems with the explosives but nobody seemed really interested and we unloaded them the following morning with the minimum of fuss. I must admit I was quite glad to see it disappearing up the road on lorries. We topped up with fresh water and lubricating oil so at least I felt a bit more at ease and could have a nice long shower. I even managed to get ashore on the first evening for a lovely seafood meal with Fred Roberts, the cargo superintendent. We didn't have a lot of cargo for Dubai but we did have a lot of heavy containers for Basrah but these were all in the wrong places on board and they had to be moved so we could discharge them using our own cranes. This took us a lot of extra time but everything was completed in a day and we got orders to sail as soon as possible for Basrah. This was a real bind as we had received a message in the afternoon that several reliefs for officers and some boxes of urgent engine parts would arrive at noon the following day. Some of the officers were well overdue their leave so the mood on board was not good. The only bright light was the fact that the 2nd mate was one of those expecting a relief and the mix up was all due to his miscalculation.

We sailed up the Gulf to the entrance to the Shatt al Arab waterway where we were told to anchor. I hated going to Iraq and

Basrah especially as the river was pretty tortuous and I never felt safe whilst there. After twelve hours a pilot boarded and instead of heading up the river we set off west along the coast. When I asked him where the hell he was going he replied we were going to Umm Qasr. I'd never heard of it and on examining the chart it appeared to be a tiny village in the middle of nowhere and on top of that it was getting dark and the water was getting quite shallow and as there were no navigational aids I was getting pretty concerned. The pilot then announced that we had missed the tide and would have to anchor for six hours, which we did. When it got light next morning we found we were anchored just off a brand new port. We berthed at breakfast time under brand new container cranes realising that all our work shifting the containers in Dubai had been for nothing, as they never ever intended to use the ship's cranes. Things didn't go smoothly, though, as they were commissioning the cranes and all the port equipment and training the crane drivers so there were numerous breakdowns and mishaps. We sailed the following morning and headed down to our next port, which was Shuwayk in Kuwait where we had to anchor for three days waiting for a berth. At least it gave us a bit of respite to do some repairs and the officer reliefs and the engine spares eventually caught up with us.

We berthed at noon on the 17th September and I was hoping for a nice quiet time but it was not to be. All our safety equipment had to be inspected by a government surveyor to make sure it was all in working order. I have to admit that not everything was perfect and if we had been warned of the survey we would have been a bit more thorough with our checks. The surveyor was a young Indian bloke on his first survey on his own and was determined to do everything by the book. On top of this we were changing the Pakistani crew so we had no one available to turn out the lifeboats or rig fire hoses. When the new crew arrived it was even worse as they were unfamiliar with the ship and it turned into total chaos. Pete Young, the 1st mate, spent all his time trying to placate the surveyor and if it had been left to me I would have strangled the bastard.

We had week of this and by the end the surveyor was threatening to detain the ship despite our efforts. He eventually issued our certificate with two pages of conditions attached and we sailed ten days later 30 miles along the coast to Mina al Ahmadi where we anchored and discharged some huge steel pipes onto barges. This went pretty smoothly and just as I was thinking our luck was changing Pete Young knocked on my door to tell me the carpenter had fallen off one of the pipes and broken his leg. We had quite a job extricating him and got him taken ashore on a tug where it was confirmed his leg was broken so we had to pay him off. Pete had gone ashore with the carpenter and when he returned he had several telexes and some mail. One of the telexes advised that our next cargo would be loading sugar in Mauritius for Liverpool. This would be a brilliant trip as sugar was an easy load and Mauritius was a great place. At least this brightened everyone up.

We staggered on round the Gulf discharging in Dammam, Bahrain and finished off in Abu Dhabi. By this time I was quite looking forward to a leisurely passage down to Mauritius and the trip to Liverpool where we should hopefully sort out most of the mechanical problems. When the agent came down with our clearance just before sailing he handed me a telex saying our next employment was loading in the Mediterranean back to the Gulf so it was a real downer. We sailed from Abu Dhabi on the 1st October and headed back towards Suez.

If I'd thought the previous run was bad it was nothing to this passage. On the first morning the drinking water pump failed so we had to get our drinking water by lowering buckets into the tank. It was just as well there was plenty of beer on board.

The following is an extract from my diary for Saturday 7th October:

Having problems with generators overheating. Air conditioning and fans and non-essential lights turned off.

Greaser's cabin flooded with water from faecal tank. Bailed out and moved him to another cabin.

Gyro compass overheats and inaccurate. Set up fans around it and improved.

Proceeding at 88rpm (three quarter speed) due to abnormal vibration on forward turbo blower.

Main engine using excessive amounts of fresh water.

29

4/E Ahmad switches on water for a personal shower despite being on water rationing – had to be reprimanded.

Chief steward complaining of heavy cockroach infestation in storerooms.

1400-1515 Stopped to repair main engine fuel pipe.

Electrician goes on drinking spree and causes irritation to others with the noise from his cabin. Will deal with him tomorrow.

And so it went on.

The trip up to Suez took two days longer than normal due to all the breakdowns. Morale on board was pretty good considering, though all the engineers were too knackered to complain.

We arrived at the south end of the Canal at noon on the 11th October and anchored to await our transit. We'd only been anchored three hours when everything went quiet. Our only remaining generator had failed due to the cooling pump blowing up. The engineers promptly set about changing the pump with one from the broken generators but for some reason it wouldn't fit so we ended up stuck at anchor for two days until they repaired the original pump. The only positive thing to come out of this was that we were able to take on copious amounts of fresh water from barges (at great expense but I was beyond caring). At least everyone could have a decent shower and get some washing done.

We finally cleared the north end of the Canal mid October and we brightened up considerably when we were told to proceed to Venice to start loading. I'd never been there but was really looking forward to it.

We staggered our way up to Venice and went straight alongside. It was a fantastic entrance as we passed along in front of St Mark's Square – all the lights were coming on in the cafés and shops. We berthed right in the centre of town and it was amazing standing on deck watching all the vaporettos and gondolas moving around on the still water. I'd missed my tea with all the messing around picking up the pilot and entering port so I was over the moon when the ship's agent invited me ashore for a meal. I was half expecting pizza but it was a fantastic meal with all the trimmings and I staggered back on board well after midnight more than slightly under the weather.

The 1st mate, Pete, had organised for his wife to join him in the first port so she turned up the following morning and I got some pangs of conscience about my wife slaving away at home looking after the house and kids while I was really enjoying life so I phoned home and arranged for her to join as soon as possible. The day got even better when the agent appeared with a case of the best local wines for me to sample. One of the company engineering superintendents also arrived to supervise all our repairs and soon the ship was crawling with shipyard workers and electricians trying to sort our problems out.

We just had 200 tons of ceramic tiles to load so the only fly in the ointment was that we'd only be in Venice for a short while but just as we finished loading the cargo the agent appeared full of apologies saying that we'd be stuck in port for another two days as all the tugs were on strike. It got better by the minute. We had one slight problem in that the 2nd mate managed to drop a three ton hatch lid down the hold when they were closing the hatch. Luckily it missed all the newly loaded crates of tiles and wasn't too badly damaged. We then had two full days with nothing much going on so were able to wander ashore all round Venice. The agent gave us some passes for water taxis so we got around all over the place. I only wished Diane had been there.

On the morning of the 22nd October the tugs went back to work so we sailed at breakfast time the short distance across to Trieste. It wouldn't have been a big problem to sail without tugs but I wasn't going to miss out on a couple of days looking round Venice. It was only four hours across the top of the Adriatic and we were all tied up again by teatime and were told that we'd only start loading the following morning so had time to wander round the marinas and see the sights. Again there was only 300 tons of cargo to load – mainly tiles and cartons of blankets – which was no problem at all. The stowage of cargo and organisation of the load was done by a firm of planners in Rotterdam. When I went up the following morning to telephone and resolve a few queries I found myself talking to Bas Veiveen, who I'd worked with before. He said he was having a nightmare with our cargo as it was changing by the minute. He was over the moon when I volunteered to do the planning and gave me carte blanche as long as I kept him in the picture. I really enjoyed cargo planning and there was a real satisfaction when a ship was properly loaded and all the cargo safely stowed.

There were no problems with the Trieste cargo and we started loading that morning. Diane arrived late in the evening somewhat miffed at being propositioned by the taxi driver but otherwise happy to be there. She brightened even more the following morning when the agent appeared with yet another case of local wine for our consumption. We finished loading the following afternoon and set sail for Livorno. The ship seemed to be working a lot better after the repairs and we actually had two of the three generators fully operational for the first time since I joined. The ship then decided to go for other things and the main radio transmitter blew up so we couldn't send any messages and then the steering gear failed and we started going round in circles. We eventually sorted it and set off again.

Our route took us through the Straits of Messina between Italy and Sicily. It is very narrow with some strong currents and really busy with loads of fishing boats and ferries not to mention all the other vessels transiting the Straits. Nowadays ships have to pick up a pilot to go through but in those days it was unregulated. I'd organised the 1st mate to call me just as we approached and he rang me at six in the morning to say we were nearly there. I was sitting on the side of the bed, half asleep, putting my socks on when Diane asked what all the Italians were shouting about. I said it would just be some argument on the quay. A minute later she rolled over and pointed out that we were at sea. I don't think I've ever got from my cabin to the bridge as fast. When I got there Pete was making some tea and he explained we'd passed through a fleet of fishing boats that weren't carrying any lights but he'd managed to avoid sinking any. I think he'd learnt quite a few Italian swear words in the process.

We had a great passage through the Straits just as dawn was breaking. It was flat calm with not much traffic and Mount Etna even had some spectacular streams of red hot lava running down the side. It was then up past Stromboli to our next port of Livorno where we berthed in late October. Quite a lot of our cargo hadn't arrived yet but we managed to load some huge sheets of marble for some sheik's palace in Abu Dhabi.

The following day was Sunday and as no cargo was available we had the day off so Diane and I with the 1st mate and his wife took the train up to Florence for a look around. It takes quite a bit to impress me but I was totally overawed by the Uffizi Gallery. We only had two hours there but it was amazing standing looking at all these famous paintings. We made a bit of a mistake on the return journey and caught the diretto which we assumed would be the direct train. Three and a half hours later we arrived back in Livorno having stopped in every village and farmyard on the way. Actually we found it really interesting seeing the local countryside and their way of life. We rewarded ourselves with a ginormous pizza in Livorno and a couple of bottles of Chianti. A day to remember.

Loading resumed on the Monday with more marble and a huge consignment of woollen blankets, which seemed odd for the Arabian Gulf. I took Diane up to Pisa to fly home in the afternoon. She wasn't too happy and wanted to stay on for longer but brightened up a bit when we had a wander round the Leaning Tower and the Basilica.

We sailed at noon the following day and set off for Valencia passing through the strait between Sardinia and Corsica. The islands looked really wild and rugged and uncivilised. I couldn't believe it when I passed through a few years later and it was all new buildings and hotels.

We arrived in Valencia early in the morning of the 2nd November and started loading steel bars and even more crates of tiles. I'd been to Valencia on numerous occasions and become good friends with the agent, Juan. He used to come and pick me up at nine in the morning and take me ashore for breakfast. This consisted of a huge sausage in a baguette followed by copious amounts of strong black coffee and a large brandy. I always felt I could cope with anything after that. This time I had just bought myself a new razor and was still getting used to it but inevitably cut myself quite badly most mornings. One day on the way back to the ship Juan diverted into town and took me into a sort of hardware shop. I was a bit disconcerted when the shopkeeper produced several pistols and a rifle for my inspection. Juan then explained he thought it would be lot easier to shoot myself rather than trying to cut my throat every morning. The shopkeeper and the other customers were highly amused.

Loading went very smoothly with no major breakdowns or problems. The generators also managed to keep going so all the work in Italy seemed to have paid off. The loading took five days and though I say it myself the stowage was excellent and we could see no problems to be encountered when it would be discharged. We sailed on the 7th November and headed up to Marseille arriving there the following evening. Then things started to go pear-shaped. The agent came aboard with the news that all the cargo planned for loading had been cancelled or changed and we were also now going to load in Piraeus. The only good news he had was that the dockers were on strike so we would be lying idle for a day.

Early next morning the agent brought down the lists of all the proposed cargo but he had no idea what we had to load in Piraeus so we had to have plenty of different options to hand. I began to regret volunteering to organise the cargo stowage and even more when we examined the lists. It started with over 100 tons of ammunition and grenades which involved building a large wooden spark proof magazine in one of the holds. The rest of the cargo seemed to be military vehicles and six large fire engines for Kuwait airport. There were also two complete construction cranes, which consisted of huge pieces of metal latticework and machinery. On top of this they wanted everything stowed under deck and protected from the weather. It took me and Pete, the 1st mate, nearly all day and a large quantity of cold beer to sort it out. Needless to say as the loading went on they kept changing things and cargo kept arriving in the wrong order. We loaded all the vehicles and I was very impressed by some very nippy little scout cars that were brilliant to drive.

There was no work on the Sunday and the local agent took us ashore for a meal in the old part of Marseille. It was a memorable meal not only for the obligatory bouillabaisse but the consumption of vast quantities of wine. Actually I don't think I could have eaten the bouillabaisse sober as it was full of fish eyes and whole crabs but it was delicious!

We resumed loading on Monday morning and also started to build the magazine for the explosives. It was an impressive structure and cost the price of a small house. The next day we got a message that everything was changed and we had to sail straight for the Gulf without the ammunition so we just plonked the remaining vehicles into the holds, lashed them down and sailed the following noon towards Piraeus. Two hours after we sailed we got a message cancelling the Piraeus call so we headed off towards Suez and the

Gulf.

It was a very pleasant run down through the Mediterranean and I took the ship through the strait between Sardinia and Corsica again and on through the Straits of Messina. It didn't knock many miles off the trip but it was certainly a lot more interesting and scenic. The various repairs seemed to have improved the running of the ship and we only had a couple of minor stoppages. It was an uneventful passage through the Canal and a pleasant trip round to the Gulf. Now that the ship's mechanical problems were being sorted out I started having personnel problems. The chief engineer was coming up retiring age and took very little interest in the job. Also the purser was doing his first trip and wasn't up to the task at all. It was odd too, that although the ship was running better morale seemed to go down. I had an excellent 1st mate in the form of Pete Young who managed to keep me sane but not sober.

Our first port in the Gulf was Kuwait where we berthed on the morning of the 1st December. As it was a Friday there was no work so it was a nice easy day catching up with paperwork and reading mail from home. The discharge went very smoothly apart from the removal of our unused explosives magazine. It took twice as long to dismantle as it did to build and resulted in a huge pile of timber on the quay when we left. After five days in Kuwait we nipped round the Gulf discharging in double quick time ending up in Dammam, Saudi Arabia, as our final port.

The chief engineer resolved my problem with him by falling over on deck and injuring his head. We sent him up to hospital and they kept him in so we had to leave him behind. We promoted the 2nd engineer and things showed a remarkable improvement. Our orders came through to proceed back towards Europe again so we all hoped for a load round the UK though it was obvious that we'd have to have Christmas in the Mediterranean.

We cleared the Suez Canal on the night of 22nd December and got our orders to head to Barcelona. We had a very quiet Christmas passing Malta and the cook managed to put on a really good spread. I always dreaded Christmas at sea because there was always somebody who over-imbibed and had to be reprimanded but this time everyone behaved.

We berthed in Barcelona on the 28th December and started loading steel reinforcing bars but it went pretty slowly as the bars were really long and took a lot of manoeuvring to get them into the hold. The purser was relieved but his replacement was no better and I had to warn him about his drinking on his second day, which didn't bode well. I also got a new 1st mate who turned out to be in his sixties and had previously sailed as master. I managed to fall out with him on the third day. I could see the rest of my trip being a nightmare.

On New Year's Eve I was taken out by the local agents and some of the shippers of our cargo for a slap up meal and then to a nightclub. It was a fantastic night and I was glad I wasn't paying. Somehow most of the group ended up back on the ship having a party in my day room. I was beyond caring though I did think I would have some complaints about the noise from some of the other officers in the morning. I was completely out of it by three in the morning and collapsed on my bed and left them still partying in my dayroom.

My steward would usually come in about half six in the morning with a tray of tea and toast and start cleaning my accommodation. This morning he kept knocking on my door and I thought he was going to complain about the mess but when I followed him into the dayroom not only did it look like a bomb had hit it but there were two very scantily dressed dancers from the night club asleep on the settee. Bloody hell. The girls were even more hung over than I was and took some waking up. I then had to sneak them off the ship before everyone got up. Luckily I think there had been quite a party on board while I was ashore so nobody was around. I then took the girls to the end of the jetty and found a taxi to take them home. They received some very appreciative whistles from the crews on the other ships as we walked past. I got back on board just as people were getting up and got some rather curious glances but as I was in my uniform they probably assumed I'd had an early walk or something. I think I was pretty lucky as I'm sure several of the officers would have used the incident to their advantage. The noise from the party also went unnoticed, as everybody had assumed it was from the party in the officers' bar.

We sailed early in January down to Valencia where it was back to my breakfasts of sausage, coffee and brandy. I got news that I was to be relieved in the next port, Livorno, so life started to look rosier. It took a week in Valencia to load more steel bars and a large number of crates of tiles. We seemed to have carried enough tiles to do every bathroom in the Gulf twice over and still we loaded them.

We sailed over to Livorno on the 12th January and started loading crates of marble and a few hundred tons of tinned tomatoes. Roger Mackrell appeared on the second day of loading to relieve me. The next morning I got a taxi up to Pisa and a nice flight back to Newcastle arriving in the afternoon and I was home having tea in Penrith by five o' clock. It had been an interesting trip to say the least and I just hoped the company would give me one of the newer ships next time.

CHAPTER FIVE

Mediterranean cruise

m.v. Al Farwaniah
20th March 1979 – 15 August 1979

As I'm starting to write this chapter, news is breaking of a large modern cruise liner called the *Costa Concordia* going aground and sinking off the Italian coast. It seems they were passing too close to the coast and hit a rock, which put a large hole in the hull. I just got to thinking how lucky I was in my career at sea never to have had a major incident and I have to admit that sometimes it was more by good luck that by good judgement. I shake my head now at some of the daft things I did and managed to get away with – as you will no doubt see later in this book. Anyhow back to 1979.

My leave from the *Al Sabahiah* was from the middle of January up to the middle of March so it wasn't much good weather-wise but I seemed to get a fair bit of gardening in before I got my instructions to join the *Al Farwaniah* in Malta. After all the hassle on the previous ship I was really hoping for one of the company's brand new K Class ships but not this time. The *Al Farwaniah* was identical to the *Al Sabahiah* but a year younger having been built in 1973 so I wasn't expecting too much. I flew out from Heathrow on the 20th March and joined the *Al Farwaniah* in drydock in Valletta in the afternoon. The ship had been there for a week and was ready to float out so was all nicely painted up. First impressions were good. All the paperwork was in order and Captain Tennant left in the evening to fly home.

The next day I had a good walk round the ship with Tom Bailey, the engineer superintendent, and was pleasantly surprised by the condition of the ship. When I met the officers I knew that was where my trouble would be. The 1st mate, Nabil, was an Iraqi and absolutely hopeless on deck but he was a really nice bloke and tried hard so it made life difficult chasing him up all the time. Incidentally, he did one of the best impressions of Elvis that I have ever seen. I reckon he should have done it for a living. The 2nd and 3rd mates were Indian and were brilliant with theory and calculations but completely useless concerning practical issues such as cargo stowage. On top of this the chief engineer seemed to be totally uninterested in the job so it had the makings of an interesting trip.

It took another two days to finish off the repairs and we sailed for Valencia on the morning of the 23rd March. It was uneventful except for the fire alarm going off at midnight on the second day. It turned out to be a tea towel catching fire on the galley stove and it was easily extinguished so everyone went back to bed. I used to wonder what it would be like to have a really serious fire on a ship because despite regular fire drills whenever the alarm went off people would rush around like headless chickens doing all the wrong things.

We berthed in Valencia and spent the morning discharging some empty containers and then prepared the holds for loading which started the following morning. We were to load round the usual Mediterranean ports for the Arabian Gulf but nothing firm had been decided except our first three ports which were Valencia, Barcelona and Livorno. Valencia was the usual steel reinforcing bars and crates of tiles so not too interesting. A new chief engineer, Chris Mileham, joined and seemed to inspire the engineers from the moment he boarded so I had just my deck officers to worry about. I got back into my old routine of sausage and coffee and brandy breakfasts and was quite sorry to sail five days later. The load had gone very smoothly with over 1,000 tons being loaded.

Our next port was Barcelona and twelve hours steaming up the coast. We had only 400 tons of steel bars to load so we berthed early in the morning of 31st March and sailed late in the evening for Livorno. It was straight into a real towser of a storm blowing from the south so we were rolling around all over the place. Just before I went to bed I looked out on deck and noticed that a 40 ton container was moving around and on closer inspection found it was just sitting on the deck totally unsecured. I dragged the 1st mate out of his bed and we had to turn the crew out to lash it down. It was quite dangerous with the ship rolling quite heavily but eventually it was sorted and the mate went to bed with a flea in his ear, as he should have checked before we sailed.

The storm had eased by the morning so the rest of the passage to Livorno was quite pleasant. We had a bit of a nightmare entering the port because just as we started to enter between the breakwaters an outgoing ferry appeared so I rang full astern to allow the ferry to depart. For some reason the engine went full ahead and we careered into the harbour with inches to spare with the ferry on one side and a large stone breakwater on the other. The Italian ferry skipper shouted something we assumed was very uncomplimentary as he squeezed past. We eventually got ourselves stopped and the ship tied up with the assistance of tugs.

Loading started straight away and it was even more crates of tiles. The second day was more interesting as we loaded several electrical transformers weighing over 200 tons apiece. The loading went very slowly as the weather was atrocious and we had to stop loading a few times as the ship was rolling too heavily against the quay. Still, I managed to get ashore for several lovely meals and on the last day the agent appeared with a two cases of local wine. Not a bad life. I'd always thought that Chianti was a cheap plonk but this stuff showed me a whole new perspective. I was converted.

Our next port was designated as Marseille and after that we would finish off loading in Venice so we were getting all round the Mediterranean on this trip. Marseille was only a quick stop as we berthed at six in the morning and sailed at three in the afternoon. All we loaded were some large boxes of military equipment, which were delivered down to the ship by the military. Nobody would tell us what it was but I think it was a complete missile tracking station. At least it wasn't explosives!

We had a pleasant trip through the Straits of Messina again and we berthed in the centre of Venice in mid April and had a nice day off as it was Good Friday. I had a wander up to St Mark's Square with Chris, the chief engineer, and his wife as it was a lovely day but I've never seen so many people milling around. We only lasted an hour especially when we found out what they were charging for a beer. When we got back we found the agent had delivered yet another two cases of wine and some boxes of Italian Easter cake so we finished off the afternoon sitting on deck in the sun drinking wine, eating cake and watching the boats in the lagoon. This was what going to sea was all about.

Next morning we were brought down to earth when the cargo appeared. It was for a refinery in Ruwais in the United Arab Emirates. It consisted of numerous pipes all welded together at funny angles with valves and gauges sticking out everywhere. It was a nightmare but eventually we had it loaded and lashed down.

Next day was Easter Sunday so there was no work again and this time we didn't venture ashore as we could see all the crowds getting off the buses and trains. In the evening Loris, the local agent, took myself, the 1st mate, chief engineer and his wife ashore for a meal. We didn't go into Venice much to our disappointment but to Mestre a small town about ten miles away. I gather that Venice was too full of tourists. The restaurant was a fantastic place with a huge open-air courtyard. Loris insisted we sat inside because of the eggles. I wondered what he was on about but didn't say anything. Halfway through the meal we noticed the people in the courtyard moving to the inside tables. Loris announced that the eggles had arrived. It turned out he meant eagles, his name for giant bloodthirsty mosquitoes attracted by the lights. The meal went on until after midnight and ended with Nabil doing his Elvis impression and getting a huge round of applause from the other diners. Loris poured us back on board about one in the morning but I was woken up at two by the local police who had arrested three of the junior engineers for fighting in a bar. They signed them over to my care and then I had to entertain the police for a couple of hours while they finished off my best whisky. I was seriously under the weather by the time I crawled into bed. It was just as well there was no cargo work the following day, which was Easter Monday. It was a miserable wet day but we spent all the day loading stores which had just arrived in a container from Liverpool. I gave a hand stowing the stores away to try and clear my hangover but it wasn't all that successful so I opted for an early night.

We resumed loading the next day and it surprised me the variety of goods we were loading. There were washing machines and fridges and a lot of lovely Italian furniture. It all went very smoothly except on the last night when I was woken at three in the morning to be told the engineers had been in another fight and one was in hospital. There wasn't much to be done so I went back to bed. The following morning Loris, the agent, appeared and somehow he already knew about the fight and had arranged for a taxi to bring the engineer back on board. I got the two other engineers up to my office and gave them both a roasting and they went back to work suitably chastened. I talked to the chief engineer and he was quite happy for me to sack the other engineer as he wasn't much good anyhow. When he eventually arrived from the hospital he had obviously picked a fight with the wrong blokes as he was missing a couple of teeth and had a fractured jaw and he was all battered and bruised. I nearly felt sorry for him but when I told him I was sacking him he became all belligerent and even started to threaten me. We got him off the ship and on his way to the airport within the hour. It was the first time I had to sack someone and it felt a bit odd but I later found out he was really unpopular on board though he'd only joined in Livorno and I'd gone up in everyone's estimation.

We finished our loading that evening and set off for the Suez Canal and the Gulf. It was quite a pleasant passage with no major problems though Chris, the chief engineer, was getting worried about the main engine overheating and the odd bit fell off necessitating a couple of short stops. It also became apparent that the ship was infested with rats. I wasn't too bothered until I saw one crawling round in my bedroom ceiling light. We also had a near miss with a drilling rig off the coast of Oman. The 3rd mate was checking flags on the bridge and not keeping the best of lookouts. When he did spot the rig it was only quarter of a mile dead ahead. He put the wheel hard over and we scraped by with only feet to spare. It was a really close one and Roger, the 3rd mate, was shaking like a leaf afterwards. There was quite a bit of verbal abuse from the rig over the VHF radio. As we were an Arab registered ship they assumed we were Arabs and the language was pretty racist. We didn't enlighten them. As the chief engineer observed afterwards, it was a fucking stupid place to be drilling for oil anyway.

We berthed in our first discharge port of Ruwais early May and then we went round Dubai, Abu Dhabi, and Damman in double quick time arriving in Kuwait ten days later. The crew on board the *Al Farwaniah* were from Sierra Leone. I liked them a lot better than the Indian and Pakistani crews as they were generally a lot harder working and a happier bunch. On arrival in Kuwait we were told that the crew were being paid off and replaced by Pakistanis who were a lot cheaper. I was really disappointed as I got on really well with the West Africans. I always hated being in Kuwait as the company head office was there and the superintendents had to come down and inspect the ships and they could always find something wrong. This time it turned into a fiasco. The African crew had just left when the supers arrived and the crew accommodation looked like a bomb had hit it as they'd just packed their bags and left. In the storerooms we found a large rat eating its way into a bag of rice. The 2nd engineer decided it was all too much for him and locked himself in his cabin with a case of beer. Two of our cranes broke down in a big way so the rest of the engineers were out working on these. The inspection was abandoned and everyone retreated to my cabin for a cold beer. When the chief steward stuck his head in the door and said there was only a cold lunch as he had no staff they all left and went ashore.

The afternoon got worse as the Pakistani crew arrived and immediately started complaining about the state of the accommodation. I'd just sorted that by paying them overtime to clean up when they found there was no dhal flour or ghee or curry spices on board because the Africans ate the same food as us. We managed to get an emergency supply from another ship and the next day we ordered in all their food requirements, which cost a fortune. It just went from bad to worse. The stevedores demanded extra money as there were rats running round in the cargo. The chief engineer found a major problem with the fuel heater so we were going to have to run the main engine on diesel instead of heavy oil, which cost four times as much. I think the supers felt sorry for us in the end because they didn't visit again. Possibly the rats scared them off.

We eventually sailed from Kuwait late on the 14th May and headed down to our last discharge port, which was Doha. There were rumours of sending the ship to India to load a cargo and I wasn't looking forward to this at all as the ship seemed to be going the same way as the previous one and falling to bits. The discharge in Doha went pretty smoothly considering that three of our cranes were out of action with no prospect of repair. The rat situation was getting really bad too and we were worried that they would chew the wiring and do some serious damage. We finished discharge six days later and just before we sailed the agent appeared with a telex telling to proceed to a little port called Sharjah in the United Arab Emirates for repairs and to fumigate the ship for the rats. I brightened up considerably as there was quite a good repair facility in Sharjah so we should be able to get most of our repairs sorted. Also if they were going to fumigate the ship for rats we would all have to housed ashore and there were some superb hotels in the area so I should be able to live the good life for a couple of days.

It only took twelve hours down to Sharjah and we berthed the following morning. Squads of repair engineers and their minions immediately invaded the ship. The fumigating team to get rid of the rats followed these. To our disappointment they announced that they would be poisoning the rats in the accommodation and fumigating all the other spaces therefore we could all stay on board. Bugger! Actually it turned out all right as I knew quite a few people on shore so I was wined and dined continuously for the week we were in port. At one stage I was dragged off to an Arab barbecue in the desert. I was dreading it as I'd heard all sorts of rumours about eating sheep's eyes and things but it turned out to be just like our barbecues back home with copious amount of cold beer. There was a job going as a pilot in Sharjah and I was seriously thinking of applying because it was really the life of riley. In the end I decided to remain as a skipper as I don't think I could have coped with the ex-pats' way of life.

After a week things were looking a lot better. We had all our cranes operational again and pipework renewed in the engineroom and Chris, the chief engineer, was in a much happier frame of mind. We had one incident just after they'd fumigated the holds when the carpenter wanted some wood from down below. He blithely removed the locks and went down one of the holds to collect some. He reappeared, much to our relief, after five minutes with his wood and announced there were loads of dead rats down there! The fumigators did a good job and cleared the ship of rats but they annoyed the cockroach population and we had a serious infestation for a couple of weeks despite constant spraying. Everything seemed to taste of insecticide and the only relief was cold San Miguel beer, which wasn't affected.

We sailed late in May and were expecting to go to India, which I wasn't really looking forward to but just before we left the agent appeared with a telex telling us to head for Suez but nothing after that. It was an uneventful passage up the Red Sea apart from the 2nd mate nearly taking a tanker out. He got too close and then blew two blasts on the whistle to indicate he was altering course to port and then altered course to starboard. We went round in a complete circle and very nearly hit it again coming back on course. The tanker was Russian and shortly afterwards he called us up on the VHF radio and subjected us to a tirade of abuse most of which was racial as we had got so close he could see the 2nd mate was Indian. It was decidedly not pc but he had a point to make. Once we cleared Suez we got instructions to head for Barcelona to load steel bars yet again. I was getting to be quite the expert around the Mediterranean. As we progressed towards Spain the port changed from Barcelona to Valencia to Cadiz and finally they decided on Algeciras just beside Gibraltar. It appeared that it was fiesta season in Spain and the company was trying to find the port with the fewest delays. They failed miserably.

We berthed in Algeciras mid morning on the 8th June. When the agent boarded he apologized that the load would take a lot longer than expected as it was fiesta time and it was very hard to get labour. It was looking good already as it seemed like a really nice port. We were berthed next to the ferry terminal where the boats left to cross the Straits of Gibraltar to Ceuta and Tangiers in Morocco. The town itself wasn't too commercialised and there were lots of lovely beaches and pleasant little bars.

They started loading the next morning, which was Saturday, but only worked until noon and that was it for the weekend. The agent appeared with several bottles of the local fino sherry, which looked more like white wine it was so light coloured. He instructed us to drink it very cold so we duly obliged and I have to admit being rather unwell the following day. Just as well it was a Sunday with nothing much going on. Monday saw them resume loading but again they stopped at noon. We were programmed to load 7,000 tons of steel bars and at this rate it would take another month. In the afternoon reliefs turned up for the 1st mate and the purser. The new 1st mate was Mike Winkworth who was the same age as me and had served his apprenticeship with the British India Company, which was a really prestigious company. He made my life such a lot easier because Nabil, nice bloke that he was, was utterly useless on deck and needed checking all the time. The new chief steward also seemed pretty efficient so my last month on board had the makings of a good time.

We actually got four full days loading after this so things were looking up but on Friday it was the fiesta proper and everyone knocked off for four days. The agent gave me a couple of tickets for a bullfight on the Saturday so Mike and I wandered up. All the pageantry was spectacular but the killing of the bull and it being dragged out of the ring by horses really put me off. I think we left halfway through and adjourned to a local bar. The following three days were also very pleasant just wandering round the town and we got taken out for a couple of really nice meals which improved the situation even more.

We were having problems with two of our hydraulic cranes so the company organised for an engineer from the makers to come and sort them out. He turned out to be a young Dutch bloke and a great character. He was ensconced in a four star hotel just out of town so we would wander up there in the evening and sit on a lovely open veranda overlooking the Straits of Gibraltar and put the world to rights over one or two cold beers. Thinking back I can't remember ever paying for the beer so he must have put it on expenses.

They resumed loading again on the Wednesday and at last we seemed to be loading at a decent rate and in the end we finished the following Wednesday. Our next port was supposed to be Barcelona and the agent said there would be long delays there as their fiesta would start on the day we arrived. It had the makings of a really relaxing load. Just after we sailed from Algeciras we got a message to proceed to Valencia instead, which was a bit of a disappointment. Mind you I always preferred Valencia to Barcelona so it wasn't all bad.

We berthed in Valencia on the 22nd June and the agent there greeted us with the news that most of the cargo was being sent down from Barcelona but as it was fiesta time it would take twice as long as usual to load. Ah well.

The agent and I introduced Mike to the 'Valencia breakfast' of sausage, coffee and brandy. The loading did indeed go very slowly. They also kept changing the cargo so I was relieved Mike was there to help sort it all out. The Spanish shippers of the steel bars were really pleased that their cargo was being loaded as they had a deadline to meet in Saudi Arabia. They invited Mike and me out for a meal one night. It was a really sumptuous place a few miles out of

46

town. We felt distinctly underdressed but no one seemed to mind. The meal was fantastic but the best bit was the waitresses who were all gorgeous and wore long black dresses that were slit up to the waist at the side. I couldn't figure how the dresses stayed on. I had a huge grilled lobster and they gave me a tool like nutcrackers for breaking the claws. I was so diverted by the waitress that I inadvertently got my finger in the crackers and when I squeezed them I nearly broke my finger. The head shipper saw all this and collapsed into fits of laughter and couldn't tell the rest of the table for laughing but eventually he got everyone told including the waitress who came over and patted me on the head. Every time the shipper looked at me after that he went off into gales of laughter. It was a really good night though my finger was all swollen next morning.

We were all finished loading on Friday 29th June and getting ready to sail when we got a message that they had found 200 tons of blankets and we had to stay an extra day to load them. I never could figure out what they did with all those blankets. Our next port was programmed to be Livorno to load more tiles and marble but just before we sailed we were told to head for Trieste to load a mystery cargo.

On this passage I was unable to do the trip through the Straits of Messina, as it would actually have added distance to the passage. As we rounded the heel of Italy we got a message from the agent in Trieste saying to slow down, as we would have to anchor on arrival. We reduced to half speed and had a lovely day and a half cruising up the Adriatic in idyllic weather. We went quite close to the Croatian coast admiring all the little beaches and ports. We anchored off Trieste late on the 4th July and as it was a lovely warm night I sat out on deck for an hour or so with the chief engineer and his wife drinking cold beer and looking at all the twinkling shore lights.

The next morning the agent came out by boat bringing with him a heap of mail and details of the cargo we were going to load so at least we could figure out where it was all going. He also brought with him a new radio officer who had been waiting in a hotel ashore for over a week. Obviously people in head office had no idea where we were but he seemed to have enjoyed himself at the company's expense. I was pleased to get rid of the existing radio officer as he was bone idle and inclined to drink too much. I now found I had a really good bunch of officers with the exception of the 2nd mate and life became

47

really quite pleasant. The agent also brought out two cases of local wine so things were definitely looking up.

We had another day at anchor, which gave us plenty of time to work out where the cargo would go. The biggest part of the load seemed to be a complete bottling plant for Pepsi, which had been made in Germany. It seemed odd shipping it from Trieste but I gather it had come by barge through all the canals. There was also a lot more pipework to be loaded in Venice after Trieste for Ruwais. At least this time we knew what to expect and could leave plenty of space for it. We berthed the following morning right in the centre of Trieste beside a huge marina full of expensive yachts and motor cruisers. We were then advised that the stevedores were on holiday for three days so we could take things easy. So we had three very relaxing days except when a large lorry turned up unexpectedly from England with stores.

The weather was lovely so Mike, the 1st mate, managed to get the crew painting over the side, which smartened us up a lot. It was really pleasant just to walk ashore and through the marina admiring the yachts. It wasn't very touristy so there were some great little bars with drinks at a reasonable price. Mike managed to find a pizzeria in some back street. It was packed with locals who welcomed us with lots of advice about the best pizzas. Mike said he would like garlic on his pizza and this was met with a lot of head shaking and comments about the mad English. It had a proper wood fired pizza oven and it was good entertainment just watching them shape and form the dough. We discovered that you should only have cold beer with pizza and not wine. After that Mike and I would forego our meal on board and wander up there in the evening and fill up with Peroni beer and pizza.

They eventually started loading and were surprisingly efficient, stowing and lashing the cargo really well. We were eight days in port altogether and we sailed for Venice on the evening of the 12th July. We couldn't berth in Venice until the following evening so we had a day at anchor just off the entrance to the Venice lagoon. When we did berth we were disappointed to find that all the berths in Venice were occupied so we tied up in Marghera. Loris, the local agent, boarded on arrival with piles of documents relating to the cargo we were supposed to load but it was a real mess as some of it was cancelled and there was a huge amount of provisional bookings if there was room on board. We spent a long time sorting through it and eventually came up with a semblance of a plan so we could start loading the following morning.

We commenced loading with four gangs and the cargo was really flying in but by two o'clock in the afternoon it all came to a halt, as they'd run out of cargo. It appeared most of the stuff was coming from Germany and Austria and nobody seemed to know when it would arrive. This meant we had the weekend free and Loris kindly organised water taxis to take us over to Venice so things were brightening up. He also brought on board yet more wine. He gave me a couple of bottles of pinot grigio, which was a wine I'd never heard of, with instructions that I had to take it home with me as it was special. Needless to say it didn't make it home as it was supped one lovely evening in the Indian Ocean and I have to admit it was one of the nicest wines I have ever tasted. We resumed loading on the Monday but with only one gang so it was very leisurely. And so it carried on for the week so I was able to make several excursions up to Venice. The trouble was everything in Venice was so expensive we tended just to wander round the back streets and we found some amazing little places though we got lost quite a few times.

The company finally lost patience with the slow progress and we were instructed to sail on Tuesday the 24th July even though all the cargo hadn't arrived. By this time we'd been in port eleven days and loaded only 600 tons of cargo. There was about 400 tons of steel and the rest seemed to be children's toys and clothes from Germany.

It was four days down to Port Said at the entrance to the Suez Canal. We had to tie up to buoys in the harbour to await the start of the convoy. It turned into a disaster as the main engine failed in the middle of the harbour. Luckily we obtained the services of a couple of tugs who prevented us running aground and then pulled us to our buoys to tie up. I had to give hundreds of cigarettes and quite a few bottles of whisky to the pilot, tugs and the harbour master otherwise the engine failure would have been reported and the ship could have been seriously delayed. The fault turned out to be a pilot valve in the engine starting system (whatever that is) and I was very impressed by the engineers when they managed to make a new bit from an old generator bolt. We started the Canal transit at four the next morning and had a really quick passage so we were clear of the other end by seven in the evening. I had to stay up until three o'clock, though, as someone had obviously found oil in the Gulf of Suez and it was wall to wall with oil rigs with supply boats and barges nipping in and out of them.

It was a pleasant passage down the Red Sea but when we got out into the Indian Ocean the south west monsoon was in full swing so we had four days of heavy rolling before we turned north round Oman when it got pleasant again.

The engineers were having all sorts of problems with the cooling system on the main engine so we had to reduce speed to just over half to stop the engine overheating. It was really quite enjoyable cruising along in lovely weather with the sea like a mirror. I got a message from the company saying I was being relieved on arrival in Kuwait. This created a bit of a problem with all these lovely bottles of wine that I'd been given as we weren't allowed to land with alcohol in Kuwait so I took the decision to make the best of it and consume them there and then. We had a barbecue on deck and had quite a memorable evening though somewhat regretted it the following morning.

Our first port of discharge was Ruwais with oil drilling equipment which went very smoothly, then it was up to Damman in Saudi Arabia for two days discharging steel then on up to Kuwait. My relief, John Holmes, arrived the next day and after handing over I was on my way home arriving back in the UK on the 15th August. Looking back it had been a very enjoyable trip and I was sorry to leave as there was a cracking bunch of officers on board which had made my life such a lot easier.

CHAPTER SIX

Running to the Far East

m.v. Al Muharraq
17th November 1979 – 15th March 1980

I had a very pleasant relaxing leave after the *Al Farwaniah*. I went down to the office in Liverpool for a day for a debrief about the voyage and was nicely surprised to find they were very pleased with me and the way the voyage had gone. I reminded them that I always seemed to end up on the old wrecks with all their inevitable problems but it seemed I'd got a reputation for sorting out problems and I should take it as a compliment. I resigned myself to being stuck on the old Behzitsa class for a while to come. After my five months on the *Al Farwaniah* I was due about two and a half months leave and I was surprised to get an extra fortnight. It turned out that they had too many skippers on the books. My joining letter came through instructing me to join the *Al Muharraq* in Hong Kong on the 17th November. This was excellent as not only was the weather starting to turn really wintery at home but also the *Al Muharraq* was one of the newest ships in the company being less than six months old. A few days before I was due to leave one of the marine superintendents phoned me up and asked if I wouldn't mind taking some certificates out to the ship and he would post them to me before I left. He also congratulated me on getting one of the new K Class vessels but also for joining the 'flag ship'. I assumed that this meant that the *Al Muharraq* was the best ship in the fleet but was later to find out it was nothing of the sort.

I flew out to Hong Kong on the 16th November arriving there

about eight in the evening. I loved landing in Hong Kong as the airport is in the centre of the city and surrounded by mountains. It felt like we were flying down the main street as we came in to land. I assumed I would join the ship straight away but instead I was taken to a five star hotel on Hong Kong Island for the night. I was picked up from the airport in the hotel limousine, which was a white Rolls Royce. My room was huge with a fantastic view of the harbour and I could see the *Al Muharraq* moored to buoys loading from barges. I had just settled down when there was a knock at the door and it was a maid enquiring whether I would like anything to eat or drink. I opted for a seafood salad and some white wine. It arrived shortly afterwards and the salad was something else with lobster and all the trimmings and a bottle of chilled chardonnay that must have cost a fortune. I sat on the veranda consuming it and thought I could cope with a life like this all the time.

Next morning after a splendid breakfast I was taken out to the ship by launch. I relieved Andy Cameron and he gave me the impression that he couldn't get off soon enough. He left after lunch and I had a wander round to see what the 'flag ship' looked like. Everything looked brand new and it all seemed to be working. She had nearly finished the Far East load and only had Singapore to go before heading off to the Red Sea to discharge. Everything was looking good and then I started to meet the officers. There was a real mixture. The 1st mate and 2nd mate were Indian but of different castes and would hardly speak to each other. The 3rd mate was Bahraini and was by far the brightest of the bunch. The engineers were nearly all Indian and on top of that we had three Arab cadets who hated each other and seemed to go out of their way to make trouble. When I went down for the evening meal there was an atmosphere you could cut with a knife and absolutely no conversation apart from the Irish radio officer, who never stopped talking, ever. This had the makings of a great trip. I had an early night beginning to regret asking for this type of vessel.

We spent the next day loading cargo from barges. It seemed to be mostly clothing and footwear from Mainland China. We finished loading in the evening and sailed out into a full northerly gale. Luckily the wind was from astern but there was a huge swell and we were rolling around a lot. There were some ominous bangs and crashes from inside the hatches and I expected to see some damage but everything seemed all right when we got a chance to have a look around.

We arrived in Singapore three days later and berthed in the container port to load 30 containers. It should have taken a couple of hours but it became apparent that Steve, the 1st mate, hadn't a clue what was going on so it took over six hours and a lot of shouting and swearing before they were all on board and securely lashed. We then shifted into the middle of the harbour to anchor and load drums of chemicals and drilling equipment from barges. Thankfully this went smoothly and we sailed a few hours later. We were to discharge in three ports in the Red Sea – Jeddah, Hodeida in Yemen and Aqaba, which was right up in the north in Jordan. I'd only been to Jeddah before so these were new ports for me.

On the passage I found out why the *Al Muharraq* was called the 'flag ship'. It was not that it was the company's pride and joy at all. It appears that while she was loading in Japan some of the engineers met up with some officers off an Israeli ship whilst in a bar. They all adjourned to the Israeli ship to finish off the night's drinking and as our engineers were leaving they were given a bag containing Israeli pennants and flags and ashtrays with the Star of David on. When they got back on board, very much the worse for wear, they decided it would be a good idea to decorate our bar with all the flags etc. Needless to say it didn't go down very well with the Arab personnel on board who went straight ashore the next morning and phoned the head office in Kuwait. They responded by sending the captain a telex instructing him to sack anyone involved immediately and this resulted in him having to send two of his best engineers and an electrician home. The Arabs on board then took great delight in taunting the remaining officers so no wonder the ship had a bad atmosphere when I joined.

Two days before arrival at the first discharge port of Jeddah I received a message saying that four of the officers would be relieved on arrival and the three cadets were also to be paid off. This brightened me up considerably as there would be some new faces on board and we were getting rid of the cadets who really were a pain in the arse. After a fairly uneventful eleven days at sea we berthed in Jeddah on the 4th December and started discharge. The new officers joined and there was a definite improvement apart from the new 3rd mate who was Egyptian and was worse than useless. Steve, the 1st mate, suddenly improved and was actually pretty efficient and on the ball. I suspect it was because he was shortly to be relieved and was hoping for a good report.

The discharge went very quickly and only took four days with minimal problems. We sailed early in the morning on the 8th December and headed south towards Hodeida where we had to anchor off for a day awaiting a berth. I was very nervous entering as the channel was poorly charted and if we strayed outside the buoyed area we would be in danger of bouncing off coral reefs. The harbour itself was very shallow too but we managed to berth without mishap. I don't know where they got all the labour from but they flooded onto the ship and soon the cargo was flying out. I reckoned it would only take a couple of days at this rate but it didn't turn out that way. Whoever was supposed to organise the transport to take the cargo off the quay was a member of the 'Not Very Good Club'. After an hour the quay was full of cargo and we had to stop unloading. It took them about ten hours to clear the quay and then we filled it up again in a couple of hours. I could see us being here for months.

On the third day I received a visit from the commandant of the Yemeni naval base. He demanded that we use our heavy lift derrick to lift one of his patrol boats out of the water onto a barge so that they could paint the bottom. It was a real pain to change all the wires and winches round and I had no idea how we stood for insurance in case we dropped it so I told him there was no way. To be honest I didn't like his attitude either. The next day he reappeared with a telex from our head office in Kuwait instructing me to comply with all his requests or they wanted to know the reason why. We actually had loads of time to use our derrick while we were waiting for the labour to clear the quay. We ended up lifting five of his bloody boats on and off the barge. It was chaos and the naval personnel hadn't a clue. We ended up smashing off most of their radio antennas and at least two radar scanners but they were happy to get their boats painted.

The transport situation on the quay gradually improved and in the end we only took six days to discharge the cargo. On the last morning the naval commandant and two of his ratings carrying two small sacks of what appeared to be rice visited me. He came to thank me for lifting his boats. He also made a determined effort to drink all my whisky. He was very happy when he left and promised to commend my services to the company. I kicked the sacks under my settee and forgot about them.

We sailed on the morning of the 14th December and headed north towards Aqaba. I was just sitting down in my cabin and opening a pre-lunch beer when the ship heeled over violently and the main engine slowed drastically. This meant that the rudder was hard over and we were taking evasive action. I went tearing up to the bridge to find the ship going round in a tight circle with nothing else in sight. I took control and brought the ship back to her original course and asked the 3rd mate what the hell he was doing (or words to that effect). He explained he had seen a flock of seagulls dead ahead and they were standing not swimming and that seagulls didn't have very long legs so the water must be very shallow. When we looked through binoculars we could see they were standing on a sheet of plywood floating just below the surface. I was lost for words so just left him to finish off his watch while I enjoyed my cold beer.

The rest of the passage up the Red Sea was uneventful. Aqaba is situated at the very top of a narrow gulf at the top of the Red Sea. The entrance, called the Straits of Tiran, is really narrow with coral reefs right in the middle. This time it was quite an interesting trip as we passed through at midnight and the Egyptians for some reason had switched off all the navigational lights and beacons. It was a full moon, though, and we had good radars so I actually quite enjoyed conning the ship through. It was then about eight hours steaming up to Aqaba and we arrived on the morning of the 17th December. We had to anchor as all the berths were occupied and this again was a bit hairy. The sides of the Gulf were very steep so to get a decent anchorage we had to go very close to the shore. I had to anchor about 200 yards off the beach and just prayed that the wind kept blowing offshore.

We started discharging into barges the following morning and the agent came on board with the mail and lots of telexes demanding urgent replies to telexes sent to Hodeida, which we hadn't received. I had been pushing to get the chief and 2nd engineers relieved, as they were both useless and very disruptive. Instead I got a telex saying they were relieving the 1st mate, 2nd mate and an electrician. It seemed about par for the course. I organised myself a boat and went ashore to telephone the company as I felt that morale on board was bad enough without this pair undermining everything. I got through to Larry Blunt in personnel and he said he would relieve the chief engineer immediately and the 2ⁿᵈ as soon as possible so things started to brighten up especially when I found out that my new 1ˢᵗ mate was to be Mike Winkworth from the previous ship. The agent then insisted on taking me out for lunch where I had an absolutely delicious meal of huge prawns followed by some sort of goat stew with apricots and dates. This was washed down with a few ice-cold beers and I repaired back on board late in the afternoon fully at peace with the world.

The reliefs, including a new chief engineer, turned up two days later and immediately the atmosphere on board changed for the better. I'd also sailed with the new chief engineer before and although I didn't get on with him particularly well he was a cracking engineer. News came through that we were to load again in the Far East and the company wanted us to pick up some empty boxes (containers) in Aqaba before we left. The agent went into a mad panic as he was supposed to load about 50 boxes and he could only find two. On the last day they found us a berth alongside so we could load all these containers so we tied up in the port late in the afternoon. Eventually the agent managed to find ten, which we duly loaded. It actually suited us down to the ground as all the holds had heaps of timber and other debris from the previous cargo which would have taken ages to clear. We sailed early the next morning looking forward to a peaceful passage to the Far East and a nice quiet Christmas in the Indian Ocean.

But just as we cleared the Straits of Tiran the radio officer appeared with a message saying we had to divert into Jeddah on the way past and pick up some more boxes so we rushed around trying to clear the holds in readiness. We berthed in Jeddah just after breakfast on Christmas Eve and the agent there blithely told us we were to load 160 empty boxes, which is an awful lot for a general cargo vessel. We had just cleared enough space for about 50. I then had to organise some shore labour to help the crew clear some more space and thankfully they turned up quickly and actually did a really good job so by eleven o'clock we were ready to start loading. We loaded using shore container cranes so it went very quickly and by midnight we had them all loaded and lashed.

When the agent appeared with the papers it showed that the containers were manifested for Barcelona and he insisted that it was right. I was in a bit of a dilemma as I was instructed to go to the Far East and I had a cargo for Barcelona on board, which was in completely the other direction and it was now Christmas Day so it was doubtful whether I could get an answer from anyone. The other major factor was that if we remained in Jeddah for Christmas it would have to be 'dry' as the Saudi customs had locked away all our booze. It was a no brainer really and we sailed straight away and I headed south towards the Far East. We had a very quiet Christmas Day (with booze) but more enjoyable as morale on board was so much better. Even the 2nd engineer sorted himself out and even became an asset.

We eventually got a radio message two days later confirming that we were to proceed to Taiwan with the containers which was just as well as we were already 700 miles in the wrong direction if it had been Barcelona.

It was a great trip across the Indian Ocean with glassy seas and some fantastic sunsets. We passed the island of Minicoy and I altered course so we went in really close. I don't know how people could live there as nowhere looked more than a few feet above sea level. The beaches looked lovely though and some children came down and waved at us. When I looked at the echo sounder afterwards I got a bit of a shock as I was a lot closer than I intended. It would have been a nice place to be shipwrecked though.

We finally got instructions to discharge all the boxes in Keelung, in the north of the island of Taiwan and we berthed there on the 11th January. It took them half a day to unload the boxes and as our cargo wasn't ready in Japan we tied up to buoys in the middle of the harbour so we could undertake some annual surveys as the ship was now just over a year old. I was surprised how poor a state the ship was in, considering her age. We had problems with the emergency fire pump and other emergency equipment that should have been in tiptop condition. We passed the surveys all right in the end. It was miserable weather there with heavy rain all the time so nobody ventured ashore much especially as it involved a ferryboat. We sailed four days later for Nagoya in Japan.

The Japanese cargo was to be mainly steel products and we started off by loading some huge girders which went in very quickly and we sailed the next afternoon for Osaka. We'd just got up to full speed after dropping the Nagoya pilot when the main engine stopped without warning. I had to drop the anchor in a bit of a hurry as we were in serious danger of running ashore. I had a few choice words with the engineers for not warning me but I suppose they were pretty busy trying to sort things out. We got going again after an hour but ten minutes later it stopped again just as we were altering course to avoid a large ferry. It was quite close and all the passengers were waving and grinning but the ferry skipper was waving in an entirely different way. This time the engine restarted after a few minutes but I'd had enough and instead of travelling the usual ten miles off the coast I took us 20 miles off. It was a lot quieter with fewer fishing boats and a lot less traffic so I was able to go off for a quiet beer and then bed.

The rest of the load was uneventful calling at Osaka, Tokyo, Yokohama, Kobe and finishing off in Sasebo in south western Japan. We only had two days in each port so didn't get ashore much and on top of that the weather was atrocious being really cold with sleet and snow all the time. I was quite pleased to be sailing fully loaded from Sasebo early in February. The first part of the trip down the China Sea was pretty miserable, too, with a very strong north east monsoon and continuous rain but at least the wind was behind us so we weren't rolling around all over the place. Once we got to Singapore it all improved and it was lovely warm weather all the way back to the Arabian Gulf.

Just after we'd passed Singapore the chief engineer knocked on my door and calmly announced that we didn't have enough fuel to reach the Gulf especially if the first port was Kuwait, which was up at the top of the Gulf. The previous chief had supposedly worked it out and I'd accepted his figures. As I was digesting this the radio officer appeared with a message saying our first port was to be Kuwait. The words shit and fan came to mind. We sat down and worked out that if we reduced speed a little bit we just might make it. We slowed down a bit and waited for the company to question why we were going so slowly but thankfully nobody seemed to notice. So apart from worrying about the lack of fuel it was another lovely trip across the Indian Ocean.

Mike, the 1st mate, had coffee with me in my office most mornings and always pulled out one of the sacks I was given in Yemen to rest his feet on. One day he queried what was in them and I confessed I had no idea so Mike opened the corner of one of the bags and revealed some dull looking green beans. On closer examination he announced that it was, "Top bloody quality mocha coffee." The trouble was we had no way of roasting it on board so it was completely useless. When I left the ship for leave I managed to pack about six kilos into my luggage. I got it roasted in the coffee shop in Carlisle and after a bit of experimenting it turned out to be some of the nicest coffee I've ever tasted. I only wish I could have got more home.

Our strategy of travelling at reduced speed worked well and we arrived in Kuwait on the 27th February with enough fuel for at least one more day and no questions were asked. The discharge round the Gulf ports went without incident and Tom Weale relieved me on arrival in Dubai. It was good to see him again as he had been the first bloke I'd relieved when I joined the company five years earlier. I flew home on the 15th March with my suitcases bulging with mocha coffee beans.

CHAPTER SEVEN

Stuck in a war zone

m.v. Al Sabahiah
8th May 1980 – 20th November 1980

I had a very pleasant leave spending quite a lot of time in my vegetable garden planting things that would all come to fruition when I'd returned to sea. I have to admit that Diane had been slightly bemused by my suitcase full of coffee beans but when she tasted the coffee she was converted. I was due ten weeks leave but I was hoping for a couple of weeks longer as the company had an excess of captains. I was disappointed to get my joining letter the day my leave finished and even more disappointed to find I was going to do another trip on the *Al Sabahiah*. I had half expected it to have sunk by now. I had to fly out to Hong Kong to join her on the 5th May. It was a good flight out on Cathay Pacific with loads of room and good food. When I landed at ten o'clock in the morning I was told that the ship had been delayed by bad weather in Taiwan so I was booked into the five star Excelsior Hotel as per my previous trip. Again I was whisked from the airport to the hotel by white Rolls Royce. I was really looking forward to my little sojourn in Hong Kong. I arrived just in time for lunch so treated myself to a rather sumptuous meal overlooking the harbour. In the afternoon I took the ferry over to Kowloon and wandered round walking off my lunch and trying to figure out whether I could afford a new watch and camera from the duty free stores. When I got back to the hotel in the evening there was a message for me saying the ship wouldn't arrive for at least two days. I thought this was the way to start every voyage.

60

The *Al Sabahiah* eventually turned up three days later by which time I was actually starting to get bored. I'd spent quite a bit of money buying a new camera and a watch for Diane and done the usual touristy things of going to the top of the island by cable car. I'd also sampled most of the menu in the hotel restaurant and even had my own table by the window. Oddly enough the food that impressed me most was the French onion soup which was absolutely delicious – the lobsters and fillet steak weren't too bad either. One afternoon I was given a tour of the harbour in the agent's launch along with some local dignitaries. It was pretty cool with top quality champagne on tap and loads of food laid out. I was more than mellow when I got back to the hotel and even had to forego my evening meal.

I got on board the *Al Sabahiah* at eight in the morning on the 8th May to relieve Dave Griffiths. After getting the paperwork out of the way Dave showed me round. I couldn't believe that the ship was actually worse than when I'd last sailed on it. They were still having major problems with the main engine and the generators but now there were big problems on the deck with the steel hatch covers not closing properly and not being watertight. I just hoped we'd have a good passage to the Arabian Gulf without taking any seas on deck. Dave left after lunch to have a night in the Excelsior before flying home so I recommended the French onion soup.

The ship was just about fully loaded but it took two days to complete the load with lots of delays due to broken cranes and jammed hatch covers. We sailed after breakfast and headed off south down the China Sea. Luckily the weather was good and looked set fair at least until Singapore.

I always tried to get a bit of exercise by walking up and down on the Monkey Island. This is the top deck above the bridge and affords a good view all around the ship so I could see what was going on round the decks. On the third day I was ambling up and down and noticed a fishing boat on a collision course with us. The 2nd mate duly altered course to avoid it but the boat altered course back towards us. When it got closer we could see it was flying the signal flags NC that meant it required assistance so we stopped and allowed it to come alongside. It turned out to be a boatload of refugees from Vietnam trying to escape from the communist regime there. There were over 60 of them crowded on board and about half were women with small children. They looked surprisingly well considering they must have been at sea for over a week. It was our duty to pick them up even knowing they would cause us enormous problems when we tried to land them anywhere not to mention the delay to the ship and the expense. The company weren't going to be best pleased. When we had them tied alongside they shouted to ask what nationality the ship was. One of the Indian crew misunderstood and thought they were asking where the ship was built and shouted back, "Russia." The refugees' attitude changed immediately and they said they didn't want rescued after all. We gave them food, fresh water and fuel for their engine and off they went. I have no idea why they didn't want to board a Russian ship but it certainly saved me a lot of hassle and I resumed our passage with a clear conscience.

Despite being the time for the south west monsoon, which is usually bad weather in the Indian Ocean, we had a reasonable trip to Dubai, apart from numerous short stops to repair broken fuel pipes, and we arrived there a fortnight later on the 24th May. We had the usual discharge ports round the Gulf starting at Dubai followed by Dammam (Saudi Arabia), Kuwait, and finishing in Bandar Khomeini in Iran. Most of the cargo was for Bandar Khomeini and I'd heard so many bad reports about the place that I wasn't looking forward to it at all. Dubai started off all right, though, with only a few delays because of faulty cranes. Quite a few officers were relieved there, too, so there were some new faces aboard. We had two days in Dubai then it was off to Dammam where we only had one day and the discharge went very quickly using shore cranes. We nearly had a major oil spill whilst we were taking on fuel. A pipe that was used to see how much fuel was in a tank had become blocked and it was only the quick thinking of Keith Farrelly, the 3rd engineer, that saved us from pumping tons of fuel over the side. I think I'd still be in jail yet if it had happened as they always hold the master responsible.

After Damman it was up to Shuwayk in Kuwait. I was hoping for a quiet time but it was complete chaos for the five days we were there. All the Indian crew were relieved and we also had a safety survey and as the head office was close by we had various inspections by all and sundry. The only good thing that came out of it was that superintendents became aware of how bad a state the ship was in and they programmed a week in the nearby port of Shuaiba to try and affect some repairs after we had discharged. We sailed from Shuwayk on the 4th June – we would have sailed the previous evening but just as we prepared to sail there was a massive power cut which blacked out all the port and the navigation lights so we hung around all night until the power came back and eventually sailed at four in the morning.

It always surprised me how small the Gulf was because it only took twelve hours to cross over to the Iranian side so we arrived off the entrance to the Khor Musa River late in the afternoon. A pilot boarded the following morning and guided us up to Bandar Khomeini where we had to anchor as the port was congested. We remained at anchor and discharged our cargo into barges. The discharge was really efficient despite our cranes continually breaking down. In most Gulf ports the labour was from India or Pakistan and very inexperienced but here they were all Iranian and knew what they were about. I never felt completely comfortable in Iran as there were always squads of the Revolutionary Guards knocking around armed to the teeth and looking very menacing. I was never actually challenged or threatened but still, it never felt safe. I was glad when we completed cargo and sailed early in the morning on the 11th June.

Again it was just a short passage across to the Kuwaiti port of Shuaiba where we were scheduled to spend ten days sorting out all our repairs with the help of shore labour. It didn't start off too well as nobody came near us for the first day in port and the second day was a Friday which was a holiday. Eventually the superintendents arrived on the Saturday morning accompanied by gangs of engineers and fitters. Work progressed at a good pace but it was becoming apparent that quite a lot of equipment was in a pretty bad state and required spare parts that weren't available in the Gulf.

At least it felt as though things were improving as we had the air-conditioning system working again after being off for three weeks and we had a constant supply of fresh water to the taps.

Ten days later we had an engine trial and as it was satisfactory we sailed the following morning to load the next cargo in the Mediterranean. After twelve hours at sea it became apparent that the main engine was not in the best of health. One of the cylinders was moving around all over the place and we were using a lot of cooling water. I was getting very concerned as we would run out of fresh water well before we reached Suez. It was all resolved when I was woken by the chief engineer at two the following morning to be told that one of the tie bolts that held the engine together had broken completely so we'd have to put into the nearest port. We slowed down to half speed and headed towards Dubai. Just before we got there we received a message from head office telling us to divert to Sharjah, which was 30 miles down the coast. We arrived there in the evening and secured alongside.

The following morning one of the superintendents arrived from Kuwait and started organising the repairs. In the afternoon I was approached by a delegation of six of the officers all requesting to be relieved before the ship sailed. I had thought morale was reasonably high, considering, but they were all fed up with everything breaking down all the time and just wanted off. I forwarded their request to head office and unsurprisingly they were told that if they left they would be considered as having resigned from the company so it all went quiet. Head office also let me know that they were relieving the chief engineer, as he was ineffectual, and sending out Norman Hatton, who was a real live wire. He arrived the following day and I could see an immediate lift in morale in the engine room staff. Repairs were completed on the 29th June and we resumed our passage towards Suez. It was back to normal on the second day when the evaporator failed and we were unable to make any fresh water so we had to go back on water rationing.

We staggered our way up towards Suez with the steering gear breaking down every day and the radar only working intermittently. I was hopeful of filling up with fresh water at Suez but for once the authorities were highly efficient and we passed through without stopping. I figured it out that we could just reach Barcelona, which was the farthest Mediterranean port, before our water ran out.

Once we'd cleared Suez I cabled the company to ask what our first port was to be only to be told we had been withdrawn from service and were to proceed to Antwerp for permanent repairs. The company weren't at all happy when I said I'd have to divert into Gibraltar for water but they agreed so we stopped off on the way past and picked up a 100 tons of fresh water so at least we could shower again. After that it was quite a leisurely passage up to Antwerp as our berth wasn't available until the 22nd July. The radar decided to give up the ghost completely just as we got into the heaviest traffic in the Dover Strait and that made life interesting for a while but we got through without hitting anything. We berthed in a repair berth early morning on the 22nd and were greeted by Malcolm

Hedley, one of the engineering superintendents, who had been given the task of making us seaworthy again.

We ended up spending a very pleasant three weeks in Antwerp. The ship was swarming with engineers and technicians dismantling and repairing everything. At last it looked like the *Al Sabahiah* would leave Antwerp in good seaworthy condition. I got my wife, Diane, over for ten days as the weather was lovely. We managed to have a few days out and even got in a trip down to Bruges. The local agent was quite a character and he spent his time trying to educate Diane on the different cheeses available in Belgium. He brought a different cheese down to sample every day. Diane also bought a fair bit of fresh fruit when she was ashore so between them they used to drive my steward to distraction. Normally the only thing in my fridge was beer with the odd coke or tonic but when the steward brought up a case of beer for me the fridge was now full of cheese and fruit and even the odd cake. Parshotem (the steward), after a deep sorrowful sigh, could spend up to 20 minutes rearranging everything so it would all go in as he didn't want to upset me or my memsahib. It kept Diane amused and she asked to be there every time I ordered a case of beer.

There were quite a few officer changes so when we came to leave on the 16th August we had an efficient ship with a happy crew so I was quite looking forward to the remainder of the voyage. Our loading ports were to be Hamburg, Bremen, Rotterdam and finish off in Venice. I think the company must have been struggling to find a cargo as we were only scheduled to pick up about 6,000 tons when our full load was 14,000 tons. Most of the cargo was for Basrah in Iraq with only about 500 tons for Kuwait.

We started off loading in Hamburg and they managed to load about 4,000 tons of structural steel in two days, which was very impressive. It was then down to Bremen and Rotterdam where we loaded another 1,000 tons of construction materials and bags of fertiliser. Not the most interesting of cargoes but at least it was easy to load. We finished off with pallets of empty soft drink bottles to be offloaded in Kuwait. I was really looking forward to a couple of days loading in Venice but it was cancelled just as we left Rotterdam and we set off back towards the Gulf at the end of August.

Things went very well to start with but as we were going down the Channel the evaporator packed in yet again so we were not

65

making any fresh water and it looked like back to water rationing yet again. At least we had plenty of beer to drink as for some reason the company had supplied us with twice the normal amount. We passed through the Suez Canal with no problem but had to wait a day to be supplied with fresh water by barge. I was determined not to run out this time. The engineers finally got the evaporator working again a day after Suez so we ended up with loads of water in the end.

We arrived off Shuwayk Port in Kuwait on the 15th September but as we only had the pallets of empty bottles they put us to anchor and we discharged into barges. This only took a day and then we set off north to the entrance to the Shatt al Arab River to head up to Basrah. While we were in Kuwait we kept hearing news of the possibility of war between Iraq and Iran but head office assured us nothing would happen. The Iraqi pilot boarded to take us up the river and he was very nervous. It turned out the Iranians had been lobbing shells at ships on the river the day before though luckily they had all missed. There were certain sections of the river where ships had to pass at reduced speed to avoid erosion of the banks but we went flying up all the way at full speed and did the river passage in record time.

We berthed alongside in Basrah at noon on the 29th September. Everything seemed pretty normal with no signs of preparation for war or anything so we relaxed a bit and they started the discharge. When we got up the following morning we found the Iraqi navy had anchored some of its warships in the middle of the river and there were two anti-aircraft guns positioned along the quay. This wasn't looking good. The day progressed quite peacefully, actually, but I was unable to speak to anyone who knew exactly what was happening. Just before tea the air raid sirens went off and all hell let loose. All the labour ran off the ship leaving loads hanging in the air and every anti-aircraft gun in the vicinity started firing. The noise was unbelievable. It was total chaos as they were all firing in different directions and some of the shells went quite close over the ships moored alongside. After half an hour they got bored and the firing petered out. We had to make the ship safe and unhook the loads and close the hatches. The Indian crew refused to go on deck and demanded to be paid off and sent home, so the officers had to go and sort the decks out. I didn't know where I stood, as if I ordered the crew on deck and a bomb fell on one of them I wouldn't be too popular. We then were told to blackout the ship in case there were any night time raids. We didn't take it too seriously but when we were told that the guards had instructions to shoot out any visible lights we made a more determined effort.

It turned out to be a quiet night with no air raid warnings and the labour boarded again and resumed discharge at seven in the morning. An hour later there was an air raid warning and they all disappeared ashore only to return half an hour later and resume work. It went on like this all day and I could see us being stuck in Basrah for a long time. Just after three o'clock we were stood on deck watching a jet flying over the port in slow circles. Nobody was taking much interest in it until it casually dropped a bomb on the oil refinery quarter of a mile away. It was a direct hit and the refinery went up with a series of explosions and huge flames. Of course that set off all the anti-aircraft guns again but the plane just flew off in an easterly direction leaving the refinery blazing merrily.

The next day we managed to discharge only 20 tons leaving over 5,000 still on board. It was going to be a really long stay. There were warnings every hour or so and in the end we were confused as to whether it was a warning or the all clear. The refinery had turned into a huge blaze as the fire spread from storage tank to storage tank so it made a terrific target for the Iranian jets and the fact that we were not too far away was a bit disconcerting. The following day was the same again except we didn't discharge anything at all. At ten o'clock at night there was another air raid warning and we could hear aircraft flying overhead. We went outside to watch and it was pretty spectacular with all the guns firing and arcs of tracer going everywhere. When we got up the following morning the decks were covered in bits of shrapnel from the shells and some of it was quite big. We never ventured out again. The ship astern of us had a great big hole in one of its lifeboats where a shell had passed through.

I must admit I was getting a bit concerned at this stage and there was absolutely no information from our Iraqi agent. Apart from the first day he hadn't appeared so I decided to take a trip to his office. I was stopped at roadblocks numerous times but eventually found his office. He was useless and knew nothing at all about the situation so I tried phoning our head office in Kuwait but it was impossible to make a call to outside the country so I was obviously on my own. As I was about to leave a telex came in saying that the *Ibn al Haitham*, another of the company ships, had been hit by a rocket whilst in the

Iraqi port of Umm Qasr and one of the crew had been killed. The whole crew had been immediately repatriated back to Kuwait. I sent the company a quick telex explaining our situation and asking, "What about us?" but got no reply so I got a taxi back to the ship. When I got there a lorry had arrived from the *Ibn al Haitham* with all their perishable food, as they had no power to keep it cold. Most of it was unusable as it had all defrosted on the trip from Umm Qasr. My Indian crew had found out about the rocket attack and I was confronted by a large delegation demanding to be repatriated immediately. When I explained I couldn't contact the company they all went on strike and refused to work. Great. The cooks decided they would cook us meals but nothing else so at least we wouldn't starve.

Next day I made another trip to the agent's office and this time I managed to phone the head office. They were unaware of our situation and thought we were happily discharging away. They said it would all die down and things would be back to normal in a couple of days and told me our next port was to be Shuaiba in Kuwait. I was slightly reassured but as I got back to the ship two Iranian jets tried to take out the bridge over the river. They missed the bridge and all their bombs fell in the water and the only casualty was a solitary fisherman who had been fishing from a little boat in the middle of the river. The bridge was only about half a mile upstream from us so things were looking a bit dodgy and the crew were getting decidedly agitated. That evening I was visited by the skipper of a Norwegian ship moored astern of us. He had been told that a ship had been sunk in the river thereby blocking our way out. His consulate was organising the whole crew's repatriation as soon as possible. At least someone was looking out for them!

The following day it was up the agent's office again and I managed to phone head office. I talked to the Gulf controller, John Farmery, and got him to agree a reduction in crew to a minimum so we arranged a bus to take them overland to Kuwait the following day. I could already see a problem in deciding who had to remain but John said that Basrah had been declared a war zone so we were all on double pay which might change some people's attitudes. I got a taxi back to the ship and on the way back saw the Iraqi bomb disposal squad in operation. A bomb had landed in a building just off the main boulevard completely destroying it but without exploding and the tail fin was clearly visible sticking out of the rubble. A team of locals were attempting to extricate it by pulling it out on a long wire attached to a bulldozer. No attempt was being made to clear the area and I was more than pleased to get past safely.

When I got back to the ship with the news of the crew reduction there was a clear-cut division. All the officers wanted to remain and the entire crew wanted to go home. With a bit of bribery and promises of promotion we managed to get enough crew to remain. I then spent the rest of the day frantically doing accounts so the crew could be paid off the following day.

The next day was somewhat stressful as there was no news from our agent or the company and half the crew were standing at the top of the gangway with their bags all packed. It wasn't until three o'clock that a coach arrived to take them to Kuwait and then we had big problems with the local customs and immigration. Luckily I had a locker full of cigarettes and bottles of whisky so that problem was quickly resolved and the coach left late in the afternoon. That night was quiet because there seemed very few of us left but we had unlimited supplies of beer and food and the Iranians seemed to have given up bombing the port.

The discharge was still going on at a very slow pace and after ten days in port we had unloaded less than half of the cargo. At least there was something to keep us occupied.

On 4th October it started to get exciting again. During the night we could see flashes of light and heard huge explosions some distance away on the other side of the river. Then mid morning two aircraft tried to bomb the bridge again. The Iraqis had upped their game and they managed to shoot one of them down. A missile hit one of the aircraft and it came down on the other side of the river. We were beginning to wonder whether it was a good idea to be staying, though I didn't have the option. At least it improved our discharge rate as the stevedores had decided the docks were not a good place to be. My biggest problem was trying to get rid of all our garbage which was mounting up on the after deck. Not only was it our stuff but we had all the condemned meat and fish off the *Ibn Al Haitham* and it was beginning to smell really bad. Eventually after some bottles of whisky and a few cartons of cigarettes changed hands a lorry appeared. It was a horrible job getting it all onto the lorry but we got it done and the decks washed off. The lorry drove 100 yards down the quay and then tipped the lot into the river – so much for the environment!

The next week was uneventful apart from the Iranians bombing the power station and some storage tanks. 90 per cent of their bombs failed to explode and it was the physical damage caused when the bombs hit anything. Just as well I suppose. The discharge was completed on the 17th October so I blithely requested my sailing instructions from the harbour master. I was told there were no pilots and on top of that the river was blocked at a place called Devil's Gap by a burnt out Yugoslav vessel so we were going nowhere. I managed to get a telex to that effect off to head office and actually received a reply saying that the company was keeping our families informed and if the situation got really bad they would relieve us all. We did feel a bit isolated as no mail was getting through and there were no telephone lines available out of the country.

Now the cargo was unloaded there was very little to do as there didn't seem any point in trying to do any maintenance as the ship was going to be stuck here for a long time. We started to make a half hearted attempt to clean the hatches but ended up sitting on the hatch tops in the sun drinking beer and watching a couple of roller birds who had taken up residence in a hole in the main mast. They were a kingfisher blue colour and brilliant fliers and regularly looped the loop as they returned to their nest. In the evening a few of us would walk the mile or so up the road to the Shatt al Arab Hotel as we'd heard a rumour it was possible to phone home from there but it turned out to be false. It was a splendid old place built as part of the old Basrah airport. It was all art deco and the only bit open was a huge bar overlooking the runway. We were usually the only customers and the beer was awful. The barman showed us round the place one evening and it was easy to imagine what it had once been like. The control tower for the airport was built onto the roof. I'd have loved to be there when it was all going on.

After four days of lying idle the harbour master came on board and insisted we shift astern and tie up alongside another ship, as the Iraqi navy wanted our berth. I later found out that we were about the only ship with enough personnel to be able to shift. We moved back in the afternoon and tied up alongside a Greek ship which was deserted. It wasn't good as it was filthy and infested with rats and we had to climb over it to get ashore. Life was becoming a bit of drag as it had all gone quiet on the war front again.

We were visited by some Iraqi naval officers and representatives of the Red Cross who said they were arranging to sail us down the river flying the Red Cross flag. We didn't fancy the idea unless it was an absolutely huge flag. They invited me and the chief engineer ashore for a meal that evening. They were obviously on expenses as we went to this really suave place down by the river. It was looking a bit down at heel but the food was good. One corner was boarded off and several of the windows had holes in them. When we asked what had happened it turned out a couple of army officers had got drunk the previous night and had a shoot out with each other. I think one of them was killed. We decided not to return again if asked.

Over the next few days we had a wander round the port looking at the other ships and about half of them had been abandoned completely and some of them actually looked like they were sinking. We had just got back from one of our forays when we had a surprise visit by Said Noffal, one of our superintendents who had driven from Kuwait. He brought a great heap of mail with him so it was nice to catch up with things at home. He had a look round and decided it was pointless us having so many crew when all the ship really needed was someone to prevent any vandalism. It was decided that for the time being I would remain along with the 1st mate, chief engineer, 4th engineer, chief steward and any crew who wanted to stay. Two days later I paid off the extra officers and crew and they left in a minibus to Kuwait. It then got really quiet on board with just the few of us left. The Iranians had a few goes at the township of Basrah itself and every day there were loud explosions and clouds of smoke coming from the city area.

We were supposed to do tours of five months on board and as I was now coming up to six months I started agitating to get off but couldn't see anybody volunteering to come and relieve me and I was most surprised when a telex came through on the 7th November saying that they were trying to relieve me and Harry Martin, the chief steward, in a week's time. This was followed the next day by another telex to say it had all been cancelled as the Iraqis had refused permission for the new blokes to enter Iraq. Not good at all.

At least things were quietening down on the war front but we were bored out our minds. The big excitement of the day was our amble up to the Shatt Al Arab Hotel. There was very little going on in the port and more and more of the ships were being abandoned.

On the way back one evening John, the 4th engineer got talking to a couple of Iraqi girls who said they were telephonists at a local exchange and if we had any soap or shampoo they could arrange calls to the UK. As it happened we had a huge stock of good quality Lux soap on board so off he went the next night with a bag full. Half was immediately confiscated by the local customs at the gate but he managed to find the exchange and returned and hour later having had half an hour's conversation with his wife over a perfect line. Of course we all piled up the road the next day and all managed to phone home. It was good to talk to Diane and she had been told I would be home within a week so obviously the company was trying to do something.

With most of the ships on skeleton crews I decided to acquire something from of one of them as a souvenir. I tried three or four without luck. On my last try the skipper on a Yugoslav ship said he had sold the chronometer a couple of days ago but there was a really nice Plath barograph going. It was in really good condition so after a bit of bartering I left with the barograph but two bottles of whisky lighter. It took quite a bit of packing to get it into my suitcase when I came to fly home and I was bothered that taking it up to 30,000 feet might damage the mechanism but it was all right in the end.

We got another telex on the 15th November and it appeared that the company had got visas for the relieving skipper and chief steward and we would be taken off the ship on the 20th and driven by road to Kuwait and then fly home. I felt a bit guilty about leaving the others on board but there seemed very little danger now and there was still a mountain of beer to consume. John Gregson appeared on the morning of the 20th and after a very quick handover I took his transport back to Kuwait. I had a night in a hotel in Kuwait and had to go into the head office to debrief about the situation in Basrah. I think they decided to abandon the ship in the near future after hearing my tale so at least the lads on board would be getting off soon. I was also given my war bonus in cash so I ended up with a large envelope with £4,000 in £20 notes. I was sure I was going to get mugged on the way home but I got there safely and blew it all on a brand new red Ford Capri so I suppose it was all worth it in the end. I was looking forward to a nice peaceful leave and Christmas at home.

CHAPTER EIGHT

First box boat

m.v Al Shamiah
23rd January 1981 - 29th March 1981

A week after I got home I was called down to the Liverpool office for two days for a full debriefing on the situation in Iraq. They were surprised that we were so close to the action and had no idea that we were in any danger. I must admit to exaggerating a bit and at one stage I hoped I might to get an extra bonus which would have meant a bigger engine in the Capri. I thought at least I would get some extra leave out of it

Kuwait Shipping Company had decided that they needed some containerships, as that was obviously the way forward. For some reason best known to themselves instead of building some brand new vessels they opted to convert three of their oldest Russian built general cargo ships at a shipyard in Spain. They cut out the middle section of the hull and fitted a completely new piece configured for containers. It was a complete disaster as they kept the stern with the main engine and generators, which were already in a poor state. The conversion took well over a year and went way over budget but the company could now say they had three containerships and they were put to work trading between the United States and the Arabian Gulf. I had no real experience with containers but I could see which way the trade was heading so I put my name forward for a trip on one of the box boats as they were known.

I had a pleasant leave over Christmas although we got snowed in two or three times. In fact once I nearly got snowed out when I went into town with my daughter to pick her Christmas present and got stuck on the way back but we made it in the end. About halfway through my leave I got a nasty shock in the shape of a letter from the taxman asking about my war bonus. As I'd received it in cash in Kuwait I'd figured I didn't need to declare it but the taxman had other ideas. This letter was followed by one from our Liverpool office saying they had declared all bonuses paid to staff to the UK tax authorities. It was obvious that I was going to have to admit the payment and pay the tax, which was a bit of a bugger as all the money was now in the shape of my shiny new red car sitting on the drive. I then got a call from the office to say that Trevor Williams, the skipper on the containership *Al Shamiah*, wanted a relief for two months and would I go.

Although I still had six weeks leave outstanding the weather at home was still bad and, now with a large tax bill looming, I decided this was a good idea. Two days before I was due to leave I received another letter from the taxman which I opened with great trepidation. To my amazement it was from a different tax office saying that I had passed all the criteria for claiming my tax back for the previous twelve months and enclosing a sizeable cheque. I could have had the bigger engine in the Capri after all. I quickly drafted a letter to the original tax office saying that as I knew I wasn't going to pay any tax I hadn't declared the bonus to reduce the paperwork. I got a letter later on saying that it didn't work like that and in future I must declare all bonuses and they would be watching me.

I ended up flying out to Savannah to join the *Al Shamiah* on the 22nd January. I flew out with Pete Walley the 1st mate, Ray Rele the chief engineer and Les Hartney the radio officer who were all rejoining after leave. We also had Ron Crennell, the company's marine superintendent, with us, as it appeared there were numerous problems with the lashings that secured the containers on deck. We were a day early so they put us up in an hotel for the night. It looked like being a cracking night with free booze and lovely food but having the superintendent, who didn't drink, with us it rather put a damper on the evening and we all retired to bed early.

The *Al Shamiah* had berthed during the night so we all bowled aboard just after breakfast. The ship had only been in five hours and they had already completed cargo operations and we sailed an hour later. Trevor Williams decided to stay on board to explain all the problems to the superintendent so I had a peaceful two days, as we made our way up the coast, to look around and acquaint myself with the ship. I was really disappointed as I was expecting everything to be in tip top condition after the big refit but the ship seemed to be falling apart. There were major problems in the engineroom and most of the navigational equipment seemed to have faults. We berthed in Norfolk the following day and completed the cargo work in four hours. Trevor still hadn't managed to explain all the faults to the superintendent so he decided to stay on up to the next port, Baltimore. I was getting a bit fed up by now as I was stuck in a tiny spare cabin and felt completely out of the loop.

We berthed in Baltimore on the 25th January and for once had over five hours in port as only one container crane was in operation. Trevor, Ron Crennell and I got taken out for a rather splendid seafood lunch where I was introduced to Maryland crab cakes, which must be my favourite food ever. I made a bit of a pig of myself and also downed one or two more cold beers than I should have much to the disapproval of Ron. We got back on board to find that all the cargo was loaded and the ship was just about ready to sail. Trevor decided he hadn't enough time to get off so he opted to stay on until the next port which was Newark, which suited me as I'd slightly overdone the beer and wasn't really in a fit state. I also didn't blot my copy book with Ron either as I still had no responsibilities on board.

We berthed in Newark early in the morning on the 28th January and Trevor finally handed over to me. I read down the list of equipment and machinery that required repair and could see I was going to be in for one of 'those' trips. We completed cargo operations at nine in the evening and were told we had to vacate the berth immediately as it was required for another vessel. The main engine was in pieces so we had to hire tugs to move. It was blowing a howling gale with horizontal sleet but the tugs did a great job and we were soon secure in a lay-by berth. The next day was a flurry of activity on board with numerous shore engineers and technicians repairing various items of equipment. They got a surprising amount done and I was getting hopeful of a trouble free passage.

We sailed for the Suez Canal in the evening and when I checked the weather forecast was pleasantly surprised to see very few depressions around so it had the makings of a decent Atlantic crossing. Ron Crennell had decided to travel with us to Suez as he wanted to see how the deck container lashing system performed. I've a feeling he just wanted to escape from the office for a while and have a peaceful cruise. I was certainly going to have to watch my Ps and Qs. Despite there being very little wind there was quite a heavy swell running from the north and I was surprised how much the ship rolled. I had to keep adjusting the course and speed to ease the rolling.

The deck containers were secured to the deck and to each other with a device called a twist lock. The containers were stowed three high on deck and the top layer was fastened down with long iron bars. All the lashing equipment had been made in Spain when the ship was converted and they had obviously used very poor quality steel as the bars broke very easily as soon as any strain came on them. After three days of rolling the bars were failing at an alarming rate and although we'd received some new bars in the States we were rapidly running out of spares.

The following day we had to stop for an hour to repair the steering gear and do some work on the main engine and when we stopped the ship lay beam on to the swell and started rolling really heavily to about thirty degrees and we were unable to do anything about it until the repairs were finished. We could also hear the cargo inside the containers crashing around so some of it wasn't going to be in good condition when we unloaded it. I went on deck with Pete, the 1st mate, and was shocked to see the stacks of containers swaying alarmingly. I was sure some were going to fall over the side and it was really frightening seeing those containers that weighed up to 20 tons each crashing and banging around. We tried securing them with steel wires and clamps but it was too dangerous and had to give up. Thankfully the repairs didn't take as long as expected and we were able to start up again after 40 minutes. I turned the ship into the swell so we weren't rolling and we spent the next four hours lashing the containers down with anything we could find. When we resumed our course nothing was moving and by the next day the swell died down and the rolling eased. The good thing about the episode was that Ron Crennell had witnessed the performance and he dispatched a telegram to arrange stocks of the bars to be available to us in the next port.

After we passed through the Straits of Gibraltar the weather improved although the engineers were having problems with the fuel system on the main engine. We had to keep stopping to repair leaking pipes, which was a bit of a nuisance. We arrived at the north end of the Suez Canal on Friday 13th February, which didn't bode well, but we passed through very quickly and without any problems. I discovered one advantage of being on a containership was that they got priority and went through the Canal at the head of the convoy and when we got out of the other end we were ahead of everybody and didn't have the hassle of trying to overtake slower ships in the Gulf of Suez. Ron Crennell got off and flew home weighed down with all our mail.

Next stop was Jeddah where we had to anchor for a day waiting for a berth. Once we got alongside the cargo only took five hours to complete and it would have taken less if we hadn't had an argument with an over-enthusiastic Saudi customs officer. He said that the labels on our containers indicating they contained hazardous cargo were too small even though they were the international regulation size. We eventually obtained some of the Saudi regulation size but we weren't allowed on the quay to stick them on. We had to reload the containers at great expense and take them on to the next port. This was despite Pete, the 1st mate, quickly sticking our new labels on when the containers were loaded on board.

We sailed early in the morning on the 16th February and headed south. Ray, the chief engineer, was getting really worried about the main engine and showed me a list of defects. It covered two pages and I was beginning to wonder how it was working at all. We made a radio telephone call to head office and were assured that all would be sorted when we got to the Gulf and they had repair gangs waiting. All we had to do was get there! We travelled at reduced speed and with more bits falling off every day. We actually did quite a good speed, considering, because the weather was in our favour. We even had to slow down on the last day as we were ahead of schedule.

We berthed in Dubai at two in the morning on the 22nd February and started cargo operations immediately. Thankfully the company had taken notice of our problems and gangs of shore engineers boarded on arrival and started work repairing the engine. One of the biggest problems was the fuel oil heater, which had more or less disintegrated and required replacement. The main engine ran on heavy oil, which was heated to make it less dense. If we didn't have the heater we would have to run on diesel oil which cost four times as much and anyway we didn't have enough space to carry diesel. I could see there was going to be a huge delay which would cause problems as there was another containership due on our berth at five o'clock. Unbelievably they managed to fit the new heater and have it up and running just as we finished discharging. We had a mad rush getting all the engineers and their equipment off and sailed on time.

It was then an 18 hour trip up to Dammam in Saudi Arabia where again we went straight alongside and started cargo immediately. The unloading took less than four hours though we had to stay in port for an extra two hours while we took on fuel then it was off up to Kuwait at the top of the Gulf. We arrived on Kuwaiti National Day so it was a big local holiday with no work. It gave me time to catch my breath.

I hadn't realised that containerships were so different from the conventional general cargo vessels that I was used to. Firstly everything was scheduled for weeks in advance and any delay could have a huge knock-on affect costing a lot of money. There was minimal time in port so there was no going ashore or socialising as there were no breaks and we had to be sober (more or less) and on the ball all the time. The other thing that I missed was organising the stowage of the cargo. It was now all in coloured metal boxes and we had very little idea of the contents. The stowage of the cargo was all done in offices ashore though we had to check the plans as they were always trying to put extra heavy or hazardous containers where they shouldn't. The plus side of being on the box boats was that the cargo was always clean and therefore the ships were generally a lot cleaner and tidier. The other plus was that the trips were a lot shorter as it was recognised that work on board was a lot more intensive and stressful. I was now halfway through my first trip and couldn't decide yet whether I wanted to stay on the box boats or return to general cargo.

Cargo work started the next morning and it was a lot slower than previous ports. Kuwait didn't have a dedicated container berth with gantry cranes but just unloaded the containers using conventional cranes, which involved labourers climbing around hooking the boxes on. It took twice as long as the gantry cranes with their automated hooking system. At least it gave us some time to do further repairs in the engineroom.

78

Two of the engineer superintendents came on board to look round the engineroom and were somewhat shocked at the state of everything. We pointed out that we were on a fixed schedule and couldn't afford to be breaking down all over the place so after much discussion it was decided we would stop off in Sharjah at the bottom of the Gulf for three days and get the major repairs done. I couldn't see us getting much done in three days but at least it was a start.

We eventually sailed from Kuwait on the 27th February having achieved very little apart from unloading the full containers and refilling ourselves with empty ones. Our next port was a tiny little place called Ras al Mishab on the Kuwaiti/Saudi Arabian border. It had only been open a few months and was just a jetty sticking out into the sea to service a new oil refinery that had been built there. It only took us five hours to get there. As we approached the berth the wind suddenly started blowing hard onto the shore and as there were no tugs available I decided discretion was the better option and anchored until the wind eased. It took twelve hours before I decided it was safe enough to berth and we finally tied up at eight in the morning. Like Kuwait they didn't have a container gantry so although we only had about 30 containers to discharge it took over a day. All this time lost was coming off our repair time in Sharjah so we were pushing them to hurry all the time. Just as everything was looking good we found four heavy containers which should have been discharged in Kuwait. We had to tear around to get permission to land them and organise the company to send transport down to come and pick them up. By this time it was too dark to sail as they hadn't got round to fitting navigational lights in the port so we had to wait until six the following morning before we could leave. We then scurried down the Gulf and berthed in Sharjah early on 3rd March.

As we suspected, our repair time had been shortened by a day but at least the company had organised a large gang of shore engineers to assist and two truckloads of spare parts arrived. As containerships have no cranes and very little deck machinery I found myself with not much to do apart from finishing up the previous month's accounts, which didn't seem to balance.

On the second day I was invited ashore by the harbour master, Abdul Wahab, for a meal and a drive along the coast. We went up to a small port called Ras al Khaimah where they were building dhows using traditional means. All the frames and planks were shaped by hand using an adze, which must have been razor sharp. There were several shipwrights standing on a huge piece of timber and shaping it into a keel. I don't know how they didn't chop their feet off but I did notice several of them were a couple of toes short. It was absolutely fascinating and I could have stayed for hours. He then took me to his home where his wife had cooked up a delicious lamb stew with some sort of fragrant rice. It was then back to the ship stopping off for a couple of cold beers in one of the many British style pubs that were opening all over the place. Not a bad way to spend a day at all. When I got back on board I did feel somewhat guilty as all the engineers were sitting on deck having a well-earned beer and they were absolutely knackered. They were also filthy, as they had to change a turbo charger rotor and were covered in a mixture of carbon and oil.

We had to sail early the next morning to try to keep up with our schedule. The chief engineer was still pretty unhappy about the state of the engine but off we went towards Suez. The ship did seem to have a better feel about it and now we were a lot lighter as we were only carrying empty containers and we motored along at a pretty good speed. Two days before Suez the engine started to give problems again. The scavenge, which is where the engine exhausts into, kept catching fire. Unburnt fuel and lubricating oil were getting in somehow. We had to slow down drastically to put it out every time it caught fire. It looked really spectacular at night with a huge spout of flames and sparks shooting out of the funnel. We managed to get to Suez on time despite the speed reductions but obviously we were going to have problems on the passage to the States.

We passed through Suez early in March without too much trouble. The pilot complained that the containers were too high and he couldn't see where he was going. He threatened to stop the ship until he could have a second pilot to assist him. It cost me two bottles of whisky and a carton of cigarettes to dissuade him. After that everything went smoothly and we cleared the northern end at ten in the evening. The next day went well with only one minor fire so I was beginning to hope for a good passage.

It was not to be. The next day we had four fires so it was obviously getting worse and then at midnight we had a serious fire. It was getting to the stage where the whole engine might catch fire and it took quite a bit of extinguishing. The engineers had decided that number four cylinder was the problem so we stopped and dismantled the engine to see what we could find. The piston was completely knackered with all the rings destroyed and the inside of the cylinder was also very badly scored. We replaced the piston with a spare and were underway again in less than twelve hours but it meant we had to have a really good passage to arrive in Savannah on time. We passed through the Straits of Gibraltar the next morning and I couldn't believe the amount of traffic. A Greek bulk carrier going the wrong way through the separation zones didn't help and we had to reduce speed for quite a while until everything cleared.

Once clear of the Straits the weather deteriorated and we started rolling around quite a bit. At least all the containers were empty so we didn't have any problems with the lashing bars breaking. The wind and seas then swung round to the west so we were heading directly into the weather and although the rolling eased we started pitching heavily so I had to reduce speed to avoid any damage. The following morning there was a fire on the ship's main switchboard and even though we put it out quickly some breakers were damaged and required replacing. We were stopped for two hours while the electricians sorted things out and when we restarted number six cylinder on the main engine started overheating drastically and we had to slow down numerous times while the engineers tried to figure out the problem. At this stage I gave up hope of arriving on time and sent messages off to all and sundry telling them we'd be a day late getting to Savannah. It wasn't well received and we got a terse message back saying we could expect to anchor for two days until a suitable slot was available on the container berth. I also got a message from the company saying Trevor was rejoining and I was being relieved on arrival in Savannah. I was hoping the two messages weren't connected.

I've always taken a keen interest in the weather and I was over the moon on the *Al Shamiah* as she had a weather fax machine, which received detailed weather maps from The States and UK every four hours. It paid off many times, as I was able to adjust the course and avoid the deep depressions and save much wear and tear on the ship. I had been watching a really deep depression developing way down south and hoping it would head off into the Caribbean but ominously it turned north and was on a collision course for us. I immediately altered course to the south to avoid it. I'm sure the other officers thought I was overreacting especially as it would add more time to the passage. I was vindicated when the depression was upgraded to a full-blown hurricane. We experienced winds of only gale force eight while ships stuck in the storm were having violent storm force eleven. There was a pretty big swell but it wasn't too uncomfortable. I then had to send off amended arrivals times again but this time there were no replies.

We eventually arrived off Savannah on the 27th March nearly three days behind our scheduled time. I was expecting to have to anchor off for at least three days awaiting a berth but to my amazement we were taken straight alongside and started cargo work immediately. It appeared that most of the other ships due to arrive had got caught up in the hurricane and we picked up an empty slot.

Trevor boarded in the afternoon and as we were just about ready to sail I decided to stay on until Norfolk, the next port. I spent the next day handing over and Trevor seemed pleased to be back. I couldn't wait to get off and I knew I was going to have to think seriously about coming back to containerships. I missed loading general cargo and all its problems and I didn't enjoy only being in port for only a few hours at a time.

We arrived in Norfolk two days later and I got off the ship just before it sailed mid afternoon and was taken to a really nice hotel not too far from Virginia Beach. I was expecting to fly home that night but the agent was having trouble getting me a flight and he told me the earliest would be noon the following day. I unpacked and had a very pleasant swim in the huge pool. I then proceeded to the restaurant where I made a pig of myself on crab cakes and a large T-bone steak. I retired to bed pretty content. Next morning I was told I'd be flying up to Washington in the afternoon and from there to London. I got to the airport only to find that all flights to Washington had been suspended as President Reagan had been shot. I couldn't figure out why they needed to close the airport so was somewhat miffed. In the end they changed my flight to New York and I flew home to Manchester, which was easier so I didn't complain too much. Diane came down and picked me up and it was a really miserable drive home in sleet and snow but it was nice to be home.

CHAPTER NINE

Short trip to Japan

m.v Ibn al Roomi
7th April 1981 – 11th June 1981

After I'd been home a week I got a call to go down to the company's Liverpool office for a debrief. I wasn't sure what to expect but it turned out they were more than pleased with my performance and wanted to know if I'd like to be on containerships permanently. Being diplomatic I just said I would go wherever I was sent – secretly hoping it would be back to the general cargo boats. As I'd only been away for two months and the normal length of trip was five months the personnel manager asked me if I'd like to take my full leave or ship out again for another three months. He caught me on the hop as I couldn't figure out which was the best option but as the weather was rubbish I said I'd like to go away again. The result was that two days later I was flying out to Shuaiba in Kuwait to join the *Ibn al Roomi*. She was one of the company's newer general cargo boats so that was a good start.

I joined on the morning of the 7th April and relieved Dia Tharwat. He was the first Arab master in the company and a really nice bloke. The ship was almost finished discharge and programmed to go out to Japan and load back for the Gulf. The company had recently changed from being Kuwait Shipping Company to the United Arab Shipping Company in which most of the Gulf States had a share. They had decided that the *Ibn al Roomi* would change from being Kuwaiti to go under the Saudi Arabian flag and once we had completed discharge we had to head down to Dammam in Saudi to complete the change of registry. I wasn't too bothered as I assumed it would just be a matter of changing the port of registry on the stern and putting up a Saudi ensign. I wondered why Dia got off in such a hurry.

The next day we were inundated with officials and office staff waving bits of paper to be signed and filling my office with reams of certificates and things. We had to have various surveys and inspections, which we passed without too much trouble as the ship was less than a year old. The only trouble was that after every survey and inspection all the people involved would gravitate to my cabin and proceed to empty my fridge of beer. Eventually we completed discharge after two days and sailed off down the Gulf to Dammam arriving at breakfast time the following day. Luckily, as it was Saudi, all the booze was sealed away so I wasn't going to have a repeat performance. Obviously things hadn't been thought through as it was a Friday and being a holiday it was impossible to contact anyone so we sat around for the day admiring the scenery.

Next morning didn't start well either as nobody came near the ship until nearly lunchtime and then various officials started arriving in dribs and drabs. Just after noon someone from the Saudi Ministry of Commerce swanned aboard and without examining any papers or certificates gave permission to change everything over to the Saudi flag. Then followed four hours of frantic activity while we changed the port of registry on everything on board. I had naïvely thought that it was only painted on the stern but quickly found out it was on hundreds of items from our individual lifejackets to life rafts and the life boats. Luckily Pete, the 1st mate, was on the ball and had made up loads of stencils of different sizes but it still took a while to get everything done. We also had to change our radio callsign so that required changing it on all the radio equipment. Eventually the officials were satisfied and we hoisted the Saudi ensign and sailed off for Japan.

Once we'd cleared the Saudi coast we opened the bond and downed a couple of well-deserved beers. After the second beer Pete Murphy observed that as it was now a Saudi ship we shouldn't really have beer on board. There was a stunned silence as no one had thought of this. After a few seconds deliberation I decided I wouldn't bring this to anyone's attention and just carry on as usual until told otherwise. This would turn out to be a really bad decision, I found, as

84

the trip progressed. The passage across the Indian Ocean was perfect with glassy seas and some fantastic sunsets. We had a few problems in that the main radio transmitter packed in so we were incommunicado for three days but we managed to get a message to the company when we passed another of our ships going the other way.

Afternoons on ships at sea are usually a quiet time with those not on duty having a quiet snooze or generally relaxing. The radio officer announced just after lunch one day that he had temporarily repaired the transmitter so I had to compose a bunch of telegrams to all and sundry to update them of our situation. As I was returning to my cabin from the radio room I heard a noise in the officers' bar, which is normally closed at this time, so I stuck my head in and was confronted by a party in full swing. It was being presided over by the chief engineer and consisted of mostly engineers, some of whom should have been working, and the 3rd mate. They were all completely legless. I blew my top and after my rant they all staggered off their respective cabins and I closed the bar. There was no point in talking to them as several were incoherent and most were past caring.

I now had a big problem as if I took any punitive action against them I would have to make an entry in the official logbook. This can be examined at any time by the authorities and I could see there would be some awkward questions as to how people had access to alcohol on a Saudi ship. I opened a can of cold beer and mulled over the situation. I talked to all the miscreants the following morning and told them that if there was a repetition of the incident I would close the bar permanently and this would obviously make them extremely unpopular with their shipmates. They all promised there would be no recurrence.

It became obvious talking to them that the chief engineer was the instigator and the main culprit. Bill was a serious alcoholic and coming up to retirement so he was going to be a problem. He was an old style chief engineer who very rarely actually entered the engineroom and then it was only onto the platform inside the top door where he could survey most of the machinery. His only work every day was to copy out the rough engine logbook made out by the engineers into a good copy for the ship's records and also provide me with the consumption of fuels and engine speed etc. This took approximately half an hour and the rest of the day was his own. He was a really good engineer, though, and could tell if anything was going wrong just by listening to the variations in engine noise. He would also anticipate problems when he was copying out the log by spotting changes in temperatures or pressures on the engine. The whole system worked but it left him an awful lot of spare time, which he filled by consuming vast quantities of alcohol. I had a quiet chat with him and explained that if there was a recurrence I would land all the booze in Japan and it would be a 'dry' ship from then on. He agreed to ease up but I doubted it.

The rest of the passage to Japan went without incident and we had great weather all the way travelling the 6,000 odd miles in under 15 days. Our first port was Moji on the south western corner and we tied up to buoys there around breakfast time on the 27th April. We only had 800 tons of huge steel girders for Kuwait to load and these were brought out on flat top barges shortly after we arrived. We were scheduled to finish off our loading also in Moji with 3,000 tons of construction steel. The local agent thought there might be difficulties so I went ashore with him the following morning to see what the fuss was about. The steel work was some sort of plant for making fertilizer out of oil by-products and was already laid out on the wharf waiting for us. It consisted of girders with angles and brackets sticking out in all directions, a couple of large hoppers and all sorts of conveyors and things. I reckoned they would need two ships to carry it all but the shipper was confident it would all fit in – I had my doubts. I was then taken for a slap up lunch accompanied by the compulsory sake wine so by the time I got back to the ship I reckoned it would all fit in easily.

We sailed in the evening and headed off along the southern coast to Yokohama arriving there the following evening. I always liked Yokohama as a port as we never berthed too far from the town so it was an easy walk to the shops (and bars). The loading went pretty slowly here, as the weather was atrocious with heavy rain all the time. I got a chance to walk into the shopping centre to see what bargains could be found in electronic goods. It was pretty disappointing as the value of the yen was increasing by the day so the only advantage was buying tax-free which was a bit of a rigmarole. When I first visited Japan in 1963 there were over 1,000 yen to the British pound and now we were getting less than 200. It was also making the beer pretty expensive and I've got a soft spot for Japanese beers. Anyhow I managed to buy a couple of electronic games for the kids and a new zoom lens for my camera.

The weather made the stay in Japan pretty miserable as it never stopped raining and although it wasn't cold we always seemed to be wandering round in wet clothes. The loading was also slow even though the cargo was mainly steel as it was pretty dangerous for the stevedores climbing around on top of it. We had three days in Yokohama then one day in Nagoya before we went to Kobe. I also liked going ashore in Kobe but this time we were tied up to buoys again miles from anywhere so not many ventured ashore as the prospect of an hour in an open ferry boat in the pouring rain would put anyone off. We received six months stores in Japan and I was surprised to see the company had replenished our beer stocks so obviously nobody in head office was too bothered. It was Asahi and Sapporro beer, which were my favourites so I wasn't going to make any waves. Even the chief engineer turned out in the rain to help get the beer on board. It took four days to load the cargo in Kobe and it was mostly electronic equipment (TVs and radios) so they had quite a problem keeping it dry during the load.

When we came to sail back to Moji again to finish up I had the choice to go through the Inland Sea or go out to sea and sail along the southern coast and back into the Inland Sea just before Moji. I hated the Inland Sea as it must be the most congested seaway in the world with everything from tiny fishing vessels to gigantic super tankers vying for space. We were allowed to take a Japanese Inland Sea pilot who was invaluable though he spent most of his time shouting abuse through a megaphone at the fishing vessels. The pilots were all retired shipmasters and very experienced but they cost the company a fortune. The pilots would always give the skipper a little brown envelope when they left as a thank you for employing them. It could contain as much as a £200 depending on how long they were on board. I had to weigh up whether it was worth accepting the bonus or taking the quiet, more relaxing, route along the coast. I went for the quiet option. I was really glad I did because just as we got to Moji we were enveloped in thick fog and had to anchor until it cleared. We heard reports of ships colliding and coasters sinking in the Inland Sea so I felt rather pleased with myself.

When the fog cleared we heaved up the anchor and berthed in

Moji on the 9th May. All the constructional steel was piled on the quay and I was sure it had doubled in size since we left but the agent assured me it hadn't. We started loading straight away and I was impressed by the professionalism of the stevedores. They had obviously loaded similar cargoes before and the huge sections seemed to swing through the air and land in exactly the right place interlocking with the other pieces. I could see problems when they would come to discharge it in the Arabian Gulf. It took them six days to get it all on board.

The weather had improved at last and I took the opportunity to have a couple of forays round the old port. The last time I had been there was in 1971 when we were stuck there with engine repairs for over a week. It hadn't changed much and I even managed to find the old bar that we used to frequent. It was really run down as the increased value of the yen had severely curbed the visiting seamen's drinking habits. Anyhow I went in for a beer and when I told the barmaid that the last time I'd been there was ten years ago she insisted on fetching the papasan or owner of the bar. It was still the same bloke though I reckon he must have been at least 120 years old. He seemed really pleased to see me though his English left a lot to be desired. After a while he produced an old photo album and after a bit of searching found some pictures of me and my mates all looking slightly the worse for wear surrounded by the hostesses and empty beer bottles. Looking at the changes in those ten years I decided that I wasn't wearing all that well myself. When I came to leave he refused to accept any money and seemed over the moon that I'd dropped in.

The next afternoon I was doing some paperwork in my office when Pete, the 1st mate, stuck his head in and said I had visitors. He showed in two lovely Japanese girls all done up in kimonos and looking really stunning. They presented me with a huge bunch of flowers, which they said was from the papasan. I invited them to have some tea, which they accepted. They had very limited English and as my Japanese is non existent the conversation was somewhat stilted with some long embarrassed silences. I was saved when the Japanese agent appeared and he seemed very impressed by them. He also explained that the papasan had sent them along for my pleasure and asked which one I wanted to go to bed with. Hmmm. I had to explain I was happily married and would have to decline. The agent couldn't believe it, insisting that my wife could never possibly find out. After a polite length of time the two girls left and I found out later that they had entertained two of the engineers so it hadn't been a wasted journey! My steward appeared later in the afternoon and spent a good hour trying to arrange the flowers in vases round the cabin. Regrettably they all fell over as soon as we sailed soaking my carpets.

The cargo was all loaded and securely lashed by teatime on Friday the 15th May and we sailed back for the Arabian Gulf. It was mediocre weather on the way south and with the full cargo of steel we rolled around a lot. Once we'd passed south of Taiwan the weather improved dramatically and we were sailing in the calm water of the South China Sea with the sun shining in a blue sky.

When out of sight of land the ship's position was determined by celestial sights using a sextant. The 1st mate would take a star sight at sunset and sunrise which was the most accurate and the 2nd and 3rd mates would take a sun sight in the morning and then combine that with a latitude obtained from the sun at midday to get the ship's noon position. I usually went up on the bridge at about half past six in the morning to let the 1st mate go and organise the day's work for the crew. Normally the star position was marked on the chart but when I went up on the morning after entering the China Sea Pete, the 1st mate, was still poring over his calculations and muttering to himself as he couldn't get anything like a position. I let him go down and said I would check through the figures but I couldn't find anything wrong. I checked his sextant for errors as well and couldn't find anything wrong there either so gave up as a bad job. When the 2nd and 3rd mates took their sights at nine o'clock they also had big discrepancies, which was really weird, so I got involved and took my own sight, which was even further out. The noon sight gave us a latitude that seemed about right but nothing else tallied. Luckily we passed close to the P&O containership *Largs Bay* which was heading up to Japan so we called them up on the VHF radio and got a good position from them.

I talked to the skipper and he was most unhappy. The previous day he had just picked up 65 Vietnamese boat people and the ship would lose days when they arrived in Japan while they were processed. The shipping companies all seem to blame the skipper when these sorts of things happen but there is no way anyone could just sail past and ignore them. He wished us luck with our navigational problem. We couldn't figure it out at all but Pete came up with the only common factor, which was the chronometer, which we all used to take the times of the sights. When we checked it we found it was three minutes out which equates to 180 miles in position terms. Patrick, the 2nd mate, had stopped the chronometer in Japan and restarted it on the wrong time. At least it was sorted and we knew where we were again.

I was just coming down off the bridge after resetting the chronometer and as I passed the chief engineer's cabin the door burst open and the electrician staggered out completely legless and unable to speak. When I stuck my head in the chief's cabin there was another of his parties going on. I broke it up and dispatched the miscreants to their cabins. There was no point in bollocking them as they were so drunk they were past caring. I had been congratulating myself on keeping the drink problem under control but it appeared they had just moved from the bar into the chief's cabin and carried on. The next morning I had them all into my cabin and read the riot act. I stopped their taps which meant they couldn't buy any alcohol on board. I also warned all the other officers not to supply them with any so there were quite a few dejected faces wandering round for a few days. It soon became obvious that Bill, the chief engineer, couldn't survive without his daily intake and he started getting shaking fits and got really depressed. In the end I relented and allowed them all six cans of beer a day so normal working resumed again.

We passed through the Straits of Singapore without a problem but when we entered the Indian Ocean the sea water temperature went up to 33 degrees Celsius which usually is only found in the Red Sea and the Arabian Gulf. We had to reduce speed to stop the engine overheating. The south west monsoon was blowing quite hard so it was a miserable slow passage across the Indian Ocean with low cloud and rain and drizzle all the time.

Our first port in the Gulf was Dammam in Saudi Arabia for which most of the constructional steel was destined. We arrived there late at night on the 31st May and they started unloading straight away. The stevedores were Pakistani and overseen by some ex Liverpool dockers. The system worked really well and I was surprised how efficiently the discharge went. It only took them three days and I had been expecting at least a week.

We sailed from there up the Gulf to Kuwait and when we got there I couldn't believe how many ships were anchored off. I found a nice spot close to the entrance channel and dropped anchor. The next morning the agent came out in a launch with all our mail and the news that we would have to wait at least a month, as there was huge congestion in the port. I had been hoping to be relieved on arrival but resigned myself to sitting out at anchor for another four weeks. It was pretty boring but at least we managed to get quite a bit of maintenance done both on deck and in the engineroom. After a week I got a message to say Bill Seybold was relieving me in three days time so I brightened up considerably. Bill arrived on time and I handed over to him. I warned him about the drinking problem but he had sailed with the chief engineer before and knew all about him. He was surprised he was still employed. I got a launch ashore in the late afternoon and flew straight to Heathrow and on to home. Looking back it was a very average trip with no major incidents.

CHAPTER TEN

Sojourn in Taiwan

m.v Ibn Rushd
4th November 1981 – 2nd April 1982

I got home from the *Ibn Al Roomi* two days before my birthday on the 14th June and had a very pleasant leave with pretty good weather throughout. I had to go down to the office in Liverpool after a couple of weeks for the usual debrief. I had to bring up the problem of the chief engineer and his drinking and the fact that the ship was now under the Saudi flag. There was a stunned silence round the table and it appeared that under no circumstances was there to be any alcohol on board and I should have transferred everything to another ship in Kuwait before we changed our flag. Somebody shot out of the room to find out where the *Ibn Al Roomi* was now and it turned out she was still at anchor off Kuwait so a quick message was sent telling Bill Seybold to transfer all the booze to another ship immediately. I bet I wasn't the most popular bloke around on the ship. The rest of the debriefing went off without a hitch, in fact I had been complimented by the staff in Japan on my interest in ensuring the safe stowage of the cargo. I went back home feeling quite chuffed with myself but feeling a bit sorry for the blokes back on the ship stuck at anchor with only coke and orange juice to drink.

I wasn't sure how much leave I was due so in the middle of August I phoned the personnel department and they told me I had at least another three weeks so I took the family away for a week on a boat round the Scottish sea lochs. I really enjoyed it even though it was a busman's holiday and the weather wasn't brilliant but at least I didn't damage the boat or anything though I did misjudge the height of the tide once and we nearly ended up aground. After a couple more weeks at home I was beginning to wonder whether the company had forgotten me but my wages kept being paid into the bank so I just kept quiet. Eventually at the end of October I got the phone call from the office. They asked me the curious question as to whether I got on with engineers to which I replied, "Of course." They then explained that there was a ship undergoing major repairs in Keelung, Taiwan, and the skipper on board was having issues with his engineers and they wanted someone more amenable and my name had been put forward. I don't know whether it was a good thing or it just meant I was a soft touch. Anyhow I flew out via Hong Kong on the 4th November and joined the *Ibn Rushd* the following morning.

It turned out that the *Ibn Rushd* had sailed out fully loaded from Keelung two months previously and whilst avoiding some local fishing boats had hit a large rock and put a pretty big hole in the hull amidships. The rock only pierced the tanks in the bottom of the hold so the ship was in no danger of sinking but was leaking fuel oil from the punctured tanks. The port authority refused to allow the ship back into Keelung whilst leaking oil and told them to anchor and they would bring them in the following morning with oil dispersal vessels alongside. The skipper must have had a brainstorm and just dropped the anchor where he was to await berthing. Shortly after midnight the junior engineer on watch in the engine room heard an odd noise so went to investigate and found a large piece of rock coming through the ship's side and the engineroom rapidly filling with water. The ship had swung round on the tide and the rock, which had holed the hull amidships, was now coming into the engineroom, which flooded with water immobilising the main engine and stopping the generators. When the tugs and oil dispersal vessels arrived the ship was in very real danger of sinking completely and they were lucky to get her into port. She then spent two weeks unloading all the cargo before being towed into drydock to repair the hull.

Once the hull had been repaired the ship was moved to a layby berth while the engines and generators were stripped down and rebuilt. She had been on the layby berth for three weeks when I joined. There was just a captain, a 1st mate and a full complement of engineers plus some extra electricians. There was nothing for the skipper to do so the bloke I was relieving decided to insist on everyone taking meals in the saloon in uniform which meant the engineers showering and changing and on top of that there was only one locally employed steward to serve the meals. It all ended in a blazing row with the skipper threatening to sack all the engineers but it ended up with him being removed and me arriving to try and calm the situation. It turned out that I had either sailed with or met all the engineers and knew them all to be cracking blokes and obviously they were good engineers or the company wouldn't have sent them out. Tom, the other skipper, left later in the afternoon and I was left to wander round the ship and see what was going on.

Externally the ship looked really good as the hull had all been repaired and repainted and there was a gang of local seamen employed painting and overhauling the deck equipment. The engineroom however was a different matter. Very little had escaped the sea water damage so everything had been stripped down and either cleaned or renewed. The main engine had moved on its mountings so that had to be realigned and secured in place. The engineers were busy doing that when I stuck my head in the engineroom so I didn't disturb them. A chief steward and a locally employed cook/steward provided meals on board. The chief steward wasn't much good but the Taiwanese cook was brilliant and could produce European food but everyone's favourites were his local dishes. I was quite looking forward to the evening meal when there was a big bang and all the lights went out. The ship was supplied with power from ashore as none of our generators were operational and it appeared the transformer on shore had been hit by a crane. This meant no power for at least five hours so everyone decided to go up town and have a meal in a hotel.

It was a great meal and I was looking forward to the stay in Keelung as there was potential for a really pleasant sojourn. After the meal we inevitably progressed to a nightclub where it was obvious the engineers were regular visitors as they all had their own bottle of spirits behind the bar. I think I got back to the ship about three in the morning very much the worse for wear and thankful that the power had been restored or I'd never have found my cabin.

The next day I was kept pretty busy as there was a gale blowing and we were in a very exposed berth so the ship was surging around and banging against the quay. The 1st mate and I seemed to spend all day replacing broken mooring ropes and resecuring the ship. Thankfully it all died down by teatime so I was able to knock off and have a couple of beers and enjoy a lovely meal of Chinese dumplings and crispy duck. Despite numerous invitations to go ashore I decided to give my liver a rest and have an early night.

During the next few days it became obvious that I had very little to do. I decided to check over all the navigational equipment and then found that the electrical supply from shore was very erratic and I'd probably do more harm than good. The only thing I could find to do was to correct the navigational charts. This was usually the 2nd mate's job but it was the sort of job I enjoyed and I felt sort of useful.

When the weekend came I decided to have an expedition round the surrounding countryside. I got a bus up to a local pagoda and had a wander about taking pictures but couldn't really find much of interest as all the signage was in Chinese. I then had quite a problem getting back to town as I couldn't remember which bus to catch and nobody seemed to speak English. I ended up getting a taxi back to the centre of town and he dropped me outside a respectable looking bar so I went in for a quiet beer. There was a Chinese girl playing classical music on the piano and she was absolutely brilliant. I stayed there for a couple of hours listening and then wandered back to the ship. That was my last foray into tourism. The area round Keelung was very industrialised and not set up for tourists at all. I should have made an effort and taken a trip up to the capital Taipei but I never seemed to get round to it even though I had virtually nothing to do.

After a month things in the engineroom were starting to get back to normal. The ship had been built on the Clyde and the company insisted that all the equipment and control gear was rebuilt as original, which meant long waits for things to be shipped out from the UK. A lot of it was actually flown out so it must have cost a fortune. We started to look forward to sailing in early December so the company arranged for the full complement of officers and crew to join. They all joined on the 5th December and I actually had a proper job to do again. It all went tits up from the start. The Pakistani crew had been sent out without Taiwanese visas so were detained at the airport and after a lot of bargaining they were allowed to join though they were not allowed to go ashore and we had to pay for an immigration guard to be on the gangway at all times to ensure this.

The next morning I had a delegation from the crew with a list of grievances as long as my arm. They were obviously disgruntled about not being able to go ashore but it appeared that their food stores were totally inadequate. They needed to get atta flour and stocks of spices to enable them to make curry. The chief steward who wasn't the brightest had forgotten to order any. Luckily there was another company ship in port so the chief steward was dispatched with a small truck to borrow enough for a couple of days until we could arrange a supply locally. What was supposed to take a couple of hours took over six and the chief steward eventually arrived back legless having been entertained on the other ship. He had to be carried up the gangway but at least the crew had some food.

I had the chief steward up the next morning and told him his fortune, which resulted in him resigning and demanding to be repatriated as he was being victimised. No sooner had he left than the radio officer knocked on the door and said all the radio equipment was inoperative as the heaters which normally kept everything dry had been switched off for the last two months so all the circuit boards were damp and corroded. He was followed by the 2nd mate who reported similar problems with the gyro compass and autopilot. Then Brian, the 1st mate, stuck his head in and asked if I wanted the good news or the bad news. It seemed that the lockers where we stored all the paint and equipment for maintaining the ship had been beautifully cleaned out and painted but the paint and equipment had vanished into thin air. It was getting better by the minute. Brian and I went ashore to see the shipyard managers to find if they could shed any light on the missing stores but to no avail. It appeared someone must have stolen it all. Incidentally when we did eventually sail we noticed several of the local fishing boats painted up very nicely in a similar shade of grey to our hull colour. Once back on board I was met by the chief engineer who reported that the main valve that shut off the compressed air for starting the engine was jammed shut and it was a big job to free it. We all adjourned to my cabin to discuss the situation over a beer.

Things didn't seem quite as bad after a couple so we wandered down to the saloon for our lunch only to find that the new cook was totally incompetent. Absolutely nothing was edible and even the salad had a peculiar taste. We retreated back to my cabin and opened another beer each. Luckily the chief steward redeemed himself and appeared shortly afterwards with a large plate of sandwiches. He also apologised for the previous day's behaviour and withdrew his resignation so the afternoon started to improve. On examining the cook's papers we found he had never been a cook before and had only been employed as an engineroom greaser. It appeared he'd paid off an official in Karachi who'd given him the job. It also turned out that one of the seamen had previously been a cook so we promoted him and demoted the cook. In the end it turned out the new cook was quite a star and produced some really good meals including a delicious Christmas dinner later in the voyage.

The rest of the afternoon was spent compiling a huge list of stores and paint to replace all the stuff that had been stolen. We sent off a lengthy telex to head office requesting everything soonest and expected a severe bollocking and an inquest into how we'd let it happen. Surprisingly when the reply came next morning they told us to obtain anything essential locally and the rest would be supplied on arrival in Japan. As it was now time for the evening meal we all wandered down to the saloon with some trepidation but it was totally unnecessary as our newly promoted cook had produced a brilliant meal and even managed a sticky toffee pudding to follow.

When I turned in that night I realised that I had enjoyed the day more than any I'd spent in the previous month lolling about with nothing to do. I felt I was being useful at last. The next few days were spent testing and checking everything we could think of. The engineers freed the compressed air valve and we had a couple of trial runs out of the main engine. On the 15th December we took the *Ibn Rushd* outside the harbour for a sea trial and apart from a few minor adjustments everything worked properly. I was pretty concerned for most of the time, though, as we had a local pilot to guide us and he took us perilously close to the rock that had caused the problem in the first place and the company would not have been impressed if I'd crunched the ship again. We tied up alongside again about teatime and the engineers opened up the bearings on the main engine and checked them and as everything looked good we were declared fit for sea. It looked as though we were going to earn our keep again.

Whilst we were being repaired we were berthed next to the fishing harbour and I spent a fair amount of time watching the comings and goings. Now and again when one of the boats sailed the crew would set off firecrackers. When I asked what this was about it was explained that if there had been an accident or problems on the previous voyage the crew would set them off to scare the bad spirits away. It was always pretty spectacular and I thought it would be a good idea to set some off when we sailed and I mentioned it to the Chinese shipyard manager. He thought it was a brilliant idea and said he would organise something when we sailed. I then forgot about it.

The following morning the ship was accepted back by the company and all our certificates issued so we were allowed to sail. It wasn't a good day for sailing as it was blowing a gale from the north and pouring with rain but it was good to be getting back to sea. As we were being pulled off the quay by tugs the air was suddenly filled with huge explosions with smoke and flames. The shipyard had done us proud. It was like World War Three starting. They had tied firecrackers and fireworks everywhere. The only trouble was nobody could hear anything so the tugs were pulling in the wrong direction and nobody could hear my orders for the wheel and the engines. We nearly collided with an incoming ferry and all the passengers were waving and cheering. Eventually it all died down and we were in control again but I made a mental note not to ask for firecrackers ever again.

Our instructions were to head up towards Osaka, as the company hadn't actually got a cargo organised for us. The weather was rubbish with a huge swell from the north so the ship was throwing itself all over the place. Even I was feeling seasick. The second morning Malcolm, the chief engineer, stuck his head in my cabin and said we'd have to stop the engine as he'd found a load of white metal in the oil filters. I was dreading it as I thought the ship would roll around even more if we were stopped but luckily it was no problem and we just bobbed up and down on the waves. It took the engineers over twelve hours to sort it out as one of the bearings had failed. When we started up again the storm had passed so life was much more comfortable. We berthed in Osaka in the afternoon of the 19th December. We stayed there for three days taking on stores and fuel and getting a new anchor and chain. Somehow they had lost one of the original anchors and all the anchor chain in the pandemonium when the ship had run aground.

On the second day the company told us that they had found a

cargo of steel for the Arabian Gulf and the first port was Takamatsu in the Inland Sea. We sailed down to there on the 22nd December and started loading straight away. It took them three days to load 6,000 tons so we ended up sailing at noon on Christmas Day which really messed up our dinner but we anchored off the next port at eight in the evening so had a really late meal and were able to have a bit of a party. The next morning we berthed in Wakajama, which is just outside Osaka Bay. It was a really boring load of steel girders and the weather was terrible. It was well below zero and sleeting most of the time so we were really glad when it was all loaded and we sailed late in the evening on New Year's Eve.

The trip down the China Sea turned out to be quite a memorable one for all the wrong reasons. It was the season for the north east monsoon and it was really blowing well setting up a huge following sea which, because of our cargo of steel, made us roll around uncomfortably all the way to Singapore. On top of that it rained almost continuously which just made life miserable. To finish things off, most of the electrical and electronic equipment failed as we progressed south. The gyro compass was the first to pack in so we were unable to use the autopilot to steer. This meant we had to have a man on the wheel steering by the magnetic compass all the time. We couldn't check the accuracy of the magnetic compass as it was overcast all the time so our navigation was very much hit and miss. One of our two radars was out of action as the scanner motor had burnt out and the other was operating in very basic mode due to the failure of the gyro compass. The echo sounder lasted two days before it blew up and the same with the electronic log, which told us our speed through the water. The China Sea is renowned for unmarked reefs and I was very relieved when we got to the Horsborough Light at the entrance to the Singapore Strait. The engineers were having a worse time than us with water pumps seizing up and pipes leaking everywhere. It seemed that ships didn't like lying round doing nothing for months on end.

After Singapore we were into the Indian Ocean where everything changed. The weather was idyllic with blue skies and the sea like a mirror. The fact that everything was still breaking down or blowing up didn't seem as important as long as we could stand on deck watching the sunset with a can of ice cold beer to hand.

Our first discharge port was Mina al Fahal in Oman. It wasn't actually a port but just an anchorage with a jetty for discharging barges. We anchored there on the morning of the 16th January and started discharging into barges straight away. It looked like it was going to be a good quick discharge but once they had filled the four barges up and towed them to the jetty to be unloaded everything stopped and we had to wait for the barges to come back. What should have taken two days to unload took over a week which was very frustrating as we had no access to the shore or repair facilities to sort out all the failed equipment. We were also running out of drinking water as although we had ten tons in a tank the valve was jammed and we couldn't access it. We had to resort to cold beer instead so life was reasonably bearable.

We sailed on the 23rd January up to Dammam in Saudi Arabia arriving there the next day. Discharge started immediately and a lot more efficiently. We received a lorry load of new electric motors, circuit boards, pumps and general spares that had been flown at great expense from the UK. There must have been a whole planeload. The ship was a hive of activity with people repairing things. The only thing we couldn't repair was the gyro compass, which was a real bind, but we were promised it would be working before we left the Gulf. The discharge went really well and they unloaded over 12,000 tons of steel in five days, which was really good going. That left only 5,000 to unload in Bahrain and Abu Dhabi.

There were rumours that we were heading to the UK to load our next cargo so we were all looking forward to that but as we finished unloading in Abu Dhabi we got a message telling us to go to Dubai for a day to sort any repairs including the gyro compass and take enough fuel to get to Japan and back so it wasn't going to be back to the UK after all.

We had our day in Dubai on the 3rd February and the company was good as their word and we got a complete new gyro plus spares. I found out that the company was claiming everything back from the insurance so no expense was spared. We sailed late in the evening and headed off east towards Japan. I was looking forward to the trip as the ship now seemed in good working order and it should be good weather all the way but of course it was not to be. We had changed most of the senior officers whilst discharging in the Gulf and it soon became obvious that there were some personality clashes and friction between officers and the Pakistani crew. I seemed to spend every day placating somebody and trying to smooth things over. I preferred life when I had problems with inanimate objects such as the gyro compass.

We passed south of Sri Lanka in early February and I was most disappointed to find that the authorities had instigated a separation zone to keep ships apart and it was twelve miles off the coast. I used to go in about two miles off just to look at the lovely coastline, as there was loads of deep water there. At twelve miles we could only just see the land. I was even more annoyed when I noticed that we seemed to be the only ship observing the new zone and everyone else was cruising along just off the coast. I vowed to ignore it on my return trip. Two days later we passed Singapore and turned north into the China Sea. I was unhappy to find the north east monsoon was still in full swing so we knew we were in for a poor trip all the way to Japan. We had to reduce speed to avoid the ship being damaged by the huge head seas.

It was a thoroughly miserable eight days up to Japan with more or less continuous rain and the ship bouncing round all over the place. At least the electronic equipment behaved itself but the personnel problems just went on and on. Every day someone knocked on my door with another grievance or complaint. One incidence comes to mind in that the catering crew were required to wear white shirts on duty which were issued by the company. One day the pantryman decided he wanted to wear a brightly coloured shirt and refused to change when told by the chief steward. I had to make a log book entry and fine him a day's pay in the end. So that's how my days were filled.

Our first port was Osaka and we berthed there in the afternoon of the 19th February. There was a huge pile of mail waiting so it was nice to catch up with things at home. The local agent appeared with the cargo plan and a list of the cargo we were to load. It certainly made interesting reading. We had six large mobile cranes to load and the shipper was insisting they were stowed below decks. We also had two specialist fire engines for Kuwait airport. The rest of the cargo seemed high value stuff like televisions, hi-fis and other electronic equipment which had to be carefully stowed to prevent damage. The Osaka cargo was mainly steel girders and that was loaded into the bottom of the holds in two days.

Next was Tokyo and for once we berthed close to the centre of town. The Pakistani crew adopted a new tactic and over half of them reported sick with a variety of disorders. Rather than send them all ashore I got a doctor to attend on board which turned out to be a bad idea. The doctor was a soft touch and gave most of them time off work and prescribed vast quantities of expensive medicine. Ah well.

After Tokyo we were hurried round Yokohama, Nagoya and Kobe and finished off in Tobata on the west coast. We managed to get all the cranes and fire engines stowed below. The shipper who delivered the fire engines gave us a demonstration of how they worked and we were really impressed with all the technology. We were even more impressed when we had a ride up and down the quay with all the lights and sirens going.

We sailed from Japan mid March and I was dismayed to find that the bloody north east monsoon was still blowing hard though it eased up after two days and thereafter it was quite a pleasant passage. After clearing the Malacca Strait I set a course to pass close to Sri Lanka but as we got closer we heard on the radio that the Sri Lankan navy was patrolling and reporting ships not complying with the separation zones so it was back to twelve miles off again. Bugger.

Our first port in the Arabian Gulf was Dammam in Saudi Arabia and just before we got there we got a message saying I was to be relieved on arrival, which brightened me up considerably. We berthed there late on the 1st April and at two the following afternoon I was on a British Airways flight to UK. It was a real relief to get off and I just hoped that the crew would settle down for Ron Philip, who relieved me, but I doubted it.

CHAPTER ELEVEN

A couple of nondescript trips

m.v Al Rumaithiah
25th June 1982 – 18th September 1982
&
m.v. Al Salimiah
6th November 1982 – 18th December 1982

I had a very pleasant leave with lovely weather but far too short. I was hoping for another extended leave but I received my instructions to join the *Al Rumaithiah* in Savannah and actually had a day less than my allocated leave. The *Al Rumaithiah* was the first ship I'd sailed in when I joined Kuwait Shipping but in those days it was a cargo ship. Since then the company had converted her to a containership so I was back on the box boats again. I joined her early in the morning on the 25th June and relieved Dave Bedford who managed to hand over and get off before we sailed mid afternoon. It was odd wandering round the accommodation and remembering what it used to be like. They'd added an extra deck to raise the bridge to enable us to see over all the containers on deck.

It was a quick trip up the coast to Baltimore the last bit of which was up the Chesapeake Bay in really thick fog. I was all for anchoring and waiting for it to clear but the American pilot said it would be no problem. Just before Baltimore we passed under a road bridge and never saw anything of it at all. We could hear the traffic overhead which felt really weird. We managed to berth all right but the cargo operations were slowed as they had trouble getting the containers to the ship because the fog was so thick. We sailed late in the afternoon and travelling north through the C&D Canal, which connects the top of Chesapeake Bay to Delaware Bay. It's quite a narrow canal but it saves over 100 miles on the passage to New York. I was pretty nervous, as the fog was really thick still. The Canal pilot brightened my day by saying there would be very little traffic to meet, as no one else was daft enough to use the Canal!

We actually had a really good passage and berthed in Newark late on the 28th June. It was really hectic. The engineers spent all night overhauling one of the pistons on the main engine and early the following morning we were inundated with stores, a delivery of lubricating oil and there was a gang of shore engineers repairing a damaged hatch lid. All this while the containers were being loaded and unloaded. Everything was complete by late afternoon and we sailed in the evening for the Suez Canal. It was back out into the fog but as we got further away from the coast it started to lift and by the following afternoon we were sailing on a calm sea with blue skies.

As I was writing up my reports of the loading I got to thinking of when I first went to sea in 1958. It used to take four weeks to unload a vessel and another four weeks to load and we had just done a complete load/unload in four days. Times were certainly changing. Gone were the weekends off and riotous nights ashore. On these containerships we were lucky to set foot on shore from the time we joined until we left. It looked like this was the way it was going to be in the future.

We had a great run across the Atlantic as the Gulf Stream was a bit further south than it usually was and it gave us an extra two knots so we were bombing along at nearly 20 knots which was the fastest I'd ever been. We got to the Suez Canal a day ahead of schedule but just missed a convoy and we had to wait 20 hours for the next one so it was all for nothing. It was an uneventful passage and we headed on down the Red Sea to Jeddah arriving there mid July. It was the usual bedlam there with the port refusing to accept some containers as they had the wrong seals on them and missing manifests so they had to open some containers to check the contents. It went pretty well, considering, and we were only in port for twelve hours and sailed late at night. Just after leaving we encountered some really poor visibility in a dust haze. There must have been a sand storm in Saudi and it left this huge cloud of fine sand in suspension in the air. It was a real pain as the radar couldn't see through it and visibility was only about half a mile. It cleared up after four or five hours but left everything coated in a fine red dust, which seemed to get everywhere.

Our discharge ports in the Arabian Gulf were Dubai, Dammam, Jubail (Saudi Arabia) and finally Shuaiba in Kuwait. We arrived in Dubai on the 21st July and we sailed from Shuaiba five days later heading back towards the States. We also lost a bit of time round the Gulf as well because Iraq and Iran were having a bit of a go at each other again and the Iranians assumed that everything heading north up the Gulf was carrying Iraqi cargo and was therefore fair game. They hit quite a few ships with Exocet missiles so we were ordered to travel only at night and blacked out which I thought was more dangerous as we were more likely to have a collision with another blacked out ship than to be hit by a missile. Exocet missiles were allegedly quite captain friendly as they travelled only about two metres above the waves and I spent almost all my time either on the bridge or in my cabin which was at least 20 metres high so I might get rattled about a bit but not actually killed.

Again it was quite a quick uneventful passage back to Suez and we transited the Canal early in August. Most of the passage across to the States was spent compiling lists of faults on board as we were programmed to drydock shortly. We were hoping for somewhere like Savannah, which was a pretty, laid back sort of place and a good run ashore. The radio officer was kept busy sending off the lists and receiving queries back from the company. Eventually they decided that as there was a lot to do, and it was very expensive in the States, they would find a cheaper option. Our ports this time were Savannah, Norfolk, Baltimore and Newark again and this time we got round in six days and we were soon heading off back across the Atlantic to Suez. I was rapidly going off the containership idea, as we never seemed to get a break at all. It wasn't hard work but just continuous. I missed being able to have a walk ashore in the evening and have a nice meal and a couple of drinks.

Again it was an uneventful passage back to Suez though I had some personnel problems to sort out. Two of the engineers were prone to making racist comments to the Sierra Leone crew, which was unusual on board ship. Mostly everybody got on pretty well. I was unable to prove anything either way but there always seemed to be something bubbling away under the surface. I was a bit biased as I

105

liked the Sierra Leone crews as they were usually easy going and hard working and I disliked the 3rd engineer intensely. One evening the two engineers came knocking on my door complaining that they their meals always seemed to be of poorer quality than everyone else's. It had been steak for the evening meal and they said that they had been served mostly fat and gristle. I promised to have a word with the catering staff but I was thinking if I made racist remarks I wouldn't make them to the people who were preparing and serving my food. I duly had a word with the chief cook and he said he would do a 'special' steak for them next time. I wouldn't have fancied eating it!

We transited the Suez Canal early in September and headed down the Red Sea to Jeddah arriving there a day later. It was the usual chaos with the cargo. This time they loaded ten containers in completely the wrong hatch so they all had to be discharged again. What should have taken four hours eventually took over twelve and we sailed at midnight. It was a nice quiet passage to Dubai apart from one evening. I was stood talking on deck with the chief engineer admiring the nice night with a fantastic full moon which seemed absolutely huge for some reason when I suddenly realised it was on the wrong side of the ship. I went tearing up to the bridge and found the Egyptian 3rd mate drinking tea on the bridge wing also admiring the moon. We found the gyro compass had failed and the ship was going round in slow circles. It was a good job there wasn't much traffic around so apart from losing time there was no damage.

As we approached the Arabian Gulf we started to get messages that looked like we were going to drydock somewhere there which wasn't good as it usually meant no air-conditioning while we were docked and there was nowhere decent to go ashore and relax. Then I got a message saying I was to be relieved in the Gulf. The company had decided that work on the box boats was considerably more demanding and reduced the trip time to three months instead of the usual five. I brightened up immediately.

We got to Dubai on the 15th September and they managed to complete the cargo operation in three hours. Bill Clague arrived on board to relieve me. There was no time to hand over so I stayed on to get everything right. Part of the problem was that I couldn't get my accounts to balance but with Bill's help I found my mistake. Bill assumed command and I had a very pleasant couple of days cruising up the Gulf with no responsibilities and a plentiful supply of cold beer. I paid off when the ship reached Kuwait on the 18th September and flew home.

I was expecting a very short leave after being away for only three months but the company had decided to give extra leave to the people who served on the box boats so I began to think I could cope with the life. Three month trips were a nice length especially with two months leave afterwards. When I went down to the Liverpool office for the usual debriefing I made it known that I wasn't at all averse to box boats. I got my joining instructions for the next ship and I was to join the *Al Salimiah* in Kuwait on the 6th November. All my hints had been to no avail as the *Al Salimiah* was one of the general cargo vessels. I joined her in the morning and relieved John Cole. The ship had just arrived from the Far East and was starting her Arabian Gulf discharge. John said he was really pleased to be getting off as he'd had a rubbish trip. He said the officers were a very mediocre bunch and took a lot of motivating and morale on board was very poor. He reckoned he spent all his time chasing people up. This had the makings of a miserable trip.

There was all sorts of activity on the ship with various surveys going on. The biggest of these was the survey of all the safety and emergency equipment on board. It can be a nightmare with things failing even though they'd been tested the day before, but for once things went well and we got our new certificate issued. The ship was also changing articles. The articles were the contract between all the officers and crew and the company. They had to be renewed every two years and it was a right hassle. I took all the papers up to the shipping master's office. He didn't even glance at them and just gave them to a clerk to file. He then took me into Kuwait City for a meal in one of the best hotels. I felt a bit conspicuous, as I had just come out in my uniform. The meal was terrific, though we had to make do with non-alcoholic wine, which was actually quite passable. We arrived back at his office about three o'clock and the new articles were waiting all correctly stamped and filled in by his clerk. The shipping master then dropped me off back at the ship. When I thought back to all the hassle I'd had changing articles previously I reckoned this was the way to do it. The only fly in the ointment was that when I got back I found the 1st mate had decided to relax in my absence and adjourned to the bar where he'd consumed large quantities of beer and he was so relaxed he could hardly speak. I had him up to my office the following morning and told him his fortune. He was in line for being promoted to master so I was sure he would take notice.

It took another two days to discharge the cargo and we sailed early in November down to Abu Dhabi at the bottom of the Arabian Gulf. The company had changed its mind about only sailing at night as the Iranians had noticed that there was always a large bunch of ships anchored off Bahrain at night and as they were stationery easy targets, fired a few missiles at them. They didn't do much damage and thankfully nobody was killed. In the end we had a good run and all we saw were a couple of American jets with twin tails flying past quite close. When we got to Abu Dhabi we were told that the Iranians also had jets with twin tails so maybe we shouldn't have been so complacent.

Previously I'd only had a day or so in Abu Dhabi as it didn't seem to import as much cargo as other Gulf ports but this time we had over 5,000 tons to discharge. I always liked Abu Dhabi as it came across as well run and everything always seemed clean and tidy. I managed a trip into the centre of town and was surprised how modern everything was. Every hotel seemed to have a theme bar be it Irish, Geordie, Cockney or Ye Olde Inn type. They all seemed to have come equipped with buxom British barmaids which made the run ashore even more pleasant.

When I got back on board there was a bit of a panic on. It seemed we had some large crates of electronic equipment on board destined for Doha, where we were due to berth after Dubai. These crates were urgently needed in Doha and had to be discharged here. When I was 1st mate I always took a keen interest in the cargo loading and kept an accurate plan of where everything was stowed. It seemed that my present 1st mate didn't share that interest and consequently nobody knew exactly where these crates were even though they were the size of large garden sheds and weighed over two tons each. People were dispatched down all the holds with torches and eventually the 3rd mate located them in number two hold behind several hundred tons of Dubai cargo. I ambled ashore to the agent's office and phoned the head office in Kuwait to tell them it was impossible. I was put through to the fleet manager and was told in no uncertain terms that the cargo had to be discharged immediately as transport was already on its way overland from Doha. Whatever was in the crates was obviously very important. I got back on board just at teatime as everyone was knocking off. When I went to organise the stevedores to do the job I was told they couldn't get any labour until eight the next morning. I was also handed a telex saying the transport was arriving from Doha with an escort at six o'clock the next morning. I was very tempted to return to the city centre and spend the evening in Ye Olde Shakespeare Pub with Julie the buxom barmaid.

I went back on board where everyone was settling down for a quiet evening on board and nobody showed the slightest interest in volunteering to help shift the Dubai cargo. I had to resort to bribery: viz. double overtime for the Pakistani crew and cases of cold beer for the officers. We divided the volunteers into two gangs – one to start right away and the other to start at midnight. Thankfully the stevedores had left a forklift truck in the hold and the 2nd electrician turned out to be a dab hand at driving it. By midnight we had well over three quarters of the cargo moved which was just as well as the forklift ran out of petrol and the gang coming on had spent the intervening hours in the bar and consequently some were more of a hindrance than a help. We eventually had the Doha crates ready to lift by five in the morning which was lucky as the transport convoy arrived shortly afterwards. It consisted of three lorries with several vehicles full of army personnel from Doha and a fleet of Abu Dhabi police cars. Very impressive. As the stevedores hadn't started work we obligingly loaded the crates onto the lorries and they shot off with sirens blaring and blue lights flashing. I'd have loved to know what was in the crates – someone suggested it was a new kitchen for the sheikh! I had breakfast and went to turn in and just as I climbed into my bunk I realised that we hadn't got a signature for the receipt of the crates, which is a cardinal sin when dealing with cargo. Sod it. At least I got a good sleep and when I got up there was a congratulatory telex from head office for our efforts. They weren't so happy when I sent in the bill for overtime and cases of beer though.

Later that day I was sitting in my office when there was a knock at the door. It was two policemen accompanied by an Arab gentleman who was obviously very important by the demeanour of the police and the amount of gold he was sporting. They all looked very serious and I was sure something had gone wrong with the Doha crates. It turned out he was the father of one of the cadets on board. As Abu Dhabi was his home I'd given him permission to have time off. It appeared he'd broken his ankle and was in hospital so the father had come to collect his belongings. That was quickly organised and I could relax again. I heard later that the cadet was seem wandering round the town the next day and it was obviously a ploy to get off the ship as he didn't like the 1st mate.

We got away from Abu Dhabi late afternoon on the 14th November and steamed the four hours down to Dubai arriving in the late evening. Discharge started the following morning with no problems. At noon several lorries appeared alongside with some engineering plant to be taken to the UK for repair. This obviously meant that our next employment was back to Europe and by some quick calculations we worked out that we'd be there over Christmas. The mood on board brightened considerably. It improved even more the next morning when we also loaded 20 empty containers for Rotterdam. From Dubai we headed up to Dammam then Doha.

Things seemed to be going remarkably smoothly. As we were going to Europe two more cadets joined in Dammam as they were going to study in the UK and this was a cheap way to get them there. We also loaded quite a lot of timber from another company ship to take back with us. The timber was used to chock off cargo when loading and would be quite a saving to the company.

We sailed up to Doha berthing there on the evening of the 18th November. The agent brought the mail and a sheaf of telexes from the office. The first one stated that we were to proceed to Japan after discharge and drydock in Innoshima in the Inland Sea. It was three days old so I presumed it had been sent before we'd loaded all the bits and pieces for the UK. I tried phoning the office the following morning but everything was closed as it was a Friday. When I got back to the ship the crew were loading two lorry loads of plywood sheets from another company ship, which were also destined for the UK. I was sure somebody in the office had mixed things up.

Next morning I was straight up to the agent's office as soon as it opened to phone the company. I got through to the fleet manager and he confirmed we were programmed for Europe with drydocking in Antwerp. This was brilliant as we would be in drydock with very little work going on over Christmas and most people would be able to get their wives over for a couple of days. I sat down in the agent's office for a while drinking coffee which for once was proper coffee. I can't cope with Arabic coffee, as it's far too sweet and not enough of it. Just as I was leaving someone shouted there was a telephone call for me and it was the fleet manager again. He'd just found out that we'd been reprogrammed and we were now definitely going to Japan. I protested that we had containers for the UK on board along with tons of company spares and timber. Also we had several cadets who were going to study at Liverpool and my final argument was that we didn't have enough fuel for a trip to Japan. Some devious bastard in the office had already pre-empted this and the fleet manager had all the answers. The containers were now to be unloaded in Japan, the spares, timber and cadets were to be transferred to the *Ibn Al Nafees* which was berthed ahead of us and we would get fuel in Dammam when we left Doha the following day. What really irked me was that the *Ibn Al Nafees* was an identical ship and had previously been going to Japan and there was no logical reason for changing things. I went back to the ship in a foul mood and told everyone the good news. Over the next few hours there were queues of people at my office door with various excuses for paying off but they were all to no avail. Everything was shifted over to the *Ibn Al Nafees* and we sailed late on the 20th November down to Dammam to pick up a 1,000 tons of fuel for the next trip. After that we had a quick stop of ten hours in Bahrain to complete our discharge and then we were off to Japan.

As we set off down the Indian Ocean I wasn't looking forward to the next few months at all. I seemed to spend all my time chasing people up and getting them to do their jobs. The chief engineer was a really good engineer but we didn't get on socially and the 1st mate was a waste of space. He was older than me and I think he resented the fact that I was skipper. In general it was really a miserable ship but it made for a quiet time in the bar, as most people seemed to prefer their own company.

As we progressed it became obvious that there was someone new in head office in charge of the ship movements. We got odd messages about future cargoes and queries that could have been worked out in the office with a bit of effort. As we rounded the bottom of India we received a long message detailing all our loading ports in Japan and stating we would start loading in Osaka at eight in the morning on the 8th December. I took great delight in sending a message straight back that this was impossible as the earliest we could arrive was the

10th. It went quiet for a bit after that. We had a very pleasant trip across the Indian Ocean and down the Malacca Strait. Once we got into the China Sea however it was the north east monsoon time again and we bounced our way north into a head sea. About three days from Japan we got a message from the personnel department saying they were relieving quite a few of the officers during the load so hopefully we'd get some happier souls on board and morale would pick up.

We drydocked at Innoshima, without any problems, on the 10th December. It was a huge yard with half of it given over to shipbuilding. Things didn't start off too well as the 1st mate hadn't bothered to make a proper list of work that needed doing so the initial meeting with the drydock personnel was a bit of a disaster. We spent most of the day running round trying to remember what was broken and required fixing. We were still adding items to the list when the meeting finished. There didn't seem much urgency and we actually had a day off on the Sunday. I had a walk ashore with my camera as it was a nice day but couldn't find much to take apart from the local castle. It was a museum full of Samurai armour and weapons but all the labels were in Japanese, which made it a bit frustrating.

Monday morning came and we were expecting a flurry of activity from the shore personnel as drydocking is expensive and the ship is kept in for the minimum amount of time. However we were greeted by two gangs of riggers erecting scaffolding round the cranes and a technician who came to service our gyro compass. We had no idea why the scaffolding was being erected so just before lunch I repaired ashore to find out what was going on. I found the shipyard manager and he explained that they were waiting for the company superintendent to authorise all the jobs and he'd had to rush off to Kobe to sort out another vessel. Nobody had any idea when he was due back but it was generally understood that there was no hurry for our vessel as the cargo had to be sorted out.

The manager then invited me out to lunch. I wanted to go back on board to change as I was in uniform but he insisted I go as I was. I felt a bit conspicuous especially as we went to a typical Japanese restaurant where there were no chairs and everyone sat cross-legged. I hate eating like this as I can never find a comfortable position but the meal more than compensated for that. The speciality was a fish called fugu, which I gathered was highly poisonous, and politely declined much to the amusement of the manager. I went for the tempura, which was absolutely delicious.

I also somewhat over-imbibed on Sapporro beer and was more than happy with life when I got back on board late in the afternoon. I explained to the crew what I'd found out and went and relaxed in my cabin. Just after the evening meal the company superintendent appeared complaining bitterly that he was starving and hadn't managed to have anything to eat all day so I got the cook to knock him up a couple of cheese sandwiches feeling slightly guilty as I was so full I hadn't bothered to have my evening meal.

After his sandwich and a beer the superintendent opened his case and brought out a whole pile of mail that had been waiting for us in Kobe and a stack of telexes from the office. The first telex said that all the officers due leave would be relieved towards the end of the loading which meant they'd all miss Christmas at home and also I'd have to put up with them for an extra two weeks at least. The second telex was our loading schedule that had us starting loading on Christmas Eve in Busan in Korea and then a whole heap of Japanese ports finishing off in Hong Kong. It was getting worse by the minute. The third telex said that I was to be relieved in three days and to fly back to the UK for leave. I couldn't believe it as I'd only been on board a month and now I was going to get Christmas at home! Then I had a bit of a panic in case I'd done something wrong and I was being sacked. The superintendent assured me I was all right and it was something to do with containerships. I spent the next three days sorting out the paperwork and trying to keep a grin off my face while all the officers were wandering round looking like thunder.

Roger Philip turned up to relieve me on the 17th December and I left the following morning. I was flying from Osaka airport so I had to catch the Shinkansen bullet train from Fukuyama to Osaka. It was a brilliantly organised trip. A taxi picked me up and took me to Fukuyama station where I was met by a lovely Japanese girl who organised a porter for my baggage and took me for a coffee while we waited for the train. Just before the train was due she took me down to the platform where the porter was waiting with my baggage. The girl explained she wasn't allowed to board the train as it only stopped for two minutes. She gave me my ticket and said that my seat was three rows down on the left. The train pulled in exactly on time and stopped with a door exactly opposite my baggage. My bags were put on board and I found my seat three rows down on the left and two minutes later we were on our way. I was really impressed. I couldn't believe how comfortable it was. There was a speedometer on the wall showing we were doing over 250 kilometres per hour. I must admit I would have liked to go a little bit slower as there was hardly time to take in the scenery. After a while a hostess appeared and gave me lunch which was noodle soup. The bowl was really full but the train was so steady it hardly rippled.

Shortly afterward we pulled in to Osaka station and I'd already prepared myself for the quick exit. When the train stopped my bags were unloaded and there was another girl waiting with a porter by the door. Then it was a taxi to the airport and a great flight home via Anchorage in Alaska. I wasn't too happy with this stopover as the runways were covered in sheet ice and I was sure we'd slide off into the snow on the side. The airport was pretty basic too and I was intrigued to see the main item for sale was Alaskan crab meat in various guises but I wasn't tempted. When I got to Heathrow I managed to catch a train just about straight away and was soon heading north to home in Penrith.

It was snowing pretty hard and as we got into Cumbria it was really thick. They announced that the line north of Carlisle was blocked and the train would be terminating in Carlisle. There was a lot of muttering from the Glasgow bound passengers as it was obvious that the roads would be blocked as well. I was getting worried in case Diane got stuck coming to pick me up but there she was at the station. We had quite a trip home but managed in the end. As long as I was safe at home for Christmas it could snow as much as it liked.

CHAPTER TWELVE

A maiden voyage on a brand new ship

m.v Al Ihsa'a
2nd February 1983 – 9th June 1983

Thankfully the company left me in peace over Christmas and I had a great time although we were snowed in once or twice. I got a call to attend the Liverpool office the first week in January but I had to put it off since we were completely snowed in. I managed to make it down the next week though. I was very curious to know what was in store for me and why they'd relieved me after only a month. I was shown into the fleet manager's office and he told me the company had been very impressed with my performance so far so they were sending me out to Korea to stand by a new containership that was being built there and to bring her out for the maiden voyage. I was over the moon. I'd never been on a maiden voyage before though I had been on some pretty new ships. Inevitably it was going to be quite a challenge as there would be plenty of problems to iron out once the ship sailed.

The company were building six large containerships in Ulsan in Korea. It was going to be the biggest ship I'd ever commanded at nearly 200 metres in length and powered by an 18,000 brake horsepower diesel engine. She could carry 2,200 containers which I thought pretty impressive, but as I'm writing this a containership has just been launched that carries 18,000 which rather puts mine in the shade. She was to have all the latest navigational aids and the engine was to be controlled from the bridge through a computer. This was a whole new ball game for me. I left the office on a real high and headed back to snowy Cumbria.

Two weeks later I was flying out to Japan. The company had decided that all prospective crew had to be educated in the equipment that was being installed so we were to fly to Osaka for three days touring the factories that made various gauges and valves for the ship. I flew out with another skipper, Bill Clague, who was also taking out a new ship, and our two 1st mates. We arrived in Osaka on the evening of the 29th January and booked into a very nice hotel in the centre. The following day was Sunday and as there was no work we did a bit of sightseeing. We got a tour round Osaka Castle which is one of Japan's most impressive. On the way back we got stuck in huge traffic jam and it turned out it was the day of the Osaka marathon and most roads were closed. There was nothing for it but to repair to the nearest bar and wait it out. That was the end of our sightseeing and we emerged from the bar long after the marathon had ended slightly the worse for wear.

The next two days were taken up touring a nearby factory being shown how hydraulic valves were made and operated and also how to operate the ballast console that controlled the ballast water on board. This was marine engineering and being deck officers we were completely out of our depth. The instructor was baffled when he asked if there were any questions and we all just sat and looked at him. Bill Clague explained the situation so the second day's instruction was confined to two hours watching valves being manufactured which we actually found really interesting. We were then all taken out for a lovely meal and a few beers and we had a wander round the shops in Osaka. We went to one of the big department stores where a bloke demonstrated and sold different tricks and illusions. I bought three but no matter how much I practiced people quickly sussed out how it was done so I didn't give up my day job. Pete Davis, my chief engineer, was brilliant at them, though, and kept us entertained especially the time he overdid some exploding powder on one trick.

The following day we all flew to Busan and were taken by minibus to Ulsan where the ships were being built. We checked into the brand new Diamond Hotel built specially for personnel standing by the ships. It was pretty luxurious though when we sailed six weeks later I knew the menu by heart. We were met on arrival by our ship's engineers who had already been there for a month. I was pleased to find I knew most of them from previous trips and they were a good bunch.

The following morning we were given a tour of the yard with introductions to all the various inspectors and surveyors whom I promptly forgot. Then we were taken down to see our respective ships. Mine was to be called the *Al Ihsa'a* and was to be registered in Saudi Arabia. This wasn't good news at all as a containership was bad enough but one without beer was going to be purgatory. I was surprised to see how close the ship was to being finished. From the quay everything looked finished but once we climbed aboard it was a different matter. There were electric cables hanging everywhere and pipes sticking out with nothing on the ends. My ship was going to be the first to sail in six weeks time and Bill's three weeks later. There seemed an awful lot to do but everybody was confident that it would happen.

We spent the rest of the day kitting ourselves out in warm working clothes: boots, gloves and hats, as it was obvious that South Korea wasn't the best place to be in January. For some reason I'd always thought of South Korea as being a warm country but this definitely wasn't the case. For the first two weeks I don't think the temperature got above minus ten and we were rapidly going off the idea of clambering around on cold steel checking fittings and equipment. Thankfully the hotel was warm and comfortable and we still thought the food was pretty good. Someone organised some cases of beer delivered to our rooms so life wasn't all that bad. We had weekends off which were pretty boring as there was absolutely nothing to do. The company, in their wisdom, had decided to give us a living allowance of about £25 a week paid in Korean won. It was a bit unnecessary as everything was paid for in the hotel. The trouble was it could only be spent in Korea as the money was useless outside the country. We made a determined effort to spend as much as we could in the local bars but we still ended with won to spare. There was a factory nearby that made sporting goods for export to the States so we used to visit that and spend the extra won there. I ended up with several pairs of trainers, two baseball mitts, a baseball bat and several balls and a rucksack. I also bought a giant stuffed Pink Panther somewhere, though I can't actually remember buying that – it must have been one of the non-shopping nights.

One weekend Bill Clague and I were taken for a sightseeing tour of Busan by a girl student who wanted to improve her English language. We visited some impressive temples and burial mounds but the weather was atrocious and sheeting down with rain the whole time. We got absolutely soaked despite buying huge umbrellas and the pair of us were really miserable but she insisted we saw everything. The final straw was when we stopped for a meal at a local restaurant. The girl insisted we ate local food so we ended up eating a sort of horse meat stew and kimchi. Kimchi is a dish made from pickled cabbage and is the most horrible thing I've ever tasted. It's like slimy cabbage leaves boiled in old diesel oil. I was never gladder to get back to the hotel afterwards and Bill and I tucked into huge peppered steaks and chips with a couple of bottles of beer to wash it down. I went down with a really bad cold the next day and didn't know whether to blame the rain or the kimchi.

Work was progressing at a good rate on the ship. All the navigational equipment was being installed and I was disappointed to find that we were being fitted out with run of the mill stuff. We got a satellite navigation system which was very basic and only gave us a position when a satellite was overhead. This meant we could go six hours without a position and then get three in ten minutes, but it was a start. We also go a Loran C receiver which gave us pretty good positions in the Red Sea and Mediterranean but not much good anywhere else. I was surprised to see it as it was quickly becoming obsolete with the improvements of the sat-nav. The radars were the latest models though and had all sorts of features such as warning us when another ship was on a collision bearing. I was very sceptical of this and was proved right on a couple of occasions when junior officers were relying implicitly on the radar and not keeping a proper lookout.

The biggest change I had to deal with was that the engine and the ancillaries were all controlled by a computer and the engine itself was operated directly from the bridge. At sea the engineroom was unmanned with everything monitored by the computer. This freed up the engineers as instead of keeping watches they were available to do the day to day maintenance and repairs. It seemed a big step forward.

As things progressed Bill and I began to get very frustrated as we could see many problems with the siting of dials and indicators and when we requested they were moved we were totally ignored. We got the feeling that the shipyard was taking the mick out of us as we always had our complaints referred to a Mr Park and we rapidly found out that every other person working in the yard was called Mr Park. I gave up in the end and just accepted things.

Finally after five weeks the day came for our sea trials. On the 21st March we all got up at four in morning and trooped on board. It was blowing a hooligan with horizontal sleet and I was really pleased I was only there as an observer and could keep out of the weather. Somebody had organised bacon butties and a large pot of coffee so I took advantage of these as we let go and sailed out into a full blown gale. For the first two or three hours I was really impressed. Everything worked perfectly and despite the huge seas we were moving comfortably. The ship steamed slowly round in circles while we adjusted the magnetic compass for errors and checked the radio direction finder. Then we set off north building up to full speed and I changed my mind about being comfortable. We bounced around all over the place and if I'd been in charge I would have called the whole thing off.

Gradually things started failing with alarms going off right left and centre. At one stage there were seven different alarms going off on the bridge and I had no idea what was what. I'm sure one was the fire alarm but nobody paid any attention to it. The Korean technicians were running round repairing faults and after a few hours peace reigned again. Thankfully the storm was passing and the seas dropped away quickly as we had to do our speed trials. These went off without a hitch and we actually exceeded the required speed. The final test was the crash stop. This was where we would be going along at full speed ahead and the engine was put full astern. I was most impressed as the computer managed it well albeit with some ominous bangs and clouds of black smoke. I just hoped I would never have to do it myself one day as it was usually the last resort before a collision or grounding. The trials took 36 hours and we berthed back in Ulsan the following afternoon. Now we were getting close to sailing!

Two days later we had the official naming ceremony. It was a bit of an anticlimax really. Several important Saudi officials attended along with the company management. One of the Saudis insisted on giving me the gold fountain pen used to sign the documents and I actually still have it somewhere. As we were Saudi registered they couldn't use champagne to name the ship and made do with orange juice or something which seem to take the importance out of the occasion. I had a hell of a job getting into my reefer uniform as I hadn't worn it for several years – I generally opted for the blue woollen jersey with epaulettes. I had to adjust the buttons on the jacket and let my trousers out with safety pins and it was most uncomfortable. After the ceremony we were all taken for a slap up meal which I couldn't really enjoy in my tight trousers. It amused Bill Clague no end.

Next day the crew and the remaining junior officers arrived and we started loading all our stores and spare equipment and the following day we moved on board. It now felt like a real ship with everything coming to life. We were scheduled to sail about six in the evening but I couldn't see that being possible with the amount of stuff we had to load and stow. On top of that we had to take on fuel and lubricating oil. I was sure it would be well into the next day before we would get away. However at three o'clock the fuel and lube oil arrived and I was told to sail and pick up any missing items when we got to Japan. We cleared the harbour at half past six and by that time our speed indicator, digital depth indicator and the bow thruster motor had all packed in. On top of that numerous doors in the accommodation had jammed shut and we had to break the locks to get through them. The alarm panel on the bridge looked like a Christmas tree there were so many lights flashing of the various alarms that were going off. This wasn't going well at all.

Our first port in Japan was Yokohama and we berthed there two days later without any major mishap. The engineers were working their way through the faults and reducing the number of alarm lights and also got the bow thruster working again. This was a transversely mounted propeller in the bow that helped manoeuvring in and out of harbour. I'd never sailed with one before and found it a great help as when the ship was loaded with containers the wind could have a huge effect. The stay in Yokohama was one mad panic from beginning to end. The cargo operation only took three hours and we had to load the remainder of our stores and spare gear. Unfortunately there was no beer, being a Saudi registered ship, which made life even more stressful. We also had a visit from the mayor of Yokohama accompanied by Miss Yokohama to welcome us on our maiden voyage. I had to give them a tour of the ship which I didn't really have the time to do. It was worth it in the end as I got a lovely kiss from Miss Yokohama and she gave me a bottle of Suntory whisky. I don't usually like whisky but I made an exception in this case and poured myself a quick tot once we'd sailed and headed off towards Nagoya.

Nagoya was more or less a repeat of Yokohama with the mayor and local officials this time accompanied by Miss Nagoya. She looked exactly the same as Miss Yokohama and even gave me an identical bottle of Suntory whisky and a similar kiss. Again, loading only took three hours and we were on our way. Then it was on to Kobe where again we had a visit from the mayor and his entourage accompanied this time by Miss Kobe who was again a replica of the previous two. I was getting seriously pissed off by this time as there was an awful lot going on and the last place I wanted to be was socialising with local dignitaries but it seemed it came with the job on maiden voyages. Again, the obligatory bottle of whisky although this time it was Yamazaki twelve year old which was rather nice. The kiss was ok, too.

Cargo was completed around teatime and I was really looking forward to two days at sea down to Taiwan to get the ship properly settled down. When we came to sail we found that the steering gear wouldn't work as a seal had blown and there was hydraulic oil spurting out everywhere. The nearest new seal was in Ulsan in Korea so it was arranged to fly it over immediately and unbelievably it arrived on board at four in the morning and we were ready to sail at six. No sooner had we cleared the berth than the steering gear failed again. This time it was a proper job and we had to anchor in a bit of a hurry just outside the breakwaters and send to Korea for a complete new hydraulic pump which again arrived in double quick time. The engineers had quite a job it as it weighed about a ton and had to be manoeuvred from a launch into position down various ladders and alleyways. Eventually it was fitted and tested and we picked up the anchor and set off for Taiwan at eight in the evening.

The weather on the way down was pleasant which gave us time to catch our breath. The *Al Ihsa'a* was fitted with a satellite communication system which meant we could send and receive telexes directly without having to send messages through radio stations. We could even phone but this was actively discouraged by the company as it cost in excess of £6 a minute. It seemed really odd being able to have instant access to people when quite often it was days before we were able to get a reply to our radio messages.

It took us three days to get to Kaohsiung on the west coast of Taiwan. We were one of the biggest container ships they had ever had in their port and we had all sorts of problems as the gantry cranes used to load us were too small. We had to load containers in the wrong places as the crane couldn't reach the far side of the ship. Apart from that everything went pretty smoothly and we sailed the following morning for Hong Kong. When we had sailed from Korea the ship had been completely empty and looked quite odd with no containers on deck and now we were filling up rapidly and started to look like a proper containership with the decks loaded with red and green containers.

It was only a short trip to Hong Kong and we berthed at the container terminal early the following morning. We lost a bit of time as we had to restow quite a few of the Kaohsiung containers that were in the wrong places. I always liked Hong Kong as a port. It was a good run ashore with some really good bars and eating places and some bargains to be had in the duty free shops. This time we were berthed a good hour away from the centre of town. On top of that we weren't allowed to walk ashore for fear of getting run over by the straddle carriers flying around moving the containers. We had to organise a minibus to take us to the gate, which was a right bind. Consequently no one ventured ashore so we were beginning to realise that there were serious disadvantages being on a box boat. Loading took 20 hours which gave us time to get some technicians on board to fix several bits of equipment that had failed on the passage from Japan. Most of it was sorted apart from our Doppler log, which if working was a great bit of kit as it gave us an accurate speed reading, but we hadn't had one before so it wasn't a great miss.

From Hong Kong we had a three day trip down to Singapore and this was a great passage with no wind and the sea like a mirror. We had been fitted with a new type of automatic steering which was designed to save fuel. The idea was good as it monitored the way the ship was moving then worked out how to keep it on course with the minimum of rudder movement. In practice this meant that instead of steering within one or two degrees of the course we meandered all over the ocean as we oscillated five or six degrees each side of the course line. The trouble was that 90 per cent of the traffic we encountered travelling down the China Sea were on more or less the same course as us so when they saw us careering drunkenly towards them they had no idea which way to go to avoid us. After several abusive VHF radio calls from the other ships, casting doubt on our parentage and asking what the hell we were doing, we switched it off and reverted to the old fashioned steering system. On top of that the chief engineer reckoned it actually increased our fuel consumption. I don't think the company was all that impressed when we sent in a report as it had cost quite a lot of money. At least it passed the time down to Singapore.

We arrived there at lunch time on the 10th April and by three the next morning we were on our way again and heading up the Malacca Strait towards the Arabian Gulf. We now had a week sailing to Dubai with good weather and few hazards so we were able to try and sort out all the problems we had. I have a list in my diary of all the bridge items that failed:

1. *Port radar inoperative (faulty gear box)*
2. *Doppler speed log not working*
3. *Digital echo sounder inoperative*
4. *Satellite communication system faulty*
5. *Faults with automatic steering*
6. *Satellite navigation system erratic*
7. *No air-conditioning on the bridge*
8. *Emergency radio receiver not working*

Actually it would have been quicker to list the equipment that was working. We did manage to get one or two things up and running again but most of them needed spare parts. The engineers were having a far worse time in the engineroom and they had to stay on watches rather than let the computer take charge as there were numerous false alarms.

The time to Dubai went surprisingly quickly and we arrived there on the evening of the 18th April. Cargo operations started straight away and were completed by five the following morning which gave us no time to get the faulty equipment fixed. After Dubai we went round the Gulf in double quick time as most of the ports were now equipped with modern container terminals and five days later we were passing outward bound through the Straits of Hormuz having fully discharged all the loaded containers and picked up about 1,000 empties. It all seemed unbelievable that six years earlier we would lie at anchor for a month before even starting to unload.

The quick turnaround meant that we were unable to get our faulty equipment repaired so we had to soldier on regardless. We'd had a few crew changes and the new chief engineer, Mick Colbrook, was determined to get the unmanned engineroom system working properly which mainly seemed to entail leaving the engineroom and seeing what failed and running down and fixing it. This meant that the console on the bridge was always flashing with alarm lights and sounding off with buzzers and sirens. Eventually they got it all up and running and the next day a system that monitored the oil in the engine failed and was unrepairable so they had to man the engineroom again.

We arrived in Jeddah on the 29th April which was a Friday. This is not a good day to arrive in an Arab port, being a holy day. The cargo operations were chaotic to say the least. The only papers relating to our cargo were locked in an office somewhere which was closed for the day. The new computer operated system on the shore had broken down and they were training some new workers to operate the trucks and straddle carriers and they kept getting lost. We should have completed operations in three hours but it was 24 hours later when we cleared and we still had two containers on board which they wouldn't accept because of the lack of paperwork. It was all very frustrating but the worst part was that normally after we sailed from Jeddah and all its hassle I could sit on deck with an ice cold can of beer and watch the sun go down and everything would be all right. In our case however being registered in Saudi, we had to make do with a can of coke, which just wasn't the same. I'd also given away the whisky I'd been given in Japan as I don't like it so it was coke or nothing.

We had a quick passage through the Suez Canal but then got orders to proceed at reduced speed to Tilbury to fit in with our schedule. It was a nice peaceful passage only troubled by really thick fog in the Straits of Gibraltar. We still continued to have problems with equipment failure but we seemed to be on top of things. We had a carbon dioxide fire extinguishing system for the engineroom and the cargo holds and when the 1st mate decided to check it out found a crucial valve missing which meant that whoever fired off the cylinders in an emergency would have been killed instantly by the gas – not good.

We got to Tilbury on the morning of the 11th May and berthed in Tilbury Docks. We were still a couple of days early for our schedule but the opportunity was taken to flood the ship with technicians and shore engineers and get everything sorted out. A lot of work was done and I felt a great deal happier with things when we sailed on the 15th for Antwerp. After Antwerp we did Rotterdam, Hamburg and Bremerhaven in double quick time and four days later we were heading down the Channel fully loaded.

While we'd been in Tilbury for four days with a bit of time to spare we'd managed to slip ashore a few times to investigate the local hostelries and I began to realise I did really miss the odd can of cold beer at the end of the day or after a job well done. I did a bit of research and found that most of the officers were of a like mind including, surprisingly, all of the Arab officers. So I figured out that we had thirteen days at sea before we got to Jeddah where booze was definitely not on the agenda. Everyone gave me a list of how much they would consume (some estimates had to be considerably reduced) and whilst in Bremerhaven arranged for a cooperative ship chandler to bring the booze on board disguised as engine spares and paid for it in cash. It was pretty risky and if we'd been caught I'd have probably ended up in a Saudi jail and I'd have lost my job. I figured it was worth it though as I had a good bunch of officers and in all the time I was on the ship nobody abused this privilege and morale was always pretty high. I can still remember Mick, the chief engineer, who drank gin, religiously marking his bottles of gin with a felt tip pen so he knew how much he could have each day. So as we progressed down the Channel, having cleared most of the traffic, it felt really civilised to crack open a can of Stella at the end of the day.

The passage out to the Gulf went really well and we charged along at 19 knots with about 95 per cent of our equipment working so I was pretty content. The engineers weren't so happy as we had loaded 20 or so freezer containers and these were in a very poor state of repair. As soon as the weather started to warm up they began to break down so the engineers were out there day and night trying to keep them going. Luckily, when we got to Dubai, we unloaded most of them before we headed up the Gulf into the real heat.

As we entered the Gulf I got a message saying I was to be relieved in Kuwait so I had a couple of days to get all my paperwork and accounts sorted out and I was relieved on arrival in Shuaiba by Bob Sutton and I flew home the following day.

CHAPTER THIRTEEN

My own ship

m.v Al Ihsa'a
20th August 1983 – 5th November 1984

June was a good month to get home as it gave me time to work in the garden and hopefully have some decent weather. After a couple of weeks I was called down to the office for the usual debrief. I went down armed with sheaves of paper detailing all the problems we'd experienced and lists of modifications that should be included in the following ships to make them work a lot better and save quite a bit of money.

My first visit was to the fleet manager who told me that I was going to be the permanent master on the *Al Ihsa'a* and that the length of voyage on the containerships was to be reduced from five months to three months with longer leaves. Normally the system was that we did a five month trip on a vessel, took our leave and then joined the next available ship. This was a whole new ball game. It meant I could organise the ship to run how I wanted it and hopefully have a regular core of good senior officers to sail with. It also meant I didn't have to drag my entire kit home with me each time as I'd be able to leave all the heavy stuff on board. The only down side to the whole thing was that I was to be permanently on a dry ship with no alcohol allowed on board but I had already sorted that side of things out.

After talking with the fleet manager I was then passed on to the personnel department to discuss any problems I'd had with the crew which was virtually none so after a quick natter, where I dropped a few hints as to which officers I'd like to have, I was finished there.

Then it was out to lunch (which was very nice) and when I got back to the office I was told that all the superintendents were either out of the office or busy so there was no-one to discuss all my modifications with. Nobody else seemed interested so I said, "Sod it," and caught the next train home arriving just in time for tea.

One of the things about containerships was that their trips had to be carefully scheduled and the ports and berths booked months in advance which caused problems if we were delayed by bad weather or mechanical breakdowns. The only good thing I could see was that I knew the *Al Ihsa'a* was due back in Tilbury on the 19th August and I would be rejoining then. Previously there had been uncertainty towards the end of my leave as to whether I'd go off straight away or manage another week or so if there were no ships around.

So duly on the 20th August I rejoined the ship in Tilbury. I was really disappointed to find that almost everyone was new as all my regular officers were on leave. We sailed the following day and went round the ports of Antwerp, Rotterdam, Aarhuis, Bremerhaven and Le Havre in seven days with no major problems. The only thing of interest, really, was that when we came to sail from Aarhuis there were no tugs available so I manoeuvred the ship out of the berth and turned round inside the small harbour. I was really pleased with myself as it was proper shiphandling which I didn't get much of a chance to do these days.

After Le Havre we had eight days to catch our breath before the Suez Canal. The ship was now running pretty well with most of the teething problems sorted out. Two days into the trip we found one of the containers leaking some sort of corrosive liquid and smelling very strongly of some sort of gas. As we had no idea what it was we cordoned it off and washed the area down. I sent a message to the company to find out what was in the container and what precautions we should take. We got a message back saying it only contained Growbags and nothing else. We begged to differ. I often wonder exactly what was in those containers and feel it must have been paradise for smugglers. We discharged the container later in Jeddah and it was accepted without question even though there was still liquid dripping from it.

We got to Suez just too late for a convoy so we had to anchor for a day to wait for the next one. We cleared the Canal the following evening and I found out one of the disadvantages of going round at

18 knots. Most ships are happy enough plodding along at 15 so when we set off down the Gulf of Suez we had to overtake at least ten other containerships while contending with the traffic coming the other way and numerous oil rigs and supply boats. It was quite hairy for a while and I was glad when we got into the open waters of the Red Sea.

We arrived at Jeddah at mid morning the following day and for once it was a smooth operation. They seemed to have got the hang of their computerised system for container handling and all our paperwork was in order, so by five o'clock we were on our way again having also topped up with 1,000 tons of fuel. We then had five days at sea round to Dubai and the Arabian Gulf. We zipped round the Gulf doing the usual ports of Dubai, Bahrain, Shuaiba and Dammam in five days but we had to drop in at Mina Qaboos in Oman to pick up 23 special containers for Jeddah. I'd have loved to know what was inside these containers as they were brought down with a military escort and all the doors were welded shut. There were no manifests for the containers and I was envisaging all sorts of problems when we tried to unload them at Jeddah. In the end they were quietly discharged as soon as we berthed with no mention of paperwork. After Jeddah it was back through the Suez Canal towards Europe.

I was now beginning to fully realise that life at sea had changed completely. We always seemed to be on the go with no time for relaxation. When I first went to sea in Port Line in 1958 the ships were usually about 12,000 tons deadweight (they could carry this amount of cargo) and there was a crew of nearly 70 on board. We could take up to a month to load cargo visiting various ports and the same to discharge and this was interspersed with nearly a month at sea. There was always time to wander ashore and see the sights (and visit the odd bar) and there was a great social life on board with always someone to sit and have a crack with. There was a lot of hard work but we also played hard too and it was a real pleasure to be at sea. Now I was in command of a 56,000 ton vessel with a crew of less than 40. Time in port was usually less than twelve hours with cargo work going on continually so there was no chance to even set foot on shore. We seemed to be on the go from the minute we set foot on board until the day we paid off. Social life was minimal as people were either working or sleeping. We were also getting an increasing number of junior officers from India and the Arab States and it was difficult to engage in conversation as we had little in common. I was becoming disillusioned with life at sea and especially containerships. The only redeeming feature was that we only did a maximum of three months at sea and then got two months leave.

When we got to Tilbury, our first European port, I was half way through my stint on board so maybe it could be worse. We arrived there on the 10th October and for once we had three days in port. There were a lot of modifications to do and stores to take on board so it was pretty busy though we did manage to get ashore for a couple of nice meals and more than one pint of decent beer. After Tilbury we went round Antwerp, Rotterdam, Aarhuis and Bremerhaven in quick succession and by the 22nd October we were outward bound towards Suez again. It was a pretty stressful passage round the Continent as there was a succession of gales passing through with two days of storm force eleven. I found the shiphandling really hard, as with all the containers on deck the ship was virtually unmanageable at slow speed. We were unable to disembark our pilot from Bremerhaven when we left so we had to stop off at Dover and let him off there. Luckily the bad weather died away once we cleared the Channel and we had a decent run to Suez arriving there on the 31st October.

After Suez it was the usual rotation of Jeddah, Dubai, Abu Dhabi, Bahrain, Shuaiba (Kuwait), Dammam, Dubai (again) and finishing off in Mina Qaboos in Oman which we managed in eleven days. It was interesting to see how some ports were adapting quickly to containerisation. When I first started on the containerships the ports would average about twelve container movements an hour which was really slow but on this passage at least two ports managed over 30 an hour which was quite impressive.

After we left Mina Qaboos we got instructions to stop off in Jeddah and pick up a load of empty containers. Someone in the office had worked it out that it was cheaper to carry the empties around on the ships rather than pay for storage in the various ports. It seemed to work out all right and it meant that it looked as though all our ships were travelling round completely full which gave a good impression to the shippers.

We berthed in Jeddah at midnight on the 22nd November only to find that nobody was expecting us. We were scheduled to load about

80 empties but no one in the terminal could find them. By noon we had loaded nine so it was decided to leave to enable us to catch the next Suez convoy. It took them another two hours to sort the paperwork out so we arrived in Suez and managed to make the convoy with only half an hour to spare.

We arrived in Tilbury on the 2nd December and I was expecting to be relieved on arrival which meant I'd be home for our wedding anniversary but things went pear shaped when whoever they had pencilled in decided to go sick so they had to find someone else quickly. In the end they found George Donnison who had never been on containerships before so I had to stay on until Antwerp to show him the ropes. As we were leaving Tilbury I was leaning over the bridge wing watching the river pilot disembark and as I stepped off the viewing platform I slipped and twisted my leg. I didn't think much of it but when I got home (on the evening of our anniversary) I decided it was bad enough to see the doctor. He said I'd got a hernia that needed operated on sooner rather than later but the waiting list was a couple of months. I could see extra sick leave coming up so I rang the company immediately. They told me I could have the operation immediately at the Dreadnought Seamen's Hospital in Greenwich. I managed to postpone it until after the New Year so I travelled down the first week in January.

On entering the hospital it was like stepping back in time about 20 years. It took ages to get admitted which involved getting name tags made on metal labels with a machine that James Watt probably invented. I was then informed that the operation would be the following morning so at least I would be out pretty soon. The surgeon visited me in the afternoon and I was a bit concerned that he was foreign and could hardly speak English so one of the nurses had to translate for him. He marked a cross on my hernia with a black felt tip pen which was a bit over the top as it was very obvious but never mind. I was then tended by a very effeminate male nurse who shaved off all my pubic hair. I got rather concerned as he seemed to hold onto my wedding tackle for a lot longer than necessary but in the end he wandered off. The evening meal was an inedible stew which was an indication of the standard of meals to follow. When the night nurse came on duty several of the patients got up and put their dressing gowns on and announced they were going to the pub across the road. I was invited but it didn't seem like a good idea. They all

131

arrived back about eleven with a carry out and proceeded to party until the early hours. The nurse took no notice of them at all and just sat and read a book.

I had the operation the next morning and at least I woke up alive and he seemed to have operated in the right area. It was really painful though. The doctor came round in the afternoon and told me, through the nurse, that everything had gone well. The bloke in the next bed had been operated on for a double hernia and he could hardly move but we were given painkillers and told it would improve. We were supposed to stay in for ten days but after a week I couldn't stand it. The food was atrocious and the standard of nursing was abysmal. I discharged myself after seven days and got the train home.

Things didn't improve. As we progressed north towards Carlisle we got into a blizzard and the train slowed to a crawl as the snow got thicker and thicker. We got into Carlisle hours late and then had a nightmare journey home by car. We only just made it as the snow was so thick, and when we eventually got home there was a power cut as the snow had brought the power lines down. We were snowed in for the next two days and when it started to melt I had to sit and watch Diane digging the car out as I was not allowed to do anything. I kept her going with mugs of coffee. Life was hard.

Despite the Dreadnought and its staff I was back to 100 per cent after a couple of weeks and when I phoned the company they were able to tell me I'd be rejoining the *Al Ihsa'a* on her return to Tilbury in the middle of March. She had been delayed by problems in the Gulf so I was getting an extra week's leave.

As promised I rejoined the *Al Ihsa'a* on the 17th March in Tilbury when she docked. We sailed the following day and charged round the usual six ports in seven days. It was really nice to clear Le Havre and catch our breath. It was a good passage out to Suez.

I had a surprise one morning when a delegation from the Sierra Leonian crew knocked on my door. Usually it was a list of grievances and complaints about their stores and working hours but this time they caught me out by requesting to do an extra trip on board as they were all due for relief when we got back to Tilbury. I was over the moon because they were a good hard-working bunch and it also meant that morale was pretty good as well. I immediately sent off a telex to the head office and told them the good news as it would save quite a lot of money on air fares and we wouldn't have the hassle of training a new crew. For once they replied immediately and said the crew would be leaving in Tilbury next visit regardless. I sometimes wondered what went on in people's heads in the office. I didn't tell the crew this until we were homeward bound as I didn't want a bolshie crowd on board for longer than necessary.

We passed through Suez on the 3rd April. I had an argument with the Canal pilot as we passed through. He announced he was feeling ill and thought we would have to anchor in the Bitter Lakes to get a relief. This meant we might drop out of the convoy and could easily lose 24 hours which would badly affect our schedule. I was just trying to work out what to do when he said that if I gave him four cartons of cigarettes he would make an effort and take the ship through. I blew my top and told him his pedigree. He wasn't too happy and for a while I thought I'd blown it and he would go sick and delay us. I could see huge problems coming up and just for some cigarettes but the 3rd mate turned out to be my saviour. He was a Jordanian and didn't seem to like Egyptians anyhow and he said he had heard what the pilot had said to me and would report him to the authorities. After a bit more grumbling the pilot agreed to carry on and we completed the transit on time.

After the Canal again it was the same routine round the Gulf and if anything it was a bit quicker as the ports got more efficient. The trips seem to be divided into mad activity with little or no time to sleep whilst we rattled round the loading ports on the Continent and the discharge ports in the Arabian Gulf. These were interspersed with periods of ten days at sea where life was boring and we caught up with sleep and completed all the mundane paperwork and maintenance. In port it was very hard to sleep with the noise of the container operations. Even with the windows shut the crashing about of the containers and the warning klaxons on the cranes and forklifts permeated everywhere. The company seemed to have stopped us calling at Jeddah on the homeward passage, which made life easier so we only had the hassle of the Suez Canal passage which usually took 24 hours. This trip saw us missing out Jeddah again so we were back at the Suez Canal on the 26th April three weeks after going through the other way.

It was an uneventful passage back to Tilbury apart an afternoon in the English Channel. We were south of the Isle of Wight when we encountered an area of really thick fog. The 2nd mate called me to the bridge because he had hundreds of small targets on the radar screen ahead of us. We had just come to the conclusion that they must be false echoes when the coastguard announced on the radio that there was a large yacht race in progress from the Solent to Le Havre. We promptly reduced speed and threaded our way through them. What really concerned me was that we could see several other large vessels ploughing on regardless. I still don't know how there weren't any yachts sunk.

We got to Tilbury on the 6th May just in time for the Bank Holiday so we had a day off with nothing to do so we all adjourned to the nearest hostelries to sample the beer. The trouble was we hadn't had a drink for a month and it seemed to affect us a lot quicker than normal and we all ended up back on board by mid afternoon slightly the worse for wear. It was back to normal at midnight when they started cargo operations with the containers crashing around.

We sailed 24 hours later and it was the usual Continental ports and soon we were heading down to Suez again. It was a nice easy trip with lovely Mediterranean weather. The only incident was where we nearly hit a small Egyptian coaster. We had a new 3rd mate on board who was Saudi Arabian and fresh from the nautical college. It was our duty to alter course but the 3rd mate just carried on and the coaster had to take violent evasive action missing us by only metres. I arrived on the bridge to find him on the VHF radio involved in a slanging match in Arabic with the coaster. I'm glad I couldn't understand Arabic! When I queried why he hadn't altered course he said it was because it was just a small coaster and we were a large containership. He didn't take it too well when I tore a strip off him and he said he would report me for insulting him when we got back to Kuwait. As it was an Arab company he was under the impression than I was working for him. Things were obviously changing at sea and not for the better.

After we cleared Suez we started to hear rumours of troubles again in the Arabian Gulf with the Iranians firing missiles and dropping bombs on ships. Nobody on board our ship seemed unduly worried. The main topic of conversation was whether it would be declared a war zone and then we would all be on double pay. We reached our first discharge port of Dubai on the 1st June and then it was the usual rush round all the ports. The Iranians had been firing missiles at foreign vessels so our passages round the Gulf were limited to travelling at night with the ship blacked out. It wasn't the brightest of ideas as we had to anchor off Bahrain to await darkness and were overflown by a two Iranian planes so we would have made an excellent stationary target had they decided to have a go. Apart from that it was uneventful and we cleared the last port on the 10th June.

As we sailed up the Red Sea looking forward to the relative calm of the passage from Suez to Tilbury the company came up with a plan to keep us busy. They wanted us to call in at Livorno in Italy and then Marseille on our homeward passage just to keep us out of mischief. It actually turned out to improve the trip. Firstly I got to pilot the ship through the Straits of Messina between Italy and Sicily which I always enjoyed and then when we arrived in Livorno our cargo wasn't ready as it had been such short notice. We had two days there which was very pleasant and the agents insisted on taking us ashore for a lovely meal and more importantly we could top up with beer and alcohol instead of having to wait until the Continent. After that we nipped across the top of the Mediterranean to Marseille where it was a disaster. One of the shore gantries broke down and we had orders to sail at noon to arrive in Tilbury on time. In the end we had to sail and leave 20 containers behind which meant they had to divert another ship in to pick them up. I think they must have lost a lot of money on that call.

We arrived at Tilbury on time on the 28th June and I paid off the next day and went home on leave. This time I had a very pleasant ten weeks with lovely weather and time with the kids on their summer holidays. I rejoined the *Al Ihsa'a* in Marseille on the 16th August which was a week earlier than I was expecting but when I got on board I found we were scheduled to drydock in Lisbon for two weeks. I quite liked the sound of this as I'd never been there and it always seemed to be an attractive place to visit. We arrived off Lisbon three days later and were told to anchor outside the port. It looked really nice ashore with bars and cafés along the seafront so we were dying to have a wander around. However it was not to be – the following morning we got a message saying the drydocking had been cancelled and we were to proceed to an anchorage in the River Thames to await further instructions. There was great disappointment all round as several of us had started to make

135

arrangements for our wives to join us in Lisbon.

We anchored off Southend four days later. As our drydock had been cancelled we were now well ahead of our schedule so we had to remain at anchor for eight days until we could drop back into our regular slot. It was really frustrating being anchored so close to the shore seeing all the flashing lights of the pubs and discos but we coped.

We berthed in Tilbury on the 31st August and then it was the mad rush round the Continental ports clearing Bremerhaven on the 9th September. We sailed out into a full north westerly gale and were unable to disembark the pilot outside the port so we had to carry him with us and drop him off at Dover as we passed. He was made up as he was on extra pay and he got all sorts of expenses for his trip home. He also made serious inroads into my limited supply of beer which was a bit of a bind. I was pleasantly surprised the next time we berthed in Bremerhaven when he brought me a case of special German beer to replace my stock. It was seriously strong stuff so I had to limit myself to one a day.

After we cleared the English Channel the weather improved greatly and we had a lovely passage down into the Mediterranean. The company were now making regular stops round the Mediterranean and this time we stopped off at Marseille and Genoa which wasn't too much of a hardship and I got to pilot the ship through the Straits of Messina again on the way to Suez. We received a message that we must make the Suez convoy of the 22nd September as we were a couple of days behind schedule. We got there just in time but the Canal surveyors who checked the ship and issued our permit to transit were in a belligerent mood and it cost me a case of whisky and numerous cartons of cigarettes to placate them. Normally I would have brazened it out but if they had delayed the ship until the next convoy I would have been in all sorts of trouble.

Again we omitted Jeddah on this occasion so it was a quick passage to the first discharge port of Dubai arriving there on the 30th September. It was then a mad rush round the Gulf doing six ports in six days which was pretty impressive. As we were leaving the Gulf we got a message saying the drydock had now been arranged for Valletta in Malta which although not as good as Lisbon would do all right.

We arrived there on the 17th October and moved straight into the drydock. As it was going to be two weeks and the skipper can normally have a relaxed time in drydock I arranged for Diane to fly out for the stay. The chief engineer, Mick, also arranged for his wife to join as well and the pair of them had a great time exploring the island from end to end using local buses. The engineer superintendent had been given a hire car for our stay in port and he wasn't happy about the way the Maltese drove so he let me use it whenever I wanted so Diane and I managed a couple of trips to places like Gozo and the city of Qom. I had a really nice relaxing fortnight with only the ship's accounts to bother about.

The main work was to sandblast large areas of the hull where the paint was already peeling off and repaint the whole hull with a new type of paint that was supposed to make us go faster as it had less resistance when going through the water. It cost a fortune and I could never figure whether it worked. I also managed to scrape a huge area of it off in Livorno, our first port, when we rubbed along a stone quay wall.

Livorno was our only Mediterranean port and we arrived there on the 30th October. Diane flew home from there in the afternoon so I travelled up with her to see the sights and have a pizza in Pisa. We sailed in the evening and headed back towards Tilbury. Just after we sailed I got a message from the company saying I would be leaving the *Al Ihsa'a* on arrival and a new permanent master would be taking over. I didn't know whether to be pleased or not. I was heartily sick of charging round the world without a break but on the other hand I had organised a cracking bunch of officers and I would really miss having them around.

We berthed in Tilbury on the 5th November and I was relieved by Bob Sutton who absolutely loathed containerships and wasn't looking forward to his stint on board. When I came to leave I couldn't believe how much stuff I'd accumulated and I had to hire a car to get it all home. It had been a shorter than usual trip but at least I had enough leave to have a good Christmas at home.

CHAPTER FOURTEEN

Back to 'proper ships' again

m.v Ibn Al Atheer
28th January 1985 – 8th June 1985

I had a really good leave with the bonus of being home over Christmas but in January the weather turned really bad with day after day of sleet and snow. We had to dig our way out of the drive a few times so when my orders came through the last week of January to join the *Ibn Al Atheer* in Kuwait it wasn't received too badly (at least by me). I was supposed to fly out on the 25th but when we set out to go the station we got the car completely stuck in a snowdrift and had to return. The company weren't best pleased and I don't think they believed me as they were nearly 100 miles away in Liverpool and there was no sign of snow there. I eventually flew out two days later and joined the *Ibn Al Atheer* out at anchor in Kuwait Bay where she was waiting for a berth. It was nice to be back on board a general cargo boat again.

Kuwait was the first discharge port and the majority of the cargo was for here. It was mainly constructional steel from the Far East and tons of electronic and consumer goods. The ship was also due for drydock on completion of discharge and the company had decided to try out a newly opened drydock in Bahrain. We had a week in Kuwait unloading continuously and for once it was a pretty efficient operation. After that we had a day each in Dammam and Doha before heading north for the short trip to Bahrain.

The drydock was amazing. It had been built to dock the largest tankers at the time so we looked very insignificant sitting in the middle. I figured they could get five ships of our size in the dock and still have room to spare. We docked on the 11th February and were expecting to be there about five days as the company had scheduled us to load again in Japan in early March. It soon became obvious that things weren't going to go according to plan as nobody came near us on the first day to even discuss the numerous repairs that were required. Eventually on the third day our company superintendent arrived and after a long meeting the repair programme was agreed and workers started to appear and the work commenced. One of the jobs was to survey the rudder and its fitments and on the second day of work it was discovered that the pintle (the bearing on which the rudder sits) was really badly worn and would require considerable work so our original five days in drydock suddenly extended to three weeks. Morale went downhill as there was absolutely nothing to do and we were miles from the town. Two days later we heard that one of the company ships had been hit by an Iranian missile that had penetrated the engineroom and killed one of the crew. It had also passed through the captain's day room causing a fair bit of damage on the way. We decided we would rather be bored out of our minds in drydock than paddling round the Gulf avoiding missiles. Luckily we were able to change films with other ships in port so life was at least bearable.

We eventually left drydock on the 3rd March, nearly a month after entering. The ship looked really good as we'd managed to get a fair bit of painting done and a lot of maintenance on the machinery. We were still expecting to head out to the Far East but just after we sailed we got a message telling us to take on fuel in Jeddah, which is in the opposite direction. We cleared the Gulf without being attacked by the Iranians and headed off west towards the Red Sea. It was a good passage with lovely weather and we managed to continue painting so the ship looked really smart.

I realised that I had a great bunch of officers on board who worked hard and also played hard. Morale was high and I was enjoying being at sea again after all the hassle on the containership. The only fly in the ointment was that the *Ibn Al Atheer* was registered under the Saudi flag again so we weren't allowed any alcohol on board. I had managed to acquire a few cases of beer on the quiet in Bahrain but as we were going to Jeddah there had to be nothing on board on arrival. We solved this by having a tremendous barbecue the night before we arrived and finished any remaining stock. It was hard but we were determined and consequently arrived in Jeddah very much hung over. It was all for nothing in the end as we anchored off the port and they sent the fuel out in a barge and the only people we saw were the barge crew. While we were refuelling we got a message from head office advising us that our next employment was loading round the Mediterranean back for the Gulf.

Our first port was to be Marina di Carrara and this provoked a rush up to the chartroom to find out where the hell it was. It turned out to be a tiny Italian port just south of La Spezia. This had the makings of a good trip. It only took seven hours to take on the 1,600 tons of fuel oil and then we were on our way towards the Suez Canal, which we transited without any problems on the 12th March.

We headed up to Marina di Carrara and I had my usual bit of fun piloting the ship through the Straits of Messina. When we arrived off the port the wind had decided to pick up to gale force from the west and I was very relieved when the pilot called us and said it was too windy to berth, as the entrance looked awfully narrow and it was a tiny port once inside the breakwaters. We anchored off for a day and berthed the following morning on the 17th March. As it was a Sunday there was no cargo work so everybody dispersed ashore to investigate the local bars. It was a great little town and seemed to be a bit of a holiday resort for Italians with loads of little bars and restaurants.

We started loading the following morning. The cargo was marble slabs, bags of gypsum and pallets of tiles. Great care had to be taken with the marble as it came in huge slabs weighing ten tons or more and we had to stow it so it wouldn't crack on the passage to the Gulf. The tiles were amazing with fantastic colours and designs and must have cost a fortune. Our only complaint was the weather, as it seemed to rain every day. Still, we got ashore for a wander most nights and got quite a taste for Chianti which was completely different from the stuff we used to get in raffia covered bottles back home. We also managed to stock up with some cases of Peroni beer so life was rosy.

One morning we got an invite up to the quarry where they were cutting the marble. It was unbelievable. They had examples of the different colours they could get, most of it being greys and whites but they also had some with gold and black streaks that looked terrific when it was polished up. The most impressive bit was the huge saw they used to cut the slabs – it just went through the marble like cheese. After the tour we were taken for a late lunch accompanied by copious quantities of wine. I promptly fell asleep when I got back on board. It took them eleven days to load 8,500 tons, which I thought was pretty good going as it was all securely stowed and lashed.

We sailed on the 27th March to Marseille arriving there the following morning. Here we loaded a completely different cargo. It was all military equipment ranging from armoured vehicles and a couple of small tanks to some large crates that looked suspiciously as if they contained missiles – probably Exocets. The manifests only stated 'Equipment Militaire' so I didn't delve too deeply. It only took us a day to load and secure everything and we were on our way again by the evening.

Our next port was Venice and our berth wasn't available until the 1st April so we ambled along at reduced speed. The weather was very pleasant so I did a little detour between the islands of Corsica and Sardinia. They looked wild and rocky though there were some lovely fishing villages nestling in the bays. I also nipped through the Straits of Messina again and I saw the whirlpools that occur at the northern entrance for the first time. They were quite dramatic and I wouldn't like to have gone close in a small boat.

We arrived off Venice early in the morning and were told to anchor because the tugs were on strike but thankfully things were quickly resolved and we berthed at noon. We weren't berthed in the actual port of Venice but in Port Marghera at the end of the Venice causeway. I'd been to Venice a few times and got on really well with the local agents so I was looking forward to our stay in port. I organised for my wife, Diane, to fly out and she arrived early in the evening. The agents and some of the shippers of our cargo took us out for a lovely meal that night. We got back to the ship considerably heavier than when we left as we both love Italian food.

It was a really varied cargo we had to load and a large portion of it was plant for oil refineries in Saudi Arabia which had been manufactured in Germany and shipped down by road to load in Venice. They were huge awkward pieces of pipework and pressure vessels that should have been put on a ship in Germany but had missed the deadline so someone figured we were the next best option. They were a nightmare to load as they had pipes and flanges sticking out everywhere. The Italian stevedores did a brilliant job of squeezing them in without any damage. Normally when I am in port I am often reluctant to go ashore in case anything goes wrong but this time I had a great bunch of officers and when the agents organised a taxi for me and Diane up to Venice I jumped at the chance. We spent all afternoon wandering around the streets and alleys just soaking up the atmosphere.

The following day we spent the whole day in Venice. I have no idea where we got to, as all the streets seem to curve one way or the other. We eventually came across the Grand Canal and Diane spotted a restaurant with seating overlooking the canal that she was sure had been in a Joan Collins film. We blithely bowled in for lunch. We ended up sitting on the veranda watching the gondolas paddling past. Diane ordered a lasagne and I decided to push the boat out and have a lobster. It was delicious but when the bill came we had a problem as I had nowhere near enough money. My lobster had cost 35,000 lire while Diane's lasagne was 1,200 lire. I had to leave her in the restaurant and leg it the agent's office to get some more money. Loris, the agent, was highly amused and suggested we go and have a few drinks in a local bar and leave Diane there but, though tempted, I had to decline. As I was hurrying back along the side of the canal clutching the money in my sweaty little hands I tripped over a bollard and as near as dammit fell into the canal much to the amusement of some locals. Diane wasn't bothered at all when I got back as she'd been sitting drinking coffee and watching the world go by. (20 years later and Diane still has the restaurant bill just to show people.)

The loading was going surprisingly well despite the complexity of the cargo. The agents had found a large consignment of mosaic tiles for Bahrain so we had to juggle the discharge ports around a bit to accommodate them. The tiles were made in Venice and were beautiful colours and fabulous designs. The shipper told me the cost of each tile was over £30 so I decided not to order any. On the last night in Venice we organised a party for the agents and stevedores which was a great success. One of the stevedores made a huge pan of spaghetti carbonara which was washed down with a large amount of local pinot grigio. There were one or two hangovers the following morning.

We sailed in the afternoon of the 5th April for our final port of Piraeus. When we arrived off the port we were advised that there was a nationwide transport strike and it was doubtful that we would berth. I had a bit of a panic as Diane was still on board and if Piraeus was cancelled she would have to remain on until the Arabian Gulf which was a good twelve days away. In the end the strike was called off and we berthed the following day. The loading was something of a disaster as although the strike was over the lorries still had to be loaded and brought to the port. Diane was made up as it gave us a chance to do some sightseeing in Athens. The local agent obligingly organised a car and driver for the day so we set off with Dave Short, the chief engineer, as company for the Grand Tour. Unfortunately all the guards and museum staff at the Acropolis were on strike for the day so we were confined to a brief wander round the outside which wasn't very satisfactory. I wasn't impressed with Athens at all as we seemed to spend most of our time stuck in horrific traffic jams and the city had a permanent yellow fug hanging over it.

Our driver reckoned he knew a good restaurant so we decided to at least have a decent meal out. It was a fantastic place down by a small harbour and the meal turned out to be excellent too. We ended up with a whole grilled fish the size of a small whale each and mountains of lovely fresh Greek salad accompanied by a couple of bottles of good local wine. It nearly made up for not seeing the Acropolis. When it came to pay I found out I'd overdone things again and had nowhere near enough money to pay the bill. Luckily Dave had an American Express card, which did nicely, otherwise Diane would have had another afternoon waiting for me to return with some money.

The loading rate improved on the third day and in the end we sailed in the evening leaving only two containers behind which were stuck in a traffic jam miles away. Diane got off safely to fly home and we set off towards the Suez Canal arriving there two days later on the 13th April. It was a smooth passage for once though I had to give out extra amounts of cigarettes to the various Canal officials as we had no manifests for the cargo loaded in Piraeus.

Our first discharge port was a brand new port in Saudi Arabia right at the southern end of the Red Sea. It was so new we didn't even have a proper chart and we were told to follow a buoyed channel for 50 miles until we got to within five miles of the port when a pilot would board and guide us in. I was quite nervous until we entered the channel. The Saudis didn't do things by halves and the buoys were huge and would have done credit to a major seaway. The pilot appeared on cue and we berthed in the afternoon of the 17th April. Everything in the port was brand new including the labour. It was total chaos as nobody seemed to know how anything worked. The cargo was mainly oil refinery equipment and none of the lorries on shore were big enough to carry it. Eventually some suitable transport appeared and we managed to discharge everything safely by the following morning and we sailed at noon.

Our next port was Dubai and we received strict instructions from the company only to enter the Gulf at night and all passages in the Gulf would be at night due to the increased number of attacks by the Iranian forces. We weren't too happy that we had a large amount of military equipment in number two hold and we were sure that the Iranians would know about it if they had any decent intelligence. We were also told to maintain radio silence so we had no idea what was going on in the Gulf. When we arrived at the Strait of Hormuz late at night on the 23rd April we found 40 odd ships at anchor and no ships seemed to be moving anywhere. We blacked the ship out as best we could and blithely sailed on. We only saw two other ships on the radar and had a lovely quiet run to Dubai where we berthed on arrival.

The Gulf discharge went very well in the end although it was extended as we could only travel between ports at night. The longest stay was in Dammam in Saudi where we unloaded most of the marble and tiles. It was really satisfying to see it loaded onto transport without any damage and we even got a congratulatory note from the receiver to say how pleased he was with his shipment. We had thankfully got rid of all the military equipment early on so we felt a bit easier. We completed discharge in Bahrain on the 14th May and got orders to proceed to Antwerp to load our next cargo. Once we were clear of the Gulf we were instructed to proceed at economical speed to reduce our fuel consumption as the oil prices were rocketing with all the trouble with Iran. Consequently we ambled along at about twelve knots instead of our usual 16 so life took on an easier pace – the only fly in the ointment being that we had no booze on board which would have made life really pleasant.

It was a really good run back with good weather all the way.

About four days from Antwerp we got a message that our cargo had been delayed and we had to find somewhere to anchor to put in five days. I opted for a nice little spot off the south coast called Lyme Bay. I made a point of sending a message to the company saying we were anchored close to Beer Head. Again it was a bit frustrating being so close to England and not being able to get ashore.

After five days swinging round on the anchor they decided our cargo was available so we heaved up the anchor and sailed up to Antwerp to berth there on the 6th June. We started loading immediately and I had a day to sort my accounts and paperwork out before I was relieved. Looking back it was one of the most enjoyable trips as master with a good reliable bunch of officers and lovely places to visit.

CHAPTER FIFTEEN

Last trips with United Arab Shipping

m.v Al Ahmadiah & Al Muharraq
20th August 1985 – 16th January 1986

I had a very pleasant leave again over the summer months. I even got an extra week's leave for some reason. When my joining instructions came I was to join the *Al Ahmadiah* in New York on the 20th August. My heart sank as this was a sister ship to the *Al Shamiah*, one of the converted container ships and reputedly in pretty poor condition. On top of that she was a training ship for Arab cadets who had a reputation for making trouble whenever they could and generally were a real pain in the arse. Thankfully there was a training officer on board in the form of Ray Ward who managed to keep them quiet most of the time. I brightened up a bit, though, when I was told I was only going for six weeks as the present skipper needed a relief for personal reasons. I flew out and joined her in Newark where she had just berthed on the start of the load round the States.

Surprisingly there was quite a lot of cargo to be discharged from the Gulf as normally we would just unload empty containers to be refilled so on this occasion we were to travel round the coast to Houston discharging the full boxes and then return up the coast loading. We set off the following morning for Baltimore. To save time we went up the Delaware Bay and through the Chesapeake and Delaware Canal to get there. It was a bad idea as we encountered thick fog as soon as we entered Delaware Bay and had to go at slow speed most of the way. On top of that there was a problem with the main engine and we had to keep stopping to repair an exhaust valve.

This was no problem out at sea but losing power in a canal is not the best. I was knackered by the time we tied up early on the morning of the 22nd. I was hoping to get a couple of hours kip but there was a knock on my door and it appeared that three of the cadets' passports had expired which made for difficulties with the immigration authorities. In the end I arranged for them to go to their embassy in Washington under guard to get them renewed. It left no time for my kip as we commenced cargo operations shortly afterwards. The cadets arrived back six hours later to report that the embassy was shut when they got there as they had an early day before the weekend. The immigration officer organised that they could remain on board but were not allowed ashore in the States and we would have to employ a guard in every port to ensure they stayed on board. I was all for paying them off and deporting them but was told by the company that they had to remain on board no matter what the expense. Cargo was completed late evening and we sailed off down the Chesapeake Bay towards our next port of Houston. This was a five day passage so at least I would have a nice quiet time for a bit.

This was not to be. A real towser of a hurricane called Elena was brewing out in the Atlantic and I had to decide whether to stop and let it cross ahead of me or go as fast as possible and see if I could beat it round Florida and into the Gulf of Mexico. Thankfully the Americans were tracking it very accurately so I decided to go full speed and outrun it. It turned out to be the right decision as it slowed down and we were well ahead of it when we arrived off Houston. It was an efficient cargo operation and in 24 hours we were sailing out into the Gulf of Mexico right into the path of Elena. Bugger. We hove to and waited to see which way it would go but the bloody thing stopped in the middle of the Gulf for a few hours before moving off north east out of our way. We had an uncomfortable passage up to New Orleans in the huge swell but we still managed to arrive on schedule. We had a day loading in New Orleans then it was back out into the very rough seas left by Elena on our way to Savannah. Thankfully by the time we had got down to the Florida Keys the weather subsided and we had a very pleasant trip north up the American coast. We got ourselves into the Gulf Stream and it gave us an extra three knots so we arrived in Savannah well ahead of schedule. We then did Norfolk, Baltimore and finished off sailing from New York towards Valencia on the 9th September.

It was a miserable trip across the Atlantic. I thought Elena might have cleared the air but there was depression after depression so it was quite a slow passage. Halfway across the mate reported that some of the containers had been broken into with the locks smashed and the seals broken. Whoever it was didn't have access to the manifests as the containers were stowed with mundane items like bags of salt and plastic plates. It was still very serious as broaching cargo is a sackable offence and on top of that we would have no end of trouble landing containers without seals.

We replaced the locks and seals from a stock we had on board and let it be known that we would be calling in the police. We also collected all the broken locks and seals and then put it about that the police would be able to get fingerprints off them. Two hours later Ray, the training officer, came to tell me he had been approached by several of the cadets to say that it wasn't them so it became obvious that it was some of the cadets. I didn't take any more action and just let them stew. Needless to say there weren't any more incidents of that nature.

It took us an extra day to get to Valencia with the continuous bad weather and we arrived there on the evening of the 19th September. It was a mad panic as we were changing eight officers including the 1st mate and the chief engineer. They were all trying to hand over to each other whilst the cargo operation was going on. On top of that two lorry loads of stores and spare equipment from the UK appeared on the quay without any prior notice so we had to load all that as well. It was all done and dusted in four hours and we were on our way again. I knew quite a few of the new officers, having sailed with them before, and I was particularly pleased to see Dave Short, the chief engineer off my previous ship.

Unlike the Atlantic the weather in the Mediterranean was perfect with no wind and warm sunny days. Life would have been peaceful if it hadn't have been for the cadets who were constantly fighting among themselves and generally being a pain. Ray Ward, the training officer, was a hero as he alternately cajoled and harassed them to try and get some work out of them. Apart from a couple of breakdowns of the main engine it was a nice smooth passage and we passed through the Suez Canal without too much trouble.

Our first discharge port was Aqaba in Jordan which puzzled me a bit as we only had ten containers to discharge and the port charges must have meant that the company was losing money. I supposed they were trying to open up another port but it didn't really make sense. We arrived there on the morning of the 26th September and had to wait half a day until a berth became available. Once we got alongside it was chaotic as only one gantry was in operation. I got a message to say I had to go ashore immediately and phone our head office in Kuwait so I got a lift up to the agent's office. It was like the Secret Service. I was taken to a separate office and the door closed. When I eventually got through to Kuwait it was a verbal message that the war in the Gulf was deteriorating and we had to discharge all containers for Iraq and destroy all paperwork relating to them. When I asked which containers were for Iraq I was told nobody knew so we had to go through the cargo manifests for all the containers and look for any address in Iraq. I wandered back to the ship slightly bemused. When I got back on board (ten o'clock at night) our original ten containers had all ready been discharged and the ship was all ready to sail. I cancelled everything and started to go through the sheaves of paper that were the cargo manifests. By three in the morning we had hopefully identified all the Iraqi containers and organised for them to be discharged. Inevitably they were all underneath other containers so we ended up moving 120 containers to get at them. This took another 24 hours and ended up with a lot of frayed tempers. I was really pleased to sail at midnight the following day. We were trailed all the way down the Gulf of Aqaba by an Israeli warship which made me a bit nervous but he left us alone once we got into the Red Sea.

Our next port was Jeddah and I was worried that the delay in Aqaba would mean that we had lost our place in the schedule but luckily another ship was also delayed and we got straight in. We had a lot of hassle in Jeddah as we had quite a bit of military cargo on board and the army wanted it discharged first, onto their vehicles, and the customs officials took a hissy fit and refused to cooperate. The cargo operation came to a stop for two hours and was only resolved when a large black car with darkened windows swept onto the quay with a police escort. Whoever was inside the car didn't even bother to get out and summoned the various officials over to him. There was a lot of saluting and running about and cargo work resumed immediately. Maggie Thatcher would have been jealous. We actually made up some time in the end so when we sailed we tried for our maximum speed to try and get back on schedule. This lasted four hours until the main engine overheated and we had to slow down drastically.

It was an interesting trip to the Gulf. Every morning I had a delegation of the cadets at my door demanding that they be paid off on arrival in Dubai and then rejoin in Dubai as we came out of the Gulf as they didn't think they should be exposed to the dangers of the war. It ended up a shouting match every time and I've a feeling they were using it as an excuse to avoid work. Three days into the trip Ray Ward, the training officer, had an accident showing the cadets how to bend steel plate (or maybe that should be how not to bend steel plate) and broke his forearm. We pulled in to the port of Salalah on the south Yemini coast and sent him ashore to hospital. I was dreading trying to cope with the cadets without him and was over the moon when he was returned on board with his arm in plaster. We got to Dubai without further incident and managed to berth straight away despite being over 30 hours behind our schedule.

Dubai went very smoothly and we finished cargo by teatime on the 6th October. We had strict instructions not to sail through the middle of the Gulf in daylight so we had a night in with nothing to do. I got ashore for a lovely meal with Peter Young, one of the cargo planners, and his wife, and more than one or two beers which I regretted the following morning. From Dubai we nipped quickly round Dammam, Kuwait, Bahrain and back to Dubai in four days. The cadets created all sorts of problems and threatened to go on strike at one stage then realised that it would make no difference to anyone except themselves. Half of them managed to get paid off sick so we sailed out of the Gulf with only a few on board which pleased everyone. As we were sailing from Kuwait to Bahrain a Greek ship only 20 miles from us was hit by a missile and the captain and 3rd mate killed so we were very relieved when we cleared Dubai and headed back westwards.

We stopped off at Jeddah to pick up some empty containers then it was back through Suez and into the Mediterranean. The company were trying to expand their routes and were now offering shipment from most ports in the Mediterranean to the USA so we were programmed to stop off at Livorno, Genoa, Fos (Marseille) and Valencia on our way out. Things didn't go too well as we were delayed with bad weather and delays clearing the containers through customs. We also had to shift quite a few containers around to enable some really heavy containers to be loaded in the holds and increase our stability. We eventually cleared Valencia on the 30th October and headed off across the Atlantic. It should have been a lovely weather passage but it was a terrible trip with storm after storm and the ship rolling and bouncing around all over the place. There was a high pressure system up north and it pushed all the depressions south towards us.

We arrived in New York on the 10th November over 24 hours late but berthed on arrival as all the other ships were late too. I was expecting to be relieved on arrival but was greeted with a message that the returning skipper wouldn't be joining until Norfolk which was a week later. After New York we did a quick call at Baltimore and then headed south into the Gulf of Mexico to Houston. A day after we sailed the chief steward told me that one of the seamen had really bad tonsillitis and a temperature of 103 degrees. We radioed the US coastguard and they advised a course of penicillin. His condition gradually deteriorated and he started fitting so we asked for him to be airlifted off. The coastguard agreed and we altered course to be closer to the land. Two hours later the helicopter appeared and whipped him off to hospital in Savannah. I was very impressed by the efficiency of the operation and the seaman made a full recovery and rejoined us when we arrived back in Savannah ten days later.

As we progressed down the Florida coast it became apparent that another hurricane was forming out in the Atlantic and this looked even bigger than the previous one we'd encountered. By the time we arrived in Houston on the 17th November it was over Cuba so I knew we were going to get caught by this one. Houston didn't want us tied up in their port in case we broke loose and damaged something so they worked really hard and turned us around in double quick time. As a rule of thumb you don't want to be north west of an approaching hurricane as that is where the strongest winds and heaviest seas are experienced. We sailed out from Houston and found ourselves north west of hurricane Kate which was building in strength and heading straight towards us. I promptly set off due south at full speed to try and get away from it but the seas built up really quickly and we had to slow down to avoid damaging the ship. I was sure we were going to go straight through the middle of it but at the last minute it turned north and passed about 200 miles from us. The winds weren't too bad but the seas battered us for the next two days until we got out on the east coast again.

We arrived at Savannah more or less on time only to find the hurricane was heading back our way. The port was closed down because of the high wind and rain but eventually we got berthed in the afternoon of the 27th November.

Our seaman was returned on board none the worse for his helicopter flight. They must have been feeding him well because he was about twice the weight he was when we landed him. There was also a message from the company that I was to be relieved in the next port, which was Baltimore. Things were looking really good for being home for Christmas again.

We got to Baltimore three days later and Neil Willot relieved me as soon as we docked. There was also a message from the company saying that I wasn't going home at all but had to fly directly to Hamburg to relieve the skipper on the *Al Muharraq*. It was a real downer. I had been really looking forward to a nice quiet Christmas at home. When I got talking to the girl from the agents who was arranging my flight she said it was quite complicated as there were no direct flights to Hamburg so suggested I go via Heathrow. She then came up with the idea that I nip home for a night from Heathrow and fly to Hamburg the following day. Brilliant! She arranged all the flights including one from Heathrow to Newcastle so I'd get home quicker. From then on it all went pear shaped. The transatlantic flight from Baltimore was delayed so I missed the flight from Heathrow to Newcastle and had to catch a later one. I got home about eleven at night and then had to leave at five the next morning. I hardly saw the kids as they were asleep. When I got back to Heathrow the Hamburg flight was cancelled and the next flight was full so I had twelve hours waiting to fly.

When I got to the ship at eleven at night I was met by a very grumpy skipper who'd had to do an extra day's work. He insisted on handing over all the money and paperwork there and then so he could leave at five the following morning. Not a good start and it got worse. He reckoned it was the worst bunch of officers he'd ever sailed with. The mate had been passed over for a skipper's job so was very bitter and showed no interest and the other officers were incompetent and unreliable. On top of that the ship was

152

programmed to load large quantities of ammunition and it wasn't a good time to be carrying ammunition around the Arabian Gulf.

We sailed the following afternoon, the 28th November, down to Rotterdam. On the passage it was obvious that the previous master's assessment of the officers was correct as not only were the deck officers incompetent but really arrogant and resented any criticism of their performance. This had the makings of a great trip!

There was quite a lot of cargo to load in Rotterdam and the loading plan was extremely complicated as we had several heavy lifts of electrical equipment that could only be stowed in certain places. I had to personally intervene on several occasions when I should have been able to leave the job to the deck officers. Thankfully we had a full weekend with no cargo work so I was able to catch up. I also met up with an old colleague who I had worked with on several ships and got taken ashore for a lovely meal and a tour round Old Rotterdam. He also turned up on Sunday morning and took me ashore with his wife and son and we wandered round a street market for a couple of hours and then had lunch on a floating restaurant. The weather wasn't brilliant but at least I didn't have to think about the ship.

Work resumed on the Monday morning and everything went really smoothly so maybe my luck was changing. We sailed over to Tilbury the following day arriving there in the afternoon of the 4th December. There wasn't too much cargo to load and the majority of the work was building a huge wooden magazine in number three hold to take the explosives. It took them four days to build it and it must have cost a fortune in timber. The company must have been getting a really good freight on the explosives.

Our next port was Le Havre which went without incident until we came to sail when it became obvious that the pilot was totally inebriated. I took the ship out myself but we had a hell of a job disembarking him onto the pilot boat. I thought he was going to fall in several times but the boat crew grabbed him and got him safely into the cabin. Then it was back to Chapman Anchorage in the middle of the Thames Estuary to load the explosives. It only took four hours to load the 200 tons but we spent a further three hours securing it and lashing it down so there was no chance of it moving around. It was a mixture of industrial explosives and ammunition for discharge in Kuwait so we were going to have to take it all the way up the Gulf.

It was then off to Marseille to pick up some more explosives and I was looking forward to a peaceful week at sea. We ran into bad weather straight away and we bounced and rolled our way down the Channel and across the Bay of Biscay. On the second day out I went to the bridge to see how things were going and found the Palestinian 3rd mate sitting on the chartroom settee smoking a cigarette instead of keeping his bridge watch. I tore a strip off him which resulted in him throwing the parallel rulers at me and threatening to kill me. He reckoned it was an Arab ship and I was an Infidel and shouldn't be on board. I called up the 1st mate and we made a log entry about the incident and told the 3rd mate he would be sacked on arrival in Marseille. Luckily we had an extra 3rd mate on board, who was actually pretty efficient, so we promoted him. My only problem was that we had been told to maintain radio silence as we had all these munitions on board so I was unable to advise the company. Luckily when we got to Marseille the agent was really good and got the 3rd mate off the ship straight away and escorted to the airport by police, which didn't go down very well with him at all. He was still shouting insults at me from the police car as he was driven off. It was just twelve hours to load and then we set off again for the Gulf via Suez.

We transited the Canal on Christmas Eve and it was one of the quickest passages I've ever done. The Egyptians didn't like explosives so we went just about straight through at the head of the convoy and set off down the Red Sea. I wasn't looking forward to it but the cook managed to put on a really good Christmas dinner the following day and despite my misgivings everyone behaved themselves except the radio officer who got legless and couldn't do his watch. As we were on radio silence it didn't make much odds but I still had to have words with him the following morning.

The trip down the Red Sea went pretty well with lovely weather all the way. It was a six day passage to our first port, Salalah, in Oman. It was an odd trip, though, as I found myself quite isolated and lonely for the first time in my seagoing career. Normally I would mix with the chief engineer or the 1st mate but unfortunately I didn't get on with either of them. All the other officers were either Arab or Indian so it was difficult to hold conversations with them and the electrician was Scottish which was even worse. I spent a lot of time on my own and it would have been all too easy to console myself with booze but I managed to resist the temptation (just about).

We got to Salalah on the evening of the 30th December and had a hell of a time berthing as the wind was blowing straight off the quay. There was only one small underpowered tug and after an hour of trying I was all for giving up and anchoring outside for the night but the pilot was a determined little Omani who managed it in the end though I was sure we were going to knock one of their shore cranes down. The discharge went well and we sailed the following morning. We had a quick stop in Muscat to unload a couple of containers and then we headed up to the Gulf.

I timed our arrival at the Straits of Hormuz, at the entrance to the Gulf, at midnight and we went through blacked out. All the other ships were doing the same and it was odd looking at the radar and seeing loads of targets but nothing was visible when we looked around. We had a bit of a hairy moment when two smallish targets headed towards us with no lights but they turned out to be dhows crossing over to Sharjah. I was really pleased to berth in Dubai where we discharged for two days. After that we shot up the Gulf to Kuwait and berthed there on the 13th January. I was relieved after a couple of days and I don't think I ever been as happy to leave a ship. My relief was Malcolm Youd who was doing his first trip as skipper and I didn't envy him the trip at all.

CHAPTER SIXTEEN

Drug smuggling in the Caribbean

m.v Morant Bay
10th May 1986 – 6th August 1986

I got home on the 17th January to be greeted by thick snow everywhere. We were just about snowed in for a week only managing to get out for groceries and essentials. At least the kids enjoyed it, digging out snow holes in the drifts and building igloos. It wasn't the best time of year to be home as there wasn't much I could do outside and I'm not into decorating at all. I was also despondent about what my next appointment would be as it was obvious that life at sea was changing rapidly and not for the better. I was due seven weeks leave and two days before my leave was up the usual letter arrived with my joining instructions. I opened it with trepidation but it wasn't what I was expecting at all. It was a letter from the company saying I was redundant with immediate effect and thanking me for my service for the past twelve years. I hate using the word but I was totally gobsmacked. I had no idea that anything like this was in the pipeline. I was immediately on the phone to the personnel department and surprise, surprise, all the senior managers were on leave and unavailable to talk. I got put through to one of the marine superintendents and asked him what the score was. It appeared the head office in Kuwait had decided that British officers were too expensive and had transferred to Indian and Pakistani officers who earned a lot less. He was extremely apologetic but it wasn't his fault and in fact I think his own job was in jeopardy. He said that about 15 masters and 1st mates had been made redundant that week alone. On top of that there was to be no redundancy payment so I better start looking for a job soon. He gave me a few contacts for jobs but wasn't very hopeful as the market was now flooded with masters.

I spent the rest of the day in a bit of a daze. I was only 45 and had been expecting to finish my time with United Arab Shipping and retire when I was about 58 or so. I'd been putting a bit extra into my pension fund but now realised I couldn't touch this until I retired. I also had quite a hefty mortgage on the house so I had to find a job quickly. I got a call late in the afternoon from Rod Brockbank, one of the cargo superintendents, offering his commiserations and offering to help. He gave me quite a few contacts to try and said that if I sent my CV down he would circulate it around. It was really decent of him and it brightened me up a bit but then I realised that I didn't have a CV as I'd never needed one so I buckled down immediately and tried to come up with something presentable.

It took me most of the next day to come up with a decent CV and I felt it was pretty impressive as I had experience on a whole variety of ships. I then spent the next two months posting them off with hopeful letters to what seemed like hundreds of companies. Every morning I was there to greet the postman but I got quite depressed as most of the companies never even acknowledged my letters. I was thinking I might have to change careers and started looking in the local paper for jobs but nothing much of a maritime nature comes up in Carlisle. I got myself on the dole and I can remember the clerk doing my application asking if I'd be willing to travel for a job. I just looked at him.

Looking back through my diary I applied for a job as a paint superintendent in Dubai Dry Docks, a harbour master on Ascension Island, a pilot in Saudi Arabia, a port manager in Bahrain and a job with the Fishery Protection in the North Sea. All this on top of all the shipping companies to which I applied for a master's job. We really had to economise as well so there were very few meals out or little luxuries. Not a good leave at all.

Eventually on the 1st May I got a call from a small marine agency in Swansea asking if I had any roll on-roll off experience and how good was my ship handling. I blagged my way through even though I had virtually no ro-ro experience and to my surprise I was offered a job on a small vessel, called the *Morant Bay*, owned by the Jamaican government running between Kingston, Jamaica and Miami. The wages weren't great but at least I had a job. I only had two days to get my gear sorted before I flew out. The flight was via Miami where I had to change planes for Kingston. I was detained in Miami for four hours as I didn't have the correct visa but at least they didn't deport me. When I arrived in Kingston I was greeted by Bernie, the engineer superintendent, who informed me the ship had broken down and was still in Miami. We went out for a really nice meal and he filled me in on how the company worked (which wasn't very well). After a night's sleep I caught the plane back to Miami and this time I was allowed in as I had the right visa.

The ship was lying in port beside all the cruise liners and was a conventional ro-ro ship with one main deck accessed by a ramp at the stern and an upper deck, which was accessed by a large hydraulic lift. She looked pretty small compared to the liners but she looked in good condition. I was pleasantly surprised by the large comfortable accommodation. The ship had been built in Norway and given to Jamaica under some sort of trade agreement. There was some really good equipment on board and with twin screws and a bow thruster it was going to be a doddle to manoeuvre. For a small ship we had quite a large crew as it was used to train up Jamaican officers for their certificates and give them experience. The 1st mate, the chief engineer and I were all British and all the rest were Jamaican. We were required to wear uniform which seemed to set a standard.

I liked the Jamaicans as they were generally a happy bunch though not the most energetic. The 3rd mate was a woman called Sharon who was determined to prove she was better than a bloke and I had to admit she was really efficient.

It appeared that one of the ship's two generators had blown up and we were awaiting spares. The spares were available locally but the company had a terrible reputation for not paying bills and nobody would release the spares without money up front. Bernie arrived next day to try and chase things up but didn't have much success. Barry, who I was relieving, was supposed to stay on board until we got back to Kingston to show me the ropes but as time dragged on he got himself paid off and disappeared home after two days. When it became obvious that the generator spares weren't going to be forthcoming Bernie managed to hire a portable generator and this was loaded on board and connected up and we eventually sailed on the 10th May five days after I'd joined. Just as we sailed Bernie announced that I couldn't use the bow thruster as it used too much power for the new generator. Still I reckoned I should do all right with the twin screws.

As we sailed south through the Florida Straits it became obvious that this was going to be an interesting tour. An hour out we had to reduce to half speed as the engines were over-heating and in all the time I was on the ship we never got better than 70 per cent of full power. The engines were in an awful state. When it got daylight I found out we were putting out a huge column of black smoke from the port engine and the starboard was nearly as bad with the addition of showers of sparks. After breakfast I decided to call the office in Jamaica to tell them of our progress and advise them of an eta. When I called the American shore radio station I was told the ship was blacklisted for non-payment of bills and all service was denied. They wouldn't even let me reverse the charges. Interesting. I then tried calling through stations in Cuba, Puerto Rico, Panama and Mexico but it was the same result. Nobody had told me about this and I began to wonder if my wages were going to be paid.

It took about three days to get from Miami to Kingston – it should have taken two and a half if we'd been able to progress at full speed.

As we got close to Kingston I was able to order a pilot through the VHF radio so at least I'd have someone to guide me in as I'd never taken a ship into Kingston before. The pilot boarded and took us across the harbour where he pointed out our berth right at the eastern end of the port. He explained there was a half mile channel to navigate stern first up to the berth but said it was no problem with the bow thruster. I told him the bow thruster was out of operation so the pilot immediately handed over to me and took no further interest in the berthing. After a lot of backing and filling I managed to get the ship on the berth and received the congratulations of Bernie who was expecting to have to hire a tug at great expense. We were all tied up by late evening on the 12th May and started cargo work immediately as the ship was way behind schedule after the delay in Miami. Just before I went to bed I had a wander round and was surprised to find there were only five of us on board. The complete crew had scurried off home as soon as we berthed.

I gathered it was always the same and the company condoned it. I could then see why the ship was in such a poor mechanical state.

When we were in port where the maintenance should be done there was nobody on board to do it. I brought this up with Bernie and he said he'd been complaining about it since he joined the company but nothing was going to change. I had a feeling things were going to get worse rather than better.

The cargo was all in 40 foot trailers which were ferried on and off by tractors. From the States we brought white goods (fridges, washing machines etc), machinery, chemicals and quite a few vehicles. From Jamaica we took sugar, chilled mangoes and bananas, coffee and there were usually at least two tankers full of Tia Maria liqueur. The trailers had two legs at the front to support them when they were unhitched from the tractor unit. If the trailer was full a strong frame called a horse was placed under the front and the legs retracted as they weren't designed to take the strain when the ship was rolling around. As I walked around I noticed that the stevedores weren't bothering with using the horses so I got hold of the foreman and insisted they were all fitted. This didn't go down very well as they had to unload several trailers to fit them but in the end it was all done to my satisfaction. We only loaded 50 trailers so were just on half full when we sailed for Miami the following afternoon.

Sailing was a doddle compared to berthing as we just sailed straight out of the berth and off. It turned out to be the same as the trip from Miami – we set off nicely doing about 15 knots but after three hours we were back to eleven knots with the engines seriously overheating and clouds of black smoke coming from the funnels. The following morning Evan, the 1st mate, appeared at my door asking when we were doing the search. When I asked what search he told me we had to search the whole vessel for drugs, mainly cannabis, or ganja as it was known, as the ship had a terrible reputation for drug smuggling into the States and had been arrested and fined several times. It also seemed that a few of the crew weren't averse to making extra money this way so we had to search all the crew accommodation as well. It took the two of us over four hours getting into every nook and cranny and climbing all over the trailers. We didn't find anything – in fact I never did – but it didn't help that I had no idea what I was looking for! The pair of us were absolutely filthy when we'd finished but felt considerably better after a shower and a couple of ice cold beers. I wasn't looking forward to doing this every trip though.

We arrived in Miami a day later on 16th May and berthed mid morning and started cargo straight away. A large squad of customs officials boarded complete with a sniffer dog, which got quite excited in the crew accommodation, but thankfully they never found anything. They did find quite a large amount in one of the trailer tyres but we weren't held responsible for that. The cargo operation only took three hours and we were on our way again. It was a better load this time with over 100 trailers on board. We also loaded a selection of vehicles and a couple of trailers for Georgetown in Grand Cayman. The vehicles gave me some indication of the life on Cayman as there was a lovely little helicopter on a trailer and several high speed boats on trailers along with two brand new top of the range Cadillacs and several large Mercedes. We also had two cherry pickers mounted on lorries and some tractors. I'd never been to Georgetown before so I dug out the chart to see what the place looked like. It was just a single jetty sticking out into a bay and the crew assured me I'd have no trouble berthing even without the bow thruster.

It was an even slower trip down to Kingston with the engine catching fire a couple of times. I was beginning to think this job wouldn't last much longer. We arrived there in the evening of the 19th May and started cargo operations. It went very slowly as they only had one tractor unit to move the trailers and it managed to get two punctures and break down three times. This pleased the crew immensely as they all got extra time at home so I had quite a happy crew when we sailed the following evening.

On passage I had a brilliant idea. The hold was lit by large floodlights fitted on the deckhead and over time with bulbs failing we were reduced to less than a third of them working. It was impossible to reach the lights due to their height. I talked to the crew and we fired up one of the cherry pickers. It was a doddle. When using the cherry picker it was imperative to put down hydraulic feet to steady the vehicle and I made sure of this. I supervised the operation which was going surprisingly well and after an hour I went for a cup of coffee. When I returned they were driving round the hold with the hydraulic feet raised and the cherry picker at its full height and a crewmember changing the bulbs. They had decided it would be quicker that way. How it didn't fall over I will never know but the crewmember was the palest Jamaican I've seen for a long

161

time when he came down.

I berthed the ship in Georgetown the next morning without a problem though I was a bit concerned when I looked over the side. The water was so clear it looked only inches deep with rocks sticking up everywhere. It only took a few hours to drive all the vehicles off and we were more than impressed when the owner of the helicopter arrived and fitted the blades and took off from just beside the ship. Must be nice to have money. While we were there a large Carnival cruise ship anchored just off the port and disgorged its passengers onto the island using tenders. They were all shepherded into groups for their various activities be it snorkelling, visiting the local authentic market, listening to the town band or being bussed to other beaches. After witnessing this I vowed never to set foot on a cruise liner for a holiday. Ever.

We sailed at noon and headed off back to Miami arriving there two days later. It was a nice quick load and we sailed nearly fully loaded for once. The passage to Kingston was something of a nightmare. The starboard engine caught fire several times one of which was pretty serious. The engineers then found the lubricating oil in the engine was contaminated so we had to run on one engine for eight hours while the oil was purified. Our one and only generator started giving problems so we had to revert to the emergency generator on deck which wasn't up to the job and started overheating. This meant we had to shut down the air-conditioning and were unable to cook on the galley stoves. We made do with a barbeque which turned out to be great. One thing Jamaicans are good at is making a barbeque and having a party. We eventually arrived in Kingston a day behind schedule but nobody seemed particularly bothered. It was an uneventful load and again we sailed nearly full back up to Miami. At least we would be making some money for the company.

On arrival in Miami we were again immediately boarded by a huge squad of customs officials complete with three sniffer dogs. They must have had a tip off and I was dreading them finding a very obvious stash that I had missed. The search eventually produced quite a large quantity in a sealed container so the crew couldn't be held responsible. The authorities levied quite a big fine on the shipping company though, which seemed a bit unfair, as they had no idea what was in the containers.

Our radio transmitter had been giving us a few problems but I had resigned myself to struggling along with it and was most surprised when two technicians boarded and fitted a brand new state-of-the-art single side band transmitter and receiver. The company had got it on approval to test from some unsuspecting company and I strongly doubted that it would ever be paid for. It didn't help with our communications at all as we were still blacklisted with the shore radio stations. We could send out emergency signals, though, if we ever started to sink, which was comforting. Apart from the delay caused by the customs we had a good load and sailed over half full back towards Kingston.

For this voyage we were instructed to call in at Port au Prince in Haiti on the return leg to unload some empty containers and pick a few trailers of fresh mangoes. At least I was getting see some new ports. The Kingston call was uneventful but the Port au Prince call was a nightmare. It started as we arrived off the entrance when the main engine controls failed closely followed by the radar. We had to control the engines manually which meant using two levers for each engine (one for the engine speed and one for the propeller pitch) instead of one. I figured we would manage if we took things slowly. As we entered the breakwaters there was an explosion in the focstle and the ship blacked out completely. We drifted out of control across the harbour for ten minutes until power was restored. Just as I was getting the ship under control the 2nd mate announced there was a serious fire in the bow. It took a quarter of an hour to put this out and then I found out that the windlass was damaged beyond repair so if I had to drop the anchor I wouldn't be able to get it back on board. I then started to manoeuvre the ship slowly into the berth. Sharon, the 3rd mate, was on the engine controls and when I gave an order to go astern she put pitch on the propeller before increasing the engine revs and promptly stalled the starboard engine. I was starting to lose it by this stage and when I asked what the fuck was going on she took offence and flounced off the bridge in a huff. It was getting better by the minute.

I now only had one engine and the wind then decided to pick up and start blowing us off the berth. I instructed the 1st mate to lower the ramp onto the quay as soon as he could and this would hold us in position. Unfortunately with all the panic of the fire the engineers had forgotten to bleed the hydraulic system and when the ramp was unlatched it fell all the way open and into the water. It took a further half an hour to retrieve it and after some tricky backing and filling we got it landed on the quay in roughly the right place. We had attracted quite a crowd by this time and we got a round of applause when we eventually got secure alongside. On top of all this our eyes were streaming and really sore from something and it was made worse when we tried to rub them. It was obvious there must be something in the air. When the agent boarded he explained there had been a riot near the port and the police had used tear gas to disperse them and it was blowing our way. This was going to be one port I wouldn't forget.

The cargo operation went very quickly but just as the last trailer was coming on board a bloke appeared in my cabin asking if we could stay any longer. He was a local mango grower and was desperate to get his mangoes to market in Miami. We had unloaded ten empty trailers and he wanted to get them to his plantation and loaded and back to us. I was desperate to get more time in port to try and repair all the faults so I told him we'd wait for six hours which he reckoned was sufficient. We managed to get the engine controls sorted and the radar back in operation but the windlass was beyond repair. I was a bit reluctant to sail without it working as it meant I was unable to anchor in an emergency. After five hours waiting I was getting a bit nervous but true to his word the loaded trailers appeared on time. He was over the moon that we'd waited and insisted on presenting us with some boxes of his best mangoes. I really like mangoes and these were in a different league for their taste and texture. Once the containers were loaded I sailed gingerly out to sea. On the passage north I discovered that if mangoes are eaten in excess they act as a laxative so I spent most of the trip locked in my bathroom.

We arrived off Miami at a bad time as there were a lot of cruise ship movements so we stopped the engines and drifted until we were called in. When we started the engines the port one ran for five minutes then stopped abruptly. On investigation they found that a bearing on the propeller shaft had seized and the engine was totally out of commission. We crawled into port using one engine and a couple of tugs.

The agent came on board straight away. He was quite excited as he'd got us a full load back to Kingston and he became really

164

dejected when I told him we were going nowhere until our mechanical problems were solved. I went back with him to his office in town and phoned the company in Kingston. Nobody was available to make a decision so I adjourned to a small restaurant and had a lovely seafood meal on expenses washed down with a couple of cold beers. Refreshed I wandered back to the office and found the company had decided to send the ship 20 miles up the coast to Fort Lauderdale for repairs. I wandered back on board past the cruise liners with the passengers all milling around. I felt quite at ease as with the ship going to drydock we should get everything in working order again.

We sailed the following morning on the 10th June and proceeded very slowly up the coast on one engine and arrived in Fort Lauderdale early evening. Things seem to progress at a very leisurely pace with nobody even appearing on board until late morning. It had the makings of a long job. The following morning I had a delegation of the officers and crew at my door demanding to be paid off and repatriated to Jamaica. Normally the longest they were away from home was a week and they could obviously see the writing on the wall. They were followed by the cook who announced we were rapidly running out of food. We were due to take on stores the next time back in Kingston and had run everything down. I went ashore to phone the company and tell them what the situation was. The crew were all on yearly contracts so they would have to stay unless they paid their own fare home. Also I was told to order all necessary stores locally and pay for them from the money in the safe. At least we wouldn't starve. As I walked back to the ship I realised there was very little money in the safe so we'd have to find a new plan.

Bernie, the superintendent, arrived the following morning and started to get things moving. Technicians appeared and began overhauling the generators and the main engines and servicing the radar and the gyro compass so maybe the drydock might go a bit quicker. There was no work over the weekend so I had the opportunity to explore the port and have a look around. There were some fantastic marinas and I could have spent hours just looking at the boats. There were also lots of small bars and cafes where prices seemed quite reasonable. At least I wasn't going to be bored. On Monday morning they decided the only way to repair the seized bearing was to remove the shaft which meant drydocking so the following morning we were taken out of the water. The shipyard removed the propellers and then stopped work. When I went to find out what was happening I was told that our company owed nearly $1,000,000 from a previous docking and until this was paid no work would take place on the vessel. I've feeling they had the upper hand as we obviously couldn't go anywhere else without our propellers! It was going to be a long drydock after all.

Despite my repeated requests for money nothing was forthcoming and the food situation was starting to look a bit desperate. I talked to the shipyard managers about the problem and they were very sympathetic. It turned out the company had made a payment of $20,000 to try and get things moving, without success, and it was arranged that they would let me have $2,000 to keep us fed. We got all our stores delivered the following day and when I'd paid the bill I had $150 left for any other emergencies so that wasn't going to last long.

Five days later there was suddenly activity on our ship. We assumed the company had come up with the money and it would be all go. It was not to be. The repair yard had other work and we were in the way so we were refloated and put on a lay-by berth. The first few days were very pleasant with nice weather and absolutely nothing to do. The main trouble, though, was that we had no paint on board and nobody would supply us without money up front. This meant that we had no work for the crew as there was no point chipping and cleaning as we had no paint to cover it. With lots of time on their hands the crew got more and more agitated about being away from home and there was always someone at my door every day demanding to be repatriated. Morale was at an all time low. Bernie had ensconced himself in a rather swish hotel by the beach but after a week even he was getting bored. He bought himself a sailboard and I taught him how to sail so we spent quite a few afternoons and evenings zipping up and down in the sea in front of his hotel.

Apart from the crew hassling me my only concern was whether I was still being paid so I had to phone home regularly to make sure the money was going into my bank. Days developed into a quite pleasant but boring routine. After breakfast I would have a wander round the ship and made sure nothing else had fallen off or broken down and then I would amble over to the shipyard offices where they had a supply of really good coffee and doughnuts. This was consumed while I perused the day's papers and chatted with whoever happened to be around. Then it was back to the ship for a prelunch beer with Bernie. After lunch I went for a walk round the port and the marinas and sometimes into the huge shopping malls though I just window shopped as I didn't have any spare cash. I'd get back to the ship just before the evening meal and have a chat with the 1st mate and chief engineer though there wasn't much to discuss. In the evening I retreated into my cabin which was equipped with a huge television. The shippers of the Tia Maria had given me a dozen bottles as a thank you for looking after their cargo so I would settle down with a large tumbler of Tia Maria and ice and watch the baseball until it was time to go to bed. It wasn't such a bad life.

One afternoon as I was wandering round the port I happened to bump into a customs officer I'd got to know in Miami. He casually mentioned in conversation that if the ship ever went back to Miami it would promptly be arrested for non-payment of fines for smuggling. It was beginning to look as though the ship would never sail again. The next day I phoned our insurance company in Miami and they confirmed the warrant had been issued. I wasn't all that bothered until they said that my name was on the warrant as well so I would end up with a criminal record and not be able to enter the States again. I got hold of Bernie and we phoned the company in Kingston and they were quite unperturbed. They said they would appeal the judgement and so defer payment for at least another two years. Nobody showed the slightest concern for me. I started to get pretty worried. The following day I sent the company a telex stating that unless the fine was paid promptly I would leave the ship and repatriate myself at my own expense. They didn't even bother to reply. I had another problem in that there was no cash on the ship so I would lose any balance of wages that were due.

The ship had now been lying idle for seven weeks and we were having problems getting our laundry done and were starting to run out of fresh food again. A week after I sent my ultimatum I phoned the company in Kingston again to find out what progress had been made and they said there was nobody in the office to speak to. I then phoned our insurance company in Miami again and they said nothing had been done but customs were aware we were in Fort Lauderdale and they might execute the warrant here. Luckily while I was making these calls one of the shipyard managers was sitting in the office and heard the conversations. He agreed it was pretty serious and went off to try and sort things out. He came back an hour or so later and said the company had just paid another tranche of the debt and he would advance me $5,000 to sort things out. It was brilliant. I went back on board and organised the laundry and a load of fresh stores delivered so at least I could leave the ship in good order. I also had enough to pay myself the outstanding wages.

Next morning I went over to the offices to find out how to book a flight and found out they had a specific department for arranging travel. The girl in there was fantastic. She organised a flight back to Heathrow the following morning with Eastern Airlines for a $100 and even organised free transport down to Miami airport. I handed all the keys to the mate and left the ship at eight in the morning on the 6th August. I was pretty relieved to get on the plane and head home but I was quite worried about getting another job without a reference but at least I hadn't been arrested and I'd got my pay in my pocket.

CHAPTER SEVENTEEN

Worldwide tramping

m.v Aeneas & m.v. Arko
4th November 1986 – 13th January 1988

I arrived back home in Cumbria on the 8th August and immediately started looking for another job. The weather was really good so at least that brightened things up a bit. I'd come home with a load of dollars and when I went into the bank to change them I got a pleasant surprise as the dollar had gone up against the pound and I made an extra £150, which brightened me even further.

After a week of phoning round all my known contacts I started to get depressed again as they all said things were very quiet and nobody was optimistic. I would go to the library every Thursday to look at the job ads in Lloyd's List and I even took out a job wanted ad but with no success.

In the middle of October I finally got an interview for a master's job on a containership running back and forward between Jeddah and Port Sudan in the Red Sea. They paid my travelling expenses down to London so things looked quite positive. When I got to the office it turned out the ship was a converted rig supply boat and had some stability problems. I think if I'd been young and single I would have had a go but I was too long in the tooth now so I had to turn it down. I heard later that the ship had been arrested in Jeddah, which isn't a good place to be arrested.

After two months at home prospects of getting another master's job were starting to look quite remote so I began looking round at shore opportunities but nothing suitable was forthcoming. I decided to drop a rank and go back to being a 1st mate again at least in the short term and it would mean some money coming in. At the end of October I applied for a 1st mate's job with Transocean Maritime Agencies, which was a German company operating out of Monaco. I had to go over to Newcastle for an interview and things went very well and they promised me a job in the next three weeks or so but wouldn't put me on wages until I joined a ship. I went home quite elated, as though the wages were nothing like a master's wage, they were above average and it sounded like a well run company.

A week later I got a call to join one of their ships, called the *Aeneas*, in Antwerp where she was loading for the Great Lakes in Canada. It got even better when they said I was joining as master as I'd impressed them at the interview. I was to join the following week but first I had to travel down to Monaco for a day to meet the people in the office and see how everything worked. I flew down to Nice with all my gear and once I'd deposited most of it in left luggage I was flown by helicopter to a helipad in the centre of Monaco. An impressive way to join a company, though at one stage I thought my time was up when the French helicopter pilot started showing off by flying very low over the sea. I was put up for the night in a rather swish hotel and had my evening meal in a restaurant overlooking the harbour. I have to admit the meal wasn't all that great and I'd have preferred fish and chips sitting on the harbour wall. Next day was spent in the office being shown the paperwork and meeting the superintendents. They seemed a really nice bunch and there were quite a few Brits in the office. In the evening I returned to Nice and flew up to Antwerp to join the ship.

I relieved an Indian skipper who wasn't interested in handing over and just wanted to leave which actually suited me as I knew how things operated from my trip to the office. I got a bit concerned the following morning when I rechecked the accounts and it seemed I was $4,000 short. I eventually found it but it wasn't a good start. The ship was an 18,000 ton bulk carrier originally built for Cunard and I was pleasantly surprised as she was in really good condition. Most of the officers were British with an Indonesian crew. We sailed for Cleveland in the Great Lakes the following evening with 14,000 tons of steel coils and slabs on board. It was good to be on a proper ship again and we sailed from Antwerp on the 8th November. We had a terrible Atlantic crossing with storm after storm but managed to get across without any damage.

It was nice to get into the shelter of the Gulf of St Lawrence and after two days steaming we arrived in Montreal, which was the farthest up-river I'd ever been. We anchored for a few hours to sort out the paperwork and then set off into the St Lawrence Seaway. The first section consists of seven locks which take the ship up into Lake Ontario. It was all very efficient and I was helped by the fact that the crew had done it all many times before. I got a bit nervous meeting some of the huge lakers in the narrow canals between the locks but we managed to scrape past. Once clear of the last lock we passed through the Bay of a Thousand Islands, which was amazing. It was absolutely beautiful with the autumn colours and all the little bays with cabins and jetties. I gathered it could be a nightmare in summer when everyone was zipping about in boats. When we got into Lake Ontario proper we were told to anchor as there were no pilots available but we managed to blag it out and they allowed us to cross the lake by ourselves despite this being my first visit. Once across Lake Ontario we picked up a pilot for the transit of the eight locks of the Welland Canal to take us into Lake Erie without having to go over the Niagara Falls. We then had a twelve hour trip across the lake to our discharge port of Cleveland arriving there on the 27th November.

Discharge went very smoothly though the weather had turned really cold and I made a trip up into town to buy some cold weather gear. I even bought some earmuffs on the advice of locals though I felt a bit of a prat. Mind you I was thankful of them on quite a few occasions afterwards.

We had Sunday off and a few of us managed to see a game of American football as the Cleveland Browns stadium was only 200 yards from our berth. I really enjoyed it and the atmosphere was amazing. I was quite intrigued by the crowds all arriving well early so they could have a barbecue in the car park before the game.

We completed discharge on the 1st December and got orders to proceed to Duluth to load a cargo of wheat for Hamburg. I was certainly getting to see the Great Lakes as Duluth is as far as you can get. It took us four days to get there though we were slowed down by a terrific storm on Lake Superior. It managed to produce some pretty big waves so we were bounced around a lot as we had no cargo on board.

Once in Duluth we had all sorts of problems as the weather had turned bitterly cold (earmuffs very useful) and our ballast water was frozen in the tanks. We had to hire industrial heaters before we could pump the water out. It took two days to load us and then we were heading back through the Lakes. I couldn't believe how quick the ice was forming. We had to tie up in the Seaway for ten hours as one of the locks had become jammed with ice. I was visualising being stuck there for the winter at one stage but they managed to clear it. We stopped off at Montreal to top up on fuel then it was off back across the Atlantic. There was a large high pressure system in the middle of the Atlantic so we had to go way up north to avoid head winds. It turned out a good passage in the end with some amazing northern lights. We had Christmas dinner passing north of Scotland and it was very pleasant with nobody over-imbibing and the cook producing a very good meal.

We berthed in Hamburg early on the 28th December and started discharging the wheat with pneumatic elevators. It was a really miserable visit as not only was the weather horrific but we had to clean the holds prior to loading steel, take stores and undertake several surveys of the hull. We completed discharge at one o'clock in the morning on the 30th December and shifted across the dock to load steel coils and plates. We were due to sail in the evening of New Year's Eve and I wasn't at all happy about it as there was a force nine gale blowing outside and it was going to be a horrendous run down to Antwerp. We were also supposed to clean the holds on the passage, which would have been a nightmare. When I broached the subject with the company they were adamant that we sail but we were saved by the Hamburg pilots who refused to take us out in such atrocious weather. We ended up having a very pleasant New Year party on board and sailed the following afternoon. It was a pleasant trip down to Antwerp as the storm was now well out of the way.

As the Great Lakes were frozen over our next cargo was a full load of steel products for ports in the south eastern USA. At least we'd be heading into some decent weather. We cleared Antwerp with a full cargo of 18,000 tons of steel on the 8th January. It was an uneventful trip across the Atlantic arriving in Jacksonville on the 26th January. We then wandered south round the coast calling at Port Everglades, Mobile, and New Orleans and finishing up in Houston two weeks later.

Our next employment was a real mystery and it was only as we were sailing from Houston that we were told to head back to Mobile to load a cargo of maize for Tampico in Mexico. It was only 24 hours across the Gulf of Mexico to Mobile and when we arrived there nobody knew anything about us or our intended cargo but they let us berth alongside anyway. We then had a very pleasant few days doing nothing while the cargo was organised. Once sorted they loaded a full cargo of grain in twelve hours and off we went to Tampico arriving there on the 23rd February. They discharged the grain using canvas bags, which they emptied into railway wagons so the discharge went very slowly. I liked Tampico as it was an old fashioned port and it was very pleasant just wandering around the town. I went ashore to an upmarket restaurant one evening and had a fantastic seafood meal with all the trimmings. It was only as I was leaving that I realised it was a swish brothel. I thought the waitresses were very attentive!

It took them nearly three weeks to discharge us and then we got orders to head back to New Orleans to load another cargo of grain for somewhere in Africa. It was just a short trip across to New Orleans and we arrived there on the 12th March. Again our cargo wasn't ready so we spent five days anchored in the middle of the Mississippi. We were right at the bottom of Canal Street and it was a bit frustrating not being able to get ashore as it looked really lively. We berthed on the 17th March and again loaded in double quick time.

Whilst loading we received a huge packet of mail which had been chasing us around for nearly a month. It was good to catch up with all the news. After I'd read all my mail from home I started on the company mail. The first letter blithely informed me that after this voyage the ship was being sold and the crew signed off. I thought here we go again – back to the job hunting as soon as I get home – but the next letter announced that the company was purchasing another more modern vessel to replace the *Aeneas* so hopefully I'd be re-employed.

We sailed from New Orleans with the instruction to head for the Mediterranean so it was a bit of a mystery tour. A week out we got a message saying the discharge port would be Nador. We spent the next day scouring our charts for a port called Nador not wishing to ask the company for advice. I'd given up and was about to send a message asking where the hell it was when the 3rd mate found it. It was a tiny port in Morocco also called Mellilla. It looked too small for us and on top of that we didn't have the correct charts. I set about arranging an off limits call at Gibraltar to pick up the charts but the company had second thoughts and diverted us to Agadir on the Atlantic coast of Morocco. This turned out to be another pleasant little port. It was just opening up as a holiday destination and had loads of nice little bars and cafés.

The discharge was very easy as they just unloaded the grain onto the quay making a huge heap that they loaded into lorries with mechanical shovels. I'd hate to think what would happen if it started raining. It took them over a week to discharge us during which time we visited the bars and did all the touristy things including wind surfing and generally enjoying ourselves. Very pleasant.

Just before we sailed a Polish captain and his chief engineer who were going to take over when the ship was sold, joined us. We assumed we'd be leaving from Agadir but we got instructions to take the ship up to Lisbon for the handover. The new captain was a really nice bloke and he seemed very happy with the condition of the ship. I was surprised that he was paid about the same amount as me as I'd always thought they were paid peanuts. He was going to be away for over a year though.

We got to Lisbon on the 13th March and anchored the ship in the roads. It was an easy handover and I got off the next day. I had a night's stay in a hotel as there were no available flights and flew home to Manchester the following morning. I was a bit uncertain about my future as I didn't know whether Transocean Maritime would re-employ me, however a week into my leave I got a phone call saying they had been impressed with my performance and would be finding me another command in about two months.

I had a nice relaxing leave knowing I had a job to go to at the end of it. I seemed to spend most of my time gardening and my vegetable patch was really starting to flourish when I got orders to join the *Arko* in Antwerp on the 5th June. She was very similar to the *Aeneas* but about five years younger. She was nearly loaded with a full cargo of steel coils for the Great Lakes so I was really looking forward to that. I also knew quite a few of the officers and thought I shouldn't have many problems in that direction. The ship was chartered to carry four cargoes of steel to the Great Lakes and bring grain back to the continent each time. What I wasn't looking forward to were the North Atlantic crossings with the bad weather, icebergs and fog off Newfoundland.

Our first trip went really well, though, and we rattled across in double quick time. After our discharge in Detroit we were sent up to Thunder Bay, which is a tiny little port as far north as you can get in the Lakes. The cargo was a nightmare – 5,000 tons of peas, 2,500 tons of mustard seed, 3,500 tons of flax seed, 4,000 tons of wheat and, just to top it off, the balance, about 2,500 tons of maize. It took us ages to figure how to load it without mixing the cargo up and still keeping the ship on an even keel. It was really satisfying when we sailed with it all securely on board.

The passage back down through the Lakes was amazing as it was mid summer and everything looked lovely and everywhere we looked were pleasure craft zipping about and people enjoying themselves. As we cleared the St Lawrence River we were enveloped by thick fog and this lasted for five days until we got into the warm waters of the Gulf Stream. I hated it as there were numerous icebergs reported around and a lot of them were too small to show on the radar but could still do a lot of damage if we ran into one.

Our discharge port was Rotterdam where the grain was discharged directly into barges to be shipped inland. I could have spent all day watching the barges manoeuvring round and filling up with the different grains. The company had other ideas, though, and eight days later we were sailing out loaded with steel coils for Detroit again. Being on the same run made life quite easy as we got to know the personnel in the different ports and had the right paperwork filled out correctly. The weather wasn't as kind to us on this passage and we rolled all the way across and were really pleased to get into the calm water behind Newfoundland.

It was an uneventful passage up to Detroit and once discharged we were dispatched to Duluth at the far end of Lake Superior. On my previous passage to Duluth we'd encountered a terrific storm with huge seas but this time it was flat calm with balmy breezes all the way. A quick load in Duluth and we were off again.

We stopped at Montreal on the way out to refuel and I was sent ashore by the company to sit an exam for a pilot's licence so I could pilot my own ship anywhere in the Great Lakes. It was just an oral exam and as I'd been doing a bit of swotting up I managed to pass without too much trouble. On the way back I realised I'd missed my lunch and asked the taxi driver to drop me off somewhere nice for lunch. I must have looked well off because he dropped me at a really swish place overlooking the harbour. I thought, "What the hell," and went in. I had an absolutely delicious lunch washed down with an expensive bottle of wine. I charged it to the company and thought I might be rebuked but I never heard any more about it. I should have done it more often. I bowled back on board in a nice mellow mood and off we went down the St Lawrence.

We were to drop our river pilot off at a small port called Escoumains where the river became the Gulf of St Lawrence. While we were stopped, disembarking the pilot, the ship was surrounded by a pod of Beluga whales. There must have been about 50 of them and being white we could see them way down deep in the clear water. It was amazing. I nipped down to get my camera but of course they had gone when I got back from my cabin.

Looking at the weather synopsis there were some real crackers of storms approaching up the American coast so I decided to go north of Newfoundland through the Belle Isle Strait. It had a bad reputation for fog and icebergs and normally I wouldn't consider it. This time the weather was brilliant and the scenery was fantastic with some huge icebergs aground in the shallows. That night we had the best display of northern lights that I've ever seen. There was everything from huge curtains of green light to rays like searchlight beams sweeping the sky. We all tried taking some pictures but nothing really did it justice. We just stood on the bridge wing and absorbed the sight and felt really lucky to have experienced it. Once clear of Belle Isle we found ourselves in lovely weather with light following winds and clear skies all the way across to the Bishop Rock by which time we didn't care what the weather could throw at us for the last couple of days.

This time the discharge port was Antwerp and once we'd discharged at the silo we shifted over to another berth and loaded yet another cargo of steel coils this time for Cleveland, Ohio. We took a real hammering on the Atlantic crossing this time. There was deep depression after deep depression and the final straw was just as we were approaching Newfoundland two of the buggers joined together to form a deep deep deep depression. It was bad and we hove to heading south west into the wind. We did this for ten hours and when we got a position from the sun we found we'd actually gone backwards 15 miles. The wind gradually decreased and veered and as it did we increased speed and got heading west in the right direction at last. We eventually got into the calm waters of the Gulf of St Lawrence again and things returned to normal. It was a quick passage up to Cleveland and it rapidly became obvious that this would be our last trip of the year up the Lakes as it was November and things were turning really cold with patches of ice already on Lake Erie.

It had been an interesting time on the Great Lakes starting in June and returning every six weeks and watching the landscape and scenery changing throughout the year. Obviously, at this time of year, there were now no pleasure craft zipping about. As we were passing up the Welland Canal a group of people handed over to us some boxes which contained Christmas presents for the crew and two crates of apples from local orchards. It was a lovely gesture and the apples were delicious.

As we finished discharge in Cleveland we got news that our next employment was to be loading steel turnings or swarf in Detroit and Harridon for Bombay. It was a real disappointment as we were hoping for a trip back to the Continent where we would be relieved and get home nicely for Christmas.

Swarf is the scrap metal left when items are turned on lathes. It is a real pain as it is very dirty and contaminated with oil so has a tendency to self-combust. It was loaded with magnets on shore cranes and made a real mess as bits kept falling off as the cranes swung over the deck. The crew were constantly employed cleaning the decks. It took about four days to load and as soon as we sailed the temperature of the cargo in the holds started rocketing up much to my consternation. After two days it settled and started to cool again. We had a good run down the St Lawrence and I must admit it was nice to head south east towards Gibraltar and the warm weather instead of east into the North Atlantic.

There was quite a lot of maintenance to do around the decks so I volunteered to do the four to eight watch for the trip to Suez and release the 1st mate to work on deck with the crew. I really enjoyed it as I'd forgotten how nice it was on watch seeing the sun rising and setting every day. We did a quick run to Suez but when we got there we had to anchor for two days as no funds had been deposited with the Canal authority. We tied up in Port Said on the third day while it was all sorted out and I was driven to distraction by all the officials demanding cigarettes and bottles of whisky to facilitate our passage. According to my journal I gave away 5,000 cigarettes, ten bottles of whisky and one frozen turkey. That was the minimum I could get away with and could easily have been a lot more.

I actually got a chance to walk ashore in Port Said in the afternoon but didn't enjoy it. Everything was filthy and run down and I didn't feel safe at all. We started our transit at midnight and by four the following afternoon we were clear and heading down the Red Sea. We got instructions to stop off at Jeddah to refuel which should have taken six hours maximum but in the end we lost over 24 hours and there was some confusion about the amounts we received. Once we'd cleared Jeddah I decided to go back on watch again as it allowed the 1st mate to continue with the maintenance of the cranes.

It was a lovely passage with virtually no wind and a calm glassy sea. We arrived off Bombay mid December and we were somewhat dismayed to find hundreds of other ships at anchor awaiting berths. I found a nice spot close to the pilot station and dropped the anchor. I tried contacting the local agents but they were worse than useless with no information at all. We had been hoping to be in and out before Christmas but this was now looking very unlikely. After two days we got a message from the company saying we were definitely berthing on the 23rd December and I would be relieved shortly after so I might get home for Christmas yet! Sure enough on the 21st we got a message to heave anchor and proceed to pick up a pilot. I started to get all the accounts sorted out ready for a quick get away.

I knew it was too good to be true. We shifted to an anchorage inside the harbour and then forgotten about apart from a message from the company saying my relief would now be the 10th January. Surprisingly on Christmas Eve we got a visit from our agents who brought out all our mail and we took on some fresh stores and water but it was all really a con to ask for whisky and cigarettes. They finally left clutching their booty and we were then boarded by customs who confiscated ten bottles of whisky and several thousand cigarettes, which they said weren't on the manifest. They then said they had to seal the bond, which meant we'd have nothing to drink over Christmas. It cost more cigarettes to persuade them to leave some booze out for us. I was really beginning to hate Bombay and we hadn't actually got there yet.

Eventually we berthed alongside on the 2nd January and they started discharge using magnets on the ship's cranes. It was a nightmare as our cranes kept breaking down in the heat and they threatened to send us back out to anchor again so a few thousand cigarettes lighter we managed to stay alongside. On the third day alongside I organised 25,000 rupees (about £1,500) to be delivered for subs for the crew. I couldn't find my safe key so I hid the money in my sock drawer while I went down for lunch and when I came back it had gone. One of the agent's runners must have seen me hiding it and broke into my cabin while I was down below. I stupidly called the police but all they did was drink my beer and smoke my cigarettes. As I hadn't put it in the safe I was responsible for the loss so things were going from bad to worse. It turned out that the company had been going to give me a bonus for all my good work but they cancelled the bonus and called it quits which wasn't too bad. The new master arrived on the 12th January and I escaped the next day. I don't think I've ever been more pleased to leave anywhere.

CHAPTER EIGHTEEN

Mystery Tour

m.v. Atlantic

23rd March 1988 – 7th April 1989

I had quite a pleasant two months leave and towards the end of March got instructions to join a ship in Japan. The company had bought another vessel and this time it was a two year old Japanese built ship operated by a Chinese company. I flew out to Osaka on the 20th March and expected to join the ship there but I was met at the airport and taken to a fantastic hotel overlooking the port by a lovely Japanese girl who insisted on showing me my room and explaining where the restaurant was. I thought at one stage she was going to stay the night but no such luck. I was told to be ready by nine the next morning to be taken to the ship. I wandered down to the bar and ended up talking with two British engineers who were building a large bridge close by. It was a cracking night with a fantastic meal and I must admit to slightly over imbibing so I wasn't feeling my best when I staggered down the next morning. Yet another charming Japanese girl then took me to the railway station where I was put on a bullet train to Hiroshima. It is certainly the way to travel but it was going so fast I didn't really get a good look at the countryside as we sped through. In no time I was in Hiroshima and then a two hour taxi ride to join the ship in a small port called Tsuneishi.

The ship was called the *Atlantic Sea* and to keep it in line with the other ships' names in the company it was renamed the *Atlantic*. It made things very easy for the changeover as we just painted over the word 'sea' on everything. The big job was repainting the funnel but we managed that in two days. The ship was in really good condition with a lot of good navigational aids and at least we had cranes that worked well. After four days familiarising ourselves and changing all the certificates we set off to load steel products round the Japanese coast for the east coast of the States. It was quite a slow load by Japanese standards and it was surprising to see how work standards were deteriorating in Japan. Previously very little supervision of the loading was necessary and all the preloading plans were accepted on sight, as they usually couldn't be improved on. On this occasion, though, we had to intervene several times when the stowage or lashing required improving.

The only other fly in the ointment was the radio officer who was an alcoholic and suffering from depression. Apart from being permanently legless he caused me all sorts of problems by going missing just before we sailed from Osaka and had to be retrieved from a local bar. He was also missing in the next port but after hours of searching he was found passed out behind the radio room desk. I eventually got a replacement the day before we sailed but we had to get the local police to remove him from the ship and the last I saw of him he was standing on the quay shouting abuse at me when we sailed. He might be still there.

It was mid April when we finally sailed off across the Pacific towards the Panama Canal. Much to my annoyance we were weather routed by some people in San Francisco. Our ship was equipped with the latest weather fax machines, which gave us accurate synoptic charts every four hours so I probably had more information at my fingertips than they did. I would have taken a southerly route but they insisted on sending us on a great circle which, although shorter, took us straight through several depressions and much farther north into the cold weather. I took great delight in telling them I was unable to maintain their courses as the ship was rolling in excess of 25 degrees and we would have cargo damage.

Halfway across the Pacific we noticed that we were taking in water in number three hold. We had to pump the bilges twice a day to keep up with it. The main trouble was the cargo in the hold was coils of stainless steel which doesn't like being immersed in salt water. After several fruitless expeditions into the hold, crawling in and out of the cargo in the dark we located a crack about a foot long just below the water line on the starboard side. We put some ballast into the port side tanks to gave the ship a list and hopefully lift the crack above the water line. We then spent a couple of unsuccessful days trying to weld the crack but in the end we fitted a cement box over it, which near enough cured it. The American coastguard were obviously monitoring our messages to the company as they asked if we needed an escort in case we sank and then, when we got to Panama, insisted the I sign a document promising not to sink in the Panama Canal.

We cleared the Canal the first week in May and headed up the Caribbean towards our first port of Savannah. It was a lovely passage with blue skies, calm seas and good currents that improved our speed quite dramatically. When we berthed in Savannah we were invaded by cargo surveyors and the company's insurance agents all wanting to assess the damage. We even had four surveyors for cargo that wasn't in the leaking hold and they still insisted on checking it. Paul Sanday, our marine superintendent, also arrived to supervise repairs so things got quite hectic. It turned out that only two coils had superficial rusting so remarkably we got away with it. Once the Savannah cargo had been discharged Paul was able to repair the crack using shore repairers and we lost only twelve hours.

After that we set off up the east coast calling at Wilmington, Newport News, Baltimore, Philadelphia and finishing off in New Haven. There was only about 1,000 tons for each place so we were just in port for a few hours each time. We actually had two days in New Haven, though, and managed to get ashore a couple of times. It was a lovely little port and everything seemed really clean and well kept. There were loads of students from Yale University wandering round. I got taken out for a meal and was served up the biggest lobster I've ever seen. If it had been alive it could have eaten me. I managed, though, helped by copious amounts of cold beer. It was a nice way to end this particular part of the voyage.

Once discharged the company didn't have any employment for us so we sailed out into the Atlantic for twelve hours and then stopped the engines and just drifted around. The crew were employed giving the holds a really good clean and the engineers spent the time overhauling two pistons on the main engine. I just sat around like a tin of milk and enjoyed the weather. It certainly was a mystery tour, as we had no idea where we were going next. The best bet was up into the Great Lakes for a cargo of grain as the company had some good contacts in that area. The Indonesian crew loved it and spent all their spare time fishing and managed to catch some fairly respectable cod and something else that may have been haddock so we had a lovely barbecue on deck with freshly caught fish.

In the end we drifted for two and a half days and I was amazed to find that we'd been carried over 80 miles in a north easterly direction by the Gulf Stream in that time. As it turned out it was in the wrong direction as we received orders to head to Charleston, North Carolina to load a full cargo of wheat for ports unknown. It took us just over a day to get to Charleston arriving there on the 1st June. We then had to anchor for ten days, as the cargo wasn't ready for us. Life was very quiet and relaxing though the air-conditioning packed in on the first day and it was quite uncomfortable in the humid heat. To break the monotony I let the 3rd mate take the lifeboat away for a trip round the harbour. He managed to run aground on a sandbank with the tide going out and they had to wait nine hours until the tide rose enough to refloat them. I didn't need to bollock him when he got back as the other occupants of the boat had given him enough hassle. When we did get alongside the loading went very slowly and it took us four days to load instead of the usual twelve hours. I have a note in my diary that says I was ashore for two nice meals and bought a lifejacket! I wish I could remember what that was for.

When we sailed we were told to head for Gibraltar, as our discharge port would most likely be in Morocco or Algeria. We had a great trip across the Atlantic weather-wise and it was only as we passed Gibraltar two weeks later that we were told we would be unloading in Algiers. It was only a day and a half from Gibraltar but we were somewhat dismayed when we turned into Algiers Bay to find about 30 ships at anchor waiting to berth. I found a nice quiet corner to anchor quite close to the port. We called up the port control on the VHF radio and were told they had no information for us, which was a bit disconcerting.

I left the bridge for some lunch and when I returned I found the 2nd mate had been chatting on the VHF radio with a couple of other ships in the anchorage and it appeared that there were at least two other ships ahead of us with full cargoes of wheat and it was taking a fortnight to discharge each ship. It looked like we could be here quite a while. At least we had plenty of fresh water on board but we were running really short of fresh vegetables and dairy products. After two days I managed to get a ship chandler to attend us and bring some stores out in a boat. It was all very poor quality and he charged a fortune for delivering it out to the anchorage but it was either that or starve.

My other big concern was that we were going to run out of beer, which was even more serious. The 2nd mate came to the rescue again as he'd mentioned this in one of his chats to the other ships in the anchorage and a Norwegian ship volunteered to sell us some for US dollars as long as we could collect it. Our lifeboat was dispatched in double quick time and they returned with 50 cases of Coors beer at a really good price. Life was looking up and the crew had their fishing lines out every day so we were able to supplement our stores with some really tasty fresh fish. The cook's favourite method of cooking was the Indonesian way on a barbecue so we had several very pleasant evenings on deck eating delicious fish washed down by cold Coors beer. I suppose life could have been worse.

We'd arrived at Algiers in the middle of June and it was a month later when we managed to berth alongside a silo and start discharge. It was a really old system of evacuators and unloading was very slow. I got very frustrated with the inefficiency of the place. We were supposed to be receiving diesel oil for the generators, as we were getting really low. When I phoned the company in Monaco they said it had been delivered and they had paid for it. I went ashore the following morning to chase it up again and by chance passed a small coaster also called *Atlantic* moored by the agent's office. I walked on board and asked the skipper if he'd received any fuel oil recently and he said he'd had an unscheduled delivery two days ago and had quite a job taking it as his tanks were already quite full. Mystery solved. We contacted the fuel company and told them of their mistake and they promptly delivered our fuel later in the afternoon. I don't know how they got on retrieving their oil from the other ship.

Algiers was quite an intriguing place of two separate halves. There were some really modern areas with nice shops and cafés and other parts where I wouldn't venture even with armed guards. I had one or two lovely meals ashore trying the local cuisine. On the second occasion we had just emerged from the restaurant when there was a commotion further up the street, which turned out to be four Arabs waving swords and muskets and riding horses down the street. They were all in flowing robes and the horses looked fantastic in all their trappings. They fired off a couple of shots with the muskets and galloped off up the road. I have no idea what it was about but it was certainly dramatic and the image of them galloping off with the smoke from the musket shots in the air will always stick in my mind.

Discharge went on really slowly but at least we could see the end. I was having a shower one afternoon and when I emerged from the bathroom I was confronted by a scruffy Arab in my bedroom stuffing my watch and radio into a bag. I think he was more surprised than I was. He put his hand behind his back and I thought he was going for a knife so I tackled him and we both fell on the floor. He managed to escape and ran for the door with me chasing him. My towel fell off in the melee and I ended up chasing him into the alleyway bollock naked. The radio officer was just emerging from his cabin next door to be confronted by a naked captain chasing an Arab along the corridor. I shouted at him to grab the thief, which he did and we all fell down the stairs together to the next deck with the Arab underneath. Neither the radio officer nor I were particularly lightweight so it was a somewhat dented Arab that we handed over to the local gendarmerie. He had quite a haul on him so it was very pleasing to return the watches, wallets and other valuables to their owners. Three days later the radio officer and I were instructed to attend the local magistrates court and I assumed that it was just as witnesses but on arrival we were told that the thief was pressing charges against us for assault, which could result in a jail sentence for the two of us. A judge who only spoke French interviewed us and after half an hour of confused questions and answers he announced we were free to go but he warned us that in future we should, "Ne frappez pas le voleur," (or something like it – it had been a long time since my last French lesson) or we'd go to jail. A very relieved captain and radio officer returned on board and opened a couple of beers to celebrate.

As the discharge was nearly complete I kept pressing the company for our next employment but they had nothing definite. They were working on us going to Brazil to load steel for the Great Lakes or a cargo from Northern Spain to the Far East neither of which I really fancied. We completed discharge on the last day of July and when the agent boarded with our port clearance he gave me a telex that they'd been sitting on for three days telling us to go along the coast to Safi in Morocco to load a full cargo of phosphate for Antwerp. That suited us fine as we'd be able to get some decent stores in Antwerp and get some urgent repairs done. It was two days along the North African coast to Safi and 24 hours to load and then we were on our way to Antwerp. They also told us we'd be loading a full cargo of steel in Antwerp for the Great Lakes, which sounded good.

It was a good run up to Antwerp apart from the last part up the River Schelte, which was in thick fog. We had two Belgian pilots and they commandeered our two radars so nobody else knew what was going on or where we were. It was most frustrating and I had to trust them both implicitly although they seemed to have a few arguments about which way to go. It all went well in the end and they each left the ship, clutching a bottle of whisky for a job well done.

Surprisingly the unloading went quite slowly as the stockpile on shore was full. On the second day the company superintendent came on board and asked if I'd like a trip off even though I still had a month to go for this trip. I jumped at the chance so they promoted the 1st mate to captain and I was off and onto a plane before I knew it. It was a good time to be home as it was August and the kids would be off school and I should get at least six weeks before the ship got back from the Great Lakes.

I ended up having six weeks to the day before I rejoined the ship in Esbjerg in Denmark towards the end of September. I joined with a new chief engineer, John Carroll, radio officer and two junior engineers. We got aboard at eleven in the morning and I was somewhat surprised to find the skipper still asleep in bed. He said he'd been up all night trying to sort out the accounts but by the number of empty bottles he couldn't have done much. When I went to bed he was still trying to reconcile the accounts and when I got up in the morning he was fast asleep with the accounts still unfinished and more empty bottles lying around. I tried to give him a hand but nothing seemed to tally so I signed for the remaining money on board and he took the paperwork home with him to send off later.

On merchant ships the 2nd mate's job is to draw all the courses on the charts with the skipper's agreement and then the skipper has to check them to make sure they don't contravene any regulations and take the ship overland. My 2nd mate on this occasion was cracking Irish lad called Mark Sinnot, who I had always found very reliable so

I never got a chance to check over his courses before we sailed which was very remiss of me. When we sailed that morning I took over from the pilot outside the breakwaters and was expecting to set off in a north easterly direction up the Baltic. I was somewhat bemused to find we were heading west so there was a mad panic to find out where I was. I thought we had joined the ship in Aalborg on the east coast of Denmark whereas we had actually joined in Esbjerg on the west coast. I soon got figured out where I was and which way to go but vowed to always check the courses in future.

We assumed that we'd be heading down to Antwerp to load steel for the Great Lakes but the next morning as we approached the River Schelte to pick up a pilot we got instructions to head to Le Havre to load a full cargo of wheat for the west coast of Africa. They certainly left things until the last minute. We then went into panic mode as we had only roughly cleaned the holds expecting to load steel and now they had to be spotless to load wheat. The whole crew was put on overtime as Le Havre was only 24 hours away.

We arrived early the following morning still frantically trying to get the holds clean. The grain inspectors boarded immediately and cast a perfunctory eye down two of the holds and passed us grain ready and loading started straight away. If it had been the United States the inspectors would have still been there insisting on cleaner holds! All our stores had been sent to Antwerp and they rolled up on three large lorries the following morning. Some technicians also boarded to service the gyro compass and radars so we brightened up a bit especially as there was a large stock of Belgian beer in among the stores. With the beer came an order from the company that they were having a lot of problems with excessive alcohol consumption on their ships and in future I had to account for every can of beer and send in a report at the end of every month. I was somewhat affronted as I always felt I kept good control of the drinking on board and it was an invasion of privacy not to mention the work involved. Anyhow as long as there was a can of cold beer to drink at the end of a long day life couldn't be too bad.

The loading went pretty slowly as it appeared they were clearing out all the silos in the area in preparation for the next harvest and it became apparent why the inspectors were so lax as the quality of the wheat was rubbish. It was quite a busy time for me, though, as the superintendents from the company descended on the ship en masse and I was kept busy answering all sorts of questions. One good outcome of this was that the local agent in Le Havre insisted on taking them out to lunch every day and I got included in the invitations. The meals were at the best restaurants in town and would last from one o'clock until four with numerous wines to sample. I became a great enthusiast of French cuisine and was very sorry when we left and I had to revert to ship's food.

We sailed for West Africa (ports unknown) on the 1st October. Whilst in Le Havre the superintendents had brought back on board the previous master's accounts as nothing tallied and asked me if I'd sort them out so for the first three days I worked through them surrounded by receipts and slips of paper trying to make something out of them. I eventually sorted them out and to my delight found out that he had claimed on expenses for two cases of beer, which, surprisingly, he hadn't consumed so I rewarded myself for all my extra work.

I wasn't looking forward to discharging in West Africa, as it was becoming a dodgy place to trade because of pirates and general instability in the area. Our first port was declared as Dakar in Senegal and that wasn't too bad as I'd been there a few times and found it pretty civilised. It didn't start off very well as the customs officials managed to find an error in our bond declaration so confiscated 1,000 cigarettes and eight bottles of whisky in lieu of a fine. After that everything settled down though we had quite an argument on completion of discharge as to exactly how much had been discharged and it took another four bottles of whisky to resolve that.

We had discharged approximately 7,000 tons of our 18,000 and as we sailed we had no idea of the next port or ports but we set off southwards on another mystery tour. After a day at sea we received instruction to unload another 7,000 tons at San Pedro in the Ivory Coast. We had a bit of a panic as we didn't have the correct chart for that bit of the coast but it looked quite an easy entrance so we approached with caution keeping a good eye on the echo sounder.

We berthed with no problem and I was pleasantly surprised to find it was a lovely little port – spotlessly clean and well maintained. In the evening John, the chief engineer, and I went for a stroll into town. We walked on a footpath beside a tree-lined dual carriageway into town and couldn't understand why all the locals insisted on walking along the central reservation amongst the traffic instead of using the path. When we were nearly flattened by a huge coconut falling from the trees the reason dawned on us. We found a nice little bar and sat outside in a garden supping cold beer. I was fascinated by the weaverbirds and their nests in the trees round the garden. The nests were brilliantly constructed and the adults were zipping around feeding their young. It was very colourful and relaxing. We walked back to the ship down the central reservation.

The next day I went into town again and phoned the head office to find out if they had any more news for us. We were to discharge the remaining cargo in Abidjan and after that it was another mystery. I got a chance to phone home on a very clear line, which brightened me up a bit as everything was good there. We sailed the following morning though we had a bit of trouble just before we sailed. Just before we pulled the gangway up about 20 local women appeared from the crew quarters and ran down the gangway. The local police then arrested the ship for allowing the women on board. I actually had no idea they were on board and I usually pride myself that I know most of what's going on. It cost me a further five bottles of whisky before we were allowed to sail. At this rate we would run out whisky in the first three weeks of the voyage. Thankfully nobody on board drank it or I'd have had a mutiny.

It was just twelve hours along the coast to Abidjan and this place was as I'd feared. It was positively dangerous to wander ashore and there were plenty of stories of crew members being attacked and robbed. At least the discharge went reasonably quickly taking four days. On the last day I ventured ashore by taxi and phoned head office about which way to head when we sailed. The best they could come up with was to head west as there was a chance of loading in Tubarao in Brazil. When I got back aboard I found we had no charts for Brazil at all. The 2nd mate nipped over to a Greek ship moored astern and borrowed four charts of the area. We then traced them using greaseproof paper from the galley. We actually came up with some useable charts, which came in useful in the end.

It was the last week in October when we completed discharge and just as we sailed the agent came aboard with a telex saying to head to Tubarao in Brazil at 14 knots to load a cargo of steel for the Great Lakes. At last we were going back up the Lakes though I was wondering about the wisdom of this as it was getting pretty late in the year and we could get stuck in the ice.

It took us a week to get across the South Atlantic and the weather was unbelievably good for the whole passage. The second day out I got a radio message to say my father had died and I felt really depressed and frustrated being stuck on a ship in the middle of the South Atlantic and not able to do anything. I couldn't even send a wreath as I didn't know anything about the funeral but I assumed Diane would have it all organised.

We passed through the Doldrums and the sea was like glass with not a breath of wind. It must have been pretty demoralising on the old sailing ships just floating around becalmed for days on end. We really enjoyed it as we got loads of maintenance done on the ship and it was ace sitting out on deck at the end of the day watching the sun set with an ice cold beer in hand.

It was the end of October when we got there but we had to anchor off for four days as our berth was occupied. Once we got alongside the loading went very smoothly. The cargo was mainly large billets of steel which we would take to the rolling mills in Canada to be formed into sheets. The actual loading only took 30 hours for 18,000 tons, which was really good going, but there was quite a delay at one hatch as one of the labourers was killed when a billet fell on him. We were pretty upset but the locals just accepted it as one of those things.

Once we sailed and headed north up the Brazilian coast the weather changed for the worse. We hit depression after depression and it was really uncomfortable as we rolled around violently for the majority of the passage up to the Gulf of St Lawrence. It was coming up the end of November when we entered the Seaway and got orders to proceed to Hamilton in Lake Ontario. For some reason there was a drastic shortage of pilots with ships anchored all over the place. I was allowed to carry on, having my pilot's licence, though it was a bit hairy when we got to Hamilton and I had to berth the ship. Luckily the agent had ordered us a couple of tugs and they helped a lot though I have to admit I made a right arse of things and nearly ran aground off the berth but we got there in the end.

It was nice to be in a civilised port again and we were able to stock up on good quality meat and vegetables. The company had a nice surprise for me. The chief steward was due a relief and they decided that we didn't need a chief steward and his duties would be divided between the radio officer and myself. The radio officer got some extra money for the new duties but I had to soldier on without a rise. It was quite a panic for the first few weeks as making up balanced menus was way out of our comfort zone. Luckily the chief cook was a great little Indonesian guy with years of experience and we just let him get on with it in the end. Everybody reckoned we fed better without the chief steward though I have a feeling we spent a lot more money.

Discharge in Hamilton only took three days and again it was the last minute before our next employment was confirmed. We had to load 15,000 tons of steel coils and sheets in Cleveland and Detroit for Bombay and 2,000 tons of timber for Jeddah. It seemed odd loading steel in the Lakes as we usually brought it in but that's the way trade went.

We started loading in Cleveland the first week in December and I was getting quite concerned about getting stuck in the ice as it turned very cold and the ice seemed to be forming very quickly. The radio officer and I had to order the food stores for the next three months so that kept us occupied for quite a while. I was scared we would forget some essential items but the cook seemed happy enough. We had one panic when we discovered we were nearly out of beer. Hugh, the local agent, had a friend who ran an off licence and suggested we buy from him rather than pay the exorbitant price the ship chandler was demanding. The result was that we loaded his estate car up with 50 cases of beer and did three runs with his car just about scraping along the road. I paid cash from the ship's money so everyone was happy. It worked out really well in the end, as the company didn't know we'd got extra beer on board so we didn't have to report how much we were drinking. I felt a bit guilty later on when I got a letter from the company complimenting us on our lowered consumption, but not very.

It took them a week to load us. It would have been less but the stevedores managed to drop a 20 ton coil into one of our holds. It made a hell of a bang and put a large hole in the deck, which took two days to repair. The noise it made I thought it had gone straight through the ship's bottom.

It was the middle of November when we set off back down the Seaway. I was relieved to see that although there was a lot of ice around it wasn't thick enough to hinder us. We stopped off in Montreal to load 500 tons of timber and take on some extra fuel.

191

Then we carried on down the St Lawrence to Quebec where we loaded a further 1,500 tons of timber. It looked really poor quality timber – mainly pine – but somebody in Saudi Arabia must have ordered it. It took two days to load and then we were on our way towards Suez. I was really pleased to get away as the ship obviously hadn't been designed to operate in cold weather and we had a lot of trouble with things freezing up.

It wasn't too bad a trip, though we battled some pretty strong head winds for the first few days but thankfully there was no fog. We had Christmas Day just before passing through Gibraltar into the Mediterranean. The Christmas dinner was quite a success as the radio officer and I had managed to remember everything. The cook even rustled up some bread sauce and stuffing which I'm sure isn't part of Indonesian cuisine. Everyone behaved themselves as well and there was no excessive drinking which made life a great deal easier for me.

The Mediterranean was kind to us and we had a very pleasant passage to Suez arriving there on New Year's Day. We managed to transit the Canal without too many problems although we were 1,000 cigarettes and several bottles of whisky lighter when we cleared the southern end. It was just a day down to Jeddah and we went straight alongside and started discharge. Unloading was a disaster as the port had just recruited some more labour from Bangladesh and I don't think they'd seen a ship before never mind discharged one. To avoid any major mishaps we used the ship's crew as crane drivers but the slinging of the bundles of timber left a lot to be desired and several were dropped reducing the timber to matchwood and injuring a couple of the labourers.

I got very frustrated as we were unable to obtain any fresh stores and we were starting to run pretty low and I also needed two or three documents signed and nobody would take responsibility. I won in the end, though, as when the agents arrived at sailing time with their papers to sign I refused until they signed mine. We also got some fresh vegetables right at the end but they were of very poor quality.

After that it was off down the Red Sea towards Bombay. It was strange being back here as I'd spent over ten years with United Arab Shipping trading in this area. It was lovely being in the Indian Ocean with the light winds and warm weather. I think the Indian Ocean must be my favourite part of the world, when the monsoons aren't blowing, and it's just miles of blue skies, glassy seas and light balmy winds. Top that off with a barbecue and a can of ice cold beer and it's my idea of paradise.

As we approached Bombay we got a message telling us to anchor on arrival so nothing much had changed here. Despite being told every day that we would be berthing the next day we were stuck out there for ten days. By this time we had completely run out of fresh vegetables but the cook came up with the idea of barbecues which didn't need any veg and that seemed to work although it was a bit wearing in the end. I was starting to hate the chief steward's job and was really pleased when there was a message from the company saying they were sending us a chief steward as they'd had serious problems on the other ships.

It was the last week in January when we finally got alongside. All the stevedores boarded the ship and everything looked good for a quick discharge. Not to be. The stevedores didn't have any cutters for the steel lashing bands that secured the coils so they all left again and didn't return for ten hours. This time they had cutters but to hurry things along they decided to lift two 20 ton coils at a time using our cranes, which could only lift 20 tons at a time. After a lot of shouting we got them to lift one at a time but then they decided that rather than cut the lashings they would just lift the coils and hope the lashings would break. We ended up switching the cranes off which resulted in them all walking off the ship. I was beginning to remember why I hated Bombay.

We also had several surveys and inspections on the ship to undertake and I was dreading these. The day before the surveyor was due the 1st mate came to my cabin and asked when we'd made the big dent in the ship's side. I didn't even know we had a dent and was somewhat aghast when I saw the size of it. I had no recollection of bouncing off anything and it must have been a real bang. When we checked inside we found several frames badly bent but at least we were watertight. I was sure the surveyor would spot it and demand it was repaired before we sailed which would result in quite a delay. The surveyor was pretty thorough in his inspections of the lifeboats and radio equipment and we were all quite chuffed when he said it was one of the best ships he'd inspected.

We had the opportunity to wander ashore quite a lot but it wasn't pleasant with hundreds of kids following demanding money wherever we went. I went out with John, the chief engineer, for a meal one night. It was a delicious curry though I was a bit nervous about the cleanliness of the place. Then the day before we left we were taken by the shippers up to the Taj Mahal Hotel, reputedly the best hotel in Bombay, for a slap up meal as they were very pleased with our performance. I have to admit I preferred the curry I'd had earlier in our stay, especially when I went down with bad food poisoning the day after our slap up meal!

We actually got our next employment before we sailed this time. We were to load bulk raw sugar and manganese ore in South Africa for the Far East. It had all the making of a really long trip. They didn't want us in South Africa until the middle of February so we had about four days to waste on the way down. Hopefully the weather would be good all the way.

I was quite looking forward to the trip as we'd managed to get some half decent stores on board and I'd relinquished my catering duties. The charterers had been really pleased with our performance and just before we sailed a little man appeared with an envelope for me containing a large wad of US dollars. There was also one for the other senior officers so everyone was really happy.

We set off heading south west across the Indian Ocean at reduced speed. John, the chief engineer, came up with the idea that we should stop for a day and they could overhaul two of the main engine pistons, which seemed like a good idea. Four days out, as we were passing an island called Aldabra north of Madagascar, we got an urgent message on the VHF radio from a yacht from the Seychelles that had broken down and had to anchor behind the island. We soon found them and John went over to see if he could help. The boat had about 20 German tourists on board and they had been visiting a scientific station on the island, which monitored a rare turtle. It turned out that of their two engines, one would only go very slow and the other was stuck in reverse and they were supposed to be heading back to the Seychelles the next day. John reckoned the only solution was to change the gearboxes so at least they'd have one serviceable engine. We decided to give it a go so John and two of his engineers went over with a load of tools. It was a major job and it took them over twelve hours but they sorted it. The skipper of the yacht got his crew catching fish for us so we ended up with a freezer

194

full of lovely fresh fish. It also turned out that some government minister in the Seychelles owned the yacht and he was so pleased he said he'd organise a free holiday for John and me to the Seychelles. It sounded really good and John and I fantasised over this luxurious holiday but, perhaps unsurprisingly, we never heard anything more.

Life was really quite good apart from the fact that I'd miscalculated the beer consumption and we were going to run out before we got South Africa. But all was not lost as the next day we got a message from the company to say the first port was Durban and we could get there as soon as we liked, as there was a berth available, so off we charged. We managed to last out though it was a close thing.

We were chartered to load 10,000 tons of raw sugar in Durban for Hong Kong and then nip along the coast to Port Elizabeth to load a further 8,000 tons of manganese ore for a port in China. It meant travelling with two holds full of cargo and the other three empty, which would put considerable stress on the ship. We had a computer to work out these stresses but it inconveniently broke down halfway through our calculations and we had to wing it. By fiddling round with ballast water we just about got within limits though I was praying that we wouldn't have any bad weather between Durban and Port Elizabeth.

Loading in Durban only took two days but I was able to phone the company and tell them about the large dent in the hull. I ended up having a steaming argument with the superintendent about who was responsible for it and I was positive it wasn't me. I wasn't too happy when I got back on board. We also received a load of stores here and I thought I'd do the same about ordering beer privately but the ship chandler showed me a telex from the company telling him specifically not to sell the ship any beer for cash so obviously they'd cottoned on to me. Bugger.

The sugar load went without problem and we nipped along the coast to Port Elizabeth but had to anchor off for three days as the berth was occupied. It was just supposed to be a ten hour load but they had a major breakdown ashore and it ended up taking over 24 which was just as well. John and I had decided to nip ashore for a meal at a well-recommended restaurant and we duly arrived just after noon to find it closed. It turned out they didn't start serving until one o'clock but we got into conversation with the owner's husband who invited us to sample some of the local wine. He had some fantastic wines as far as I remember and I have no idea what we had to eat. I got back on board about four o'clock sadly very much the worse for wear. We were supposed to sail at six so I had to try and sober up quickly. I consumed gallons of strong black coffee but that didn't help much. John arrived back slightly later but in a better condition than me so he could keep an eye on me. Thankfully the shore installation broke down just then and it took them eight hours to repair it, which gave me time to sober up.

I was seriously hung-over the next morning when we sailed, though. Thankfully the departure from Port Elizabeth is straight forward and directly out into the open sea so we left without any problem but right into the path of a cyclone. Luckily it cleared away northwards pretty quickly but then the barometer started dropping again really fast so there was something else around. I took evasive action and headed off south to avoid it adding 100 miles to our trip. It passed without too much trouble but it left us very short of fuel. We were chartered to do 14 knots so we'd be in trouble if we reduced to speed to economise on fuel. We were due to refuel in Singapore and I was seriously concerned that we wouldn't make it but in the end the weather improved and with favourable currents we just did it. It was a wonder nobody from the company noticed how little fuel we'd arrived with but I got away with that one.

After Singapore we headed up to Hong Kong arriving there in the middle of March. We tied up to buoys in the middle of the harbour and it took us four days to discharge the sugar into barges. We then got orders to discharge the manganese ore in Zhanjiang in China. This caused us to scratch our heads, as we couldn't actually find it on the map. There were several ports of similar name way up north beside Shanghai but we eventually found it only twelve hours steaming from Hong Kong. It was quite a difficult approach as the buoys indicating the channel were in a completely different place to those marked on our charts. I complained bitterly to the pilot when he boarded and I later got a visit from the harbour master to apologise. He consumed the best part of a bottle of whisky and demanded a carton of cigarettes for his trouble so that didn't work out too well.

The discharge went surprisingly well considering there were three times as many chiefs as there were indians! All the officials tried to outdo each other as to how many stripes and the amount of gold braid they wore. The harbour master had the biggest pair of epaulettes I have ever seen and we reckoned he could take off if he ran fast enough.

The day after we berthed we got our instructions for the next leg of the voyage – we were to load 14,000 tons of manioc in Surabaya in Indonesia for Europe. At least we were heading home again though it would be a further six weeks. Again we didn't have the correct chart for Surabaya so we borrowed it from a Polish ship moored ahead intending to trace it but I forgot and we sailed off with it. I hope the Polish ship didn't have to go there afterwards.

We sailed from Zhanjiang towards the end of March and headed south towards Indonesia. We had only five days to clean the holds of the manganese ore before we could load the manioc, which is used to make tapioca. I still can't get my head round who would want 14,000 tons of tapioca, but there you go. The 1st mate was really switched on so the hold cleaning was completed with a day in hand.

We berthed on arrival and started loading straight away. The manioc arrived on lorries in large gunnysacks and I had visions of us being there weeks but the loading went surprisingly quickly. Surabaya was a very pleasant place after Zhanjiang with everything nice and clean and wide avenues with loads of parks. I got taken out for two or three meals by the charterers and became an avid fan of Indonesian cooking. I'd always liked satay but the locally made stuff was in a different league from what I'd had before and absolutely delicious.

I got a message to phone the company so nipped up to the agent's office where I got a lovely clear phone line for once. I got the good news that I was to be relieved in Singapore in about a week and then I was passed over to the superintendent who was still rambling on about the dent in the hull. He also mentioned that he knew we had tried to buy beer privately in Durban and told me it was definitely not allowed and he hoped my reports on the officers' drinking would be accurate in future. Smug bugger. What he didn't know was that we'd bought a supply of beer and wine privately from another ship chandler so I felt I was one up. I left the office feeling a bit depressed but soon brightened when the agent invited me out for yet another meal.

Two days into the load the 2nd mate and the 3rd engineer asked if they could have two days off and fly over to the island of Bali, which was only an hour away. They were both decent lads and the other officers said they'd cover for them so off they went. We reckoned it would take another four days at least to finish the load but the agent came aboard just after the two had left and announced that the berth was needed for another vessel and we would work round the clock and finish in two days. I had a mad panic trying to contact the two officers on Bali as it would the final straw if the ship was delayed waiting for them. The following afternoon I got a message saying they had been found in the local jail and were on their way back. It turned out that they'd had their bags pinched with all their money and passports just after they had landed. Two very dejected officers returned on board later that day, much to my relief, and we sailed the next evening.

It was only two days up to Singapore where we were stopping to refuel out at anchor. My relief boarded straight away and I was able to give him a reasonable handover in the three hours it took to fuel. I was then taken ashore by launch and flew home later that day. It was quite a good time to be getting home being the start of spring and I reckoned I had at least two months leave.

CHAPTER NINETEEN

Dredging

Arco Humber; Arco Test; Arco Axe; Arco Thames; Arco Trent
9th June 1989 – 19th December 1990

It turned out I didn't enjoy my leave at all. A week into the leave I got a phone call from the company asking why I hadn't sent my final accounts in. I told them they had been sent from Singapore by courier with all the other ship's papers. I ended up talking to the superintendent again and he started on again about the dent so I hung up on him. It was becoming obvious that I would have to find another job as he really had it in for me. One day I happened to meet up with an old schoolmate who had also gone to sea and he was working as an engineer for a company that dredged aggregates offshore and brought them ashore for the construction industry. The pay was about half what I was getting with Transocean Maritime but the rota was three weeks on and three weeks off and I'd never be far from home. I quite liked the sound of it and when I discussed it with Diane she said she'd happily find a job to supplement our income so I'd give it a try.

Rather than burn my boats completely with Transocean I decided to do one trip before my leave was up and if it was no good I'd go back deep sea. I phoned up the company that John, my friend, was working for: ARC Marine in Southampton. They ran quite a large fleet of dredgers ranging from clapped out wrecks to modern state of the art jobs. The bloke I talked to didn't sound very optimistic and I was most surprised to get a phone call two days later telling me to join the *Arco Humber* in Charlton on the Thames the following day. It was a mad panic getting my gear packed as I'd no idea what to take but I made it.

I couldn't believe the *Arco Humber* when I first saw her. She was the most ugly cumbersome ship I have ever seen and her deck was completely dominated by a huge discharging gantry that severely reduced visibility forward from the bridge. I was to sign on as extra mate to learn the ropes. Interestingly, I'd sailed with the 1st mate 20 years ago when he was 3rd mate with me, and he was rather surprised to see me. The skipper was a bloke called Bob Tanner who'd worked in dredgers all his life so I figured he would be the man to follow.

I rapidly came to the conclusion that this type of sea life was nothing like I'd encountered before. The *Arco Humber* was the oldest and largest of the ARC fleet and surprisingly was still a very efficient dredger. She could load 7,500 tons of aggregate in about seven hours and discharge it with conveyors in about four. Unlike the modern dredgers the suction pump was on board whereas in the new vessels it was situated halfway down the suction pipe which was much more efficient. The loading was done in areas licensed by the government and ARC mainly had licences in the Solent and off the East Anglian coast. These were known on board as patches and all had an identifying number.

Discharge was completed about an hour after I'd got aboard and I found out I was assigned the 1st mate's watch so he could assist on deck with other tasks. It was a very steep learning curve as there was so much equipment to master and some of it I couldn't figure out at all. We sailed late in the afternoon and I stayed on the bridge for the trip down the Thames with Bob Tanner doing the pilotage. It then became apparent that not only was I going to have to learn how to dredge but also how to pilot the ship in an out of the various ports by myself without a pilot. Deep sea we inevitably had a pilot to assist us so all I had to do was make sure he did his job right and intervene if things went pear shaped. I loved actual ship handling and I could see that this would be one side of the job I could really enjoy.

Once at sea it was like any other ship with a couple of exceptions. The huge discharge gantry was parked right in front of the bridge and caused numerous blind spots so I had to keep moving around all the time and relied on the radar more than I usually would have. The other thing was that the hold, or tank as it was known, was filled with water to keep the ship ballasted down. This was slopping around and gave the ship an odd lurching movement, which I found very uncomfortable to start with and I felt queasy for the first two or three trips. Once we started loading into the tank the aggregate displaced the water, which spilled over the side until eventually the tank, was completely full with aggregate.

I came on watch again at midnight to find us two hours into the dredge. It was surreal with all the ship's lights on and water and sand cascading everywhere. Bob Tanner was in charge of the dredge and my job was to control the position of the pipe, which was suspended from two wires on winches. Obviously I hadn't a clue what I was doing to start with but I soon got the hang of things. I then had time to watch Bob to see how things were done. There were loads of things to monitor: the position of the ship, its speed, the quality of the cargo, where it was going in the tank and when to pump the ballast water out. He also had to keep his eye on me. I finished my watch at six in the morning just as the load was completed so I got to retrieve the suction pipe and stow in on deck without damaging anything. I had breakfast and went to bed wondering whether I'd ever get the hang of this and maybe I should just stay on proper ships.

We did two more runs into Charlton, which was just upriver of the Thames Barrier, and then some runs into Flushing in Holland, which is just at the entrance to the River Schelte. This took nearly two weeks and I felt I was really starting to get the hang of things. I spent a bit of time working with the crew and even drove the discharging gantry a few times. It was a lot harder physical work than I'd been used to but there was a good bunch of lads on board and I enjoyed myself.

After two weeks the other skipper, Ron Hill, relieved Bob Tanner. He, like myself, had come from deep sea and taken up dredging to have a better family life. He'd been dredging for about four years and reckoned he was still learning. He wasn't a natural like Bob Tanner and always seemed to have to work really hard to get a decent cargo. I had a week with Ron in which we always dredged on a patch 15 miles east of Great Yarmouth and took the cargo into Flushing. It was a good run and I enjoyed taking the ship up and down a narrow channel called the Oost Gat just off the Dutch coast. The channel was only yards off the shore in places and it was quite exciting. Our last cargo was back to Charlton and I paid off there and made my way home arriving there at the beginning of July.

Transocean Maritime had been on the phone two or three times asking when I was available to join a ship and now I had a difficult decision to make as to whether to give dredging a try or go back deep sea to a job I was more comfortable in. Although the pay was substantially less the attraction of three weeks on three weeks off was very tempting. Diane had found herself a job working as an administrator for a holiday company and was really enjoying it so after three days deliberating I phoned Transocean Maritime and told them I'd found another job. I don't think they were too happy as they'd just bought another vessel and were short of senior staff. I then had another ten days at home where I must admit I started to have misgivings about my decision.

The employment with ARC seemed very casual. I got a phone call from personnel asking me to join the *Arco Axe* in Cliffe at eight in the morning the following day. They seemed surprised that I didn't know where Cliffe was and all I was told was to get a train to Strood and get a taxi to the ship. This meant I had to catch the sleeper that night from Carlisle so it was quite a rush to get myself packed and off to the station. It turned out to be a very easy journey and I got a decent sleep on the train for once.

The ship was discharging at Cliffe, which is on the Thames about five miles downstream from Gravesend. The *Arco Axe* was the complete opposite of the *Arco Humber*. She was only three months old and a state of the art design by Appledore Shipbuilders in Devon. She was a lot smaller as well only lifting 4,500 tons but could load that in less than two hours. After all the time I'd spent learning about the equipment on the *Arco Humber* everything on here was different. She discharged by pulling the aggregate out of the hold using buckets on wires into a hopper and from there via conveyors to the shore. All the monitoring equipment for dredging was computerised so there were dials and screens everywhere. This was going to be more of a challenge.

The atmosphere on board was completely different from the *Arco Humber* and I felt like an interloper. The skipper was unwilling to show me how anything worked and thinking back I have a feeling he didn't exactly know how it worked himself. I spent a lot of time reading through manuals and just observed how things went. One

202

good aspect was that we were running into the Thames all the time and I managed to get my pilotage dispensation very quickly. I really enjoyed taking the ship all the way up the river though the skipper always insisted on berthing her himself. We also did some trips up the River Medway to Rochester so I got my pilot licence for the Medway as well. Halfway through my time on board the skipper changed. Brett Farmer was a completely different kettle of fish and explained in detail how everything worked. Although I didn't get to do any actual dredging I felt I could give it a good go. I did my three weeks and went home for my three weeks leave, which took me into the middle of August. I really liked this rota system although I was still feeling a bit anxious about taking command.

I have a feeling that the company were grooming me for a skipper's job as for the rest of the year I seemed to go on every vessel that ARC owned even to the pumping station that was moored off Sizewell to provide aggregate for the building of the nuclear power station. Every vessel seemed to have it's own peculiarities and advantages. My biggest problem was that I was never assigned to the same ship twice so had to take all my gear with me every time. The advantage was that I was sailing with all the different skippers and they all had their favourite run they preferred to dredge on so I started keeping a notebook with all the different coordinates in. I also noted the best way to load the vessel and any problems I might encounter. I came across the notebook a few months ago and couldn't decipher any of it. I must be getting old. Some of the skippers were very protective of their runs and the skipper on the *Arco Axe* would cover the monitor over so I couldn't see where we were but of course he had to go to the loo sometime so...

The company specified what type of cargo they wanted and usually it was 60 per cent gravel and 40 per cent sand which was reasonably easy to do but to get a higher ratio of gravel was a lot harder as the sand was screened off back over the side and it took a lot longer to load. Also if the bottom was really sandy it was virtually impossible. I liked the full loads of sand because I could never find the good gravelly patches despite all my secret jottings. You could tell if it was a good stony cargo because it rattled a lot more as it was loaded so it was always a good sign if it was really noisy but equally it was a real pain if there was just a gentle whoosh of sand coming on board.

I managed to get Christmas at home and then I was sent to the pumping station again which suited me because it was a nice easy life. I was supposed to do three weeks there but after two weeks the pipe to the shore blew a hole in it. We stayed there for a couple of days while divers tried to repair the pipe but the weather was atrocious so we were ordered into Lowestoft to lie up and release the crew.

I had my three week leave and then got orders to join the *Arco Humber* in Flushing as master. I had a bit of a panic attack as this was the hardest ship to operate and handle but I figured the company must have talked to people and decided I was up to the job. I caught the ferry from Sheerness across to Flushing and began to have serious misgivings about my ability.

When I boarded the *Arco Humber* I found that I wasn't being dropped in at the deep end completely as Bob Tanner was remaining on board for the first week to give me a bit of guidance. He put me in charge and said he'd just sit in the background and jump in if things were going seriously wrong. I took the ship off the berth and out into the River Schelte but made a right cock of things by overcompensating, aware all the time that Bob was looking over my shoulder. At least we didn't hit anything or run aground. Then it was up to the patch off Great Yarmouth to load a cargo back for Flushing. I was left to my own devices and it actually turned out a really good load with no problems much to my amazement. Back in Flushing I managed to berth without any difficulty though there was considerable room for improvement. The receiver was very happy with the cargo because it had a lot of silica in it for some reason but sadly it was pure luck as I didn't even know there was silica to be dredged up and had no idea what it looked like. I only managed one more run with Bob as we got tangled up with a force twelve gale and had to shelter for two days. The next cargo was for a full load of sand for Middlesbrough and that suited me down to the ground as I had no problem finding sand – it was gravel that was my nemesis. The next few cargoes were all sand so maybe the company was breaking me in gently. I got more and more confident and felt I could do this job.

As we were sailing out from Middlesbrough after the last cargo the ship started to list alarmingly just as we dropped the pilot. I'm sure he thought we were going to capsize because he got off rather quickly. After some urgent investigations we found a large hole in one of our wing tanks and not only that but the valve for emptying the tank was seized solid so we couldn't pump it out. There was nothing for it but to return to port for repairs. I had quite a job convincing the harbour master that we wouldn't capsize in the channel and block the entrance to his port but eventually he relented and allowed us in. We must have made quite a sight as the banks were lined with people watching us enter leaning over at 30 degrees. It took us two days to sort out the hole and repair the valve then we were off again.

We had another three trips to Flushing and they seemed reasonably happy with my cargoes though I never found the patch of silica again. I paid off in Flushing and Bob Tanner rejoined and was pleased to see his ship still in one piece.

One perk of being master was that it was now two weeks on and two weeks off which made life much more pleasant though the two weeks at home went by in a flash. I rejoined at the end of March and was told I was now permanent master of the *Arco Humber*. Unfortunately most of our cargoes were supposed to be 60 per cent gravel into Flushing and I had a really hard time getting anything over 50 per cent. I spent most of my time in Flushing arguing over the quality of the cargo, which did nothing for my confidence. I was pleased with the ship handling side of it, though, and really enjoyed every opportunity to manoeuver the vessel.

The *Arco Humber* was getting a bit long in the tooth and we were always having problems with our discharging gear but mainly it was the discharging gantry. At the end of May, on my fourth trip, we were halfway through discharge in Flushing when one of the motor generators in the gantry blew up in a big way. We were too deep to stay on the berth over low water so we shifted across the harbour to the Town Quay to effect repairs. The motor, which weighed over two tons, had to go ashore to be rewound and this took us two days. It was going to take at least two weeks to repair the motor and the harbour master wasn't too happy about us occupying a big lump of his quay. I thought he was going to insist that we go out and anchor until the motor was ready which would have been a right bind. Instead he came up with the idea of moving us into the fishing harbour to wait. The company agreed and we moved in the following morning. It was a tight fit through the lock with only inches to spare on either side but we managed and ended up moored among loads of fishing boats, barges and pleasure craft.

As it was only the first cargo of my rota I ended up spending the remaining ten days having a nice little holiday. It was only a short walk into town with its quaint little bars and general holiday atmosphere. I had to walk to the agent's office every day to phone the company with a progress report and on the way back I would stop at the railway station and buy the day's Daily Telegraph and have a nice cup of coffee in the sunshine. I actually did a bit of work in the afternoons but after tea I would wander round the marina chatting with the various people on the decks of the barges and yachts. Then it was into town for a couple of beers and sometimes a meal of fish and chips and then amble back on board well satisfied with life. I was quite disappointed when Bob Tanner came to relieve me. I managed to persuade the company it was cheaper to fly me home from Amsterdam than take the ferry back to Sheerness and then the train home. I caught the train up to Schiphol Airport and flew over to Newcastle and was back home in Carlisle before the ferry had even sailed from Flushing.

I rejoined the middle of June and it was back on the same old run from the patch off Great Yarmouth to Flushing. Even Bob Tanner had been having problems getting decent cargoes and he reckoned that the impeller in the suction pump was getting well worn and would have to be replaced before we'd get decent cargoes again. It would normally take about nine hours to load a stony cargo but my first load took nearly twelve, which was pretty tiring as I had to be alert all the time. I was rapidly going off dredging. The company took pity on me for the rest of that trip and we took sandy cargoes into Ostend and Dunkirk though the loads were still taking over ten hours. When Bob Tanner relieved me he said the ship was going to lie up for a couple of weeks to renew the impeller and do some essential repairs which brightened me up. I rejoined in Chatham halfway through and was pleased to see all sorts of repair work under way. The impeller was completely worn away and it was a wonder we'd been able to get a cargo at all.

We sailed out after a week and the first run was to Flushing. It was the best cargo I'd loaded and I think part of that was the fact that I'd figured out that the ship's speed over the bottom was really critical – too slow and the pipe blocked up and too fast we sucked mainly water. Even Flushing complimented me on the quality. Maybe I was destined to be a dredger man after all!

Full of confidence I decided to prospect a bit and investigate other areas of the patch. I was doing rather well when there was a huge thump and a bang. We pulled the pipe up and there was a large dent in it so obviously we'd hit something. I then went back to the original run to finish off the load rather than risk further damage. When we discharged the cargo in Flushing they complained there were lumps of wood in it so obviously I'd hit a sunken wreck that wasn't marked on the chart. I found out later that I must have been the only person that didn't know of the existence of the wreck and everyone else avoided the area.

The new impeller certainly made a difference and I was getting decent loads in about seven hours so I felt I was doing all right. I was actually enjoying life but as the year progressed our workload eased as the UK was going into a recession and there was a reduced demand for aggregate for building. We sometimes anchored for a day waiting for orders and there was talk of taking ships out of service to save money. In the middle of November we were told that the ship would lie up in Middlesbrough for Christmas so we ended up taking several cargoes of sand into the Tees and the Tyne before tying up in the Tees in the middle of December. We all assumed the ship would just lie up over the Christmas period and then sail again in January but knew something was amiss when several senior personnel from the company announced they were visiting the following day.

They told us they were taking the *Arco Humber* out of service indefinitely and two other ships as well so there had to be redundancies. So that was me on my bike again as it was last in first out. They said they would be in touch if the situation improved but it was obvious to us all that the recession was getting worse if anything. I collected all my gear and paid off on the 19th December so at least I got home for Christmas.

207

CHAPTER TWENTY

Containers across the North Atlantic

m.v. Canmar Triumph
16th March 1991 – 12th August 1991

ARC Marine had given me an extra month's wages so at least I wouldn't be short of money over Christmas so I decided to relax over the festive period and start looking for another job in the New Year. I felt I was pretty employable as I was now 50 with 15 years as master and experienced in a wide variety of ships and cargoes. I was quite upbeat about getting another job in the near future. Luckily I had kept records of all my previous applications so I started sending off letters with my CV to all and sundry. I did a lot of phoning around as well and it seemed there were quite a few good jobs out there but I had to find them. I got an offer from a Barrow based company called James Fisher to skipper one of their little coasters but it was tiny with only eight crew and I felt I could do better than that even though Fishers was a great company to work for. By mid February, though, I was starting to get a bit desperate and started applying for shore jobs round Carlisle but there was nothing that really took my fancy. At the end of February I got a phone call from John Carroll, who'd been chief engineer with me on the *Atlantic*. He suggested I ring Clyde Marine, an agency in Glasgow, and mention his name, which I duly did. They didn't sound too optimistic at all and I was most surprised to be phoned up the following day to be offered a job with Anglo Eastern Management in Hong Kong as master of a containership trading across the Atlantic.

The ship was the *Canmar Triumph* built in 1989 and the same size as the *Al Ihsa'a*, which I'd commanded for United Arab Shipping for two years. The only downside was that she traded Hamburg, Le Havre to Montreal and back all the time. Containerships are always on a very tight schedule with their slots at the discharge berth booked sometimes months in advance and if ever the ship is delayed the knock-on effect is tremendous and the Atlantic is notorious for bad weather so it can be a real nightmare keeping on schedule. But the wages were good again so I decided I couldn't have everything.

I flew over to Hamburg and joined on the 16th March. The ship impressed me, as she looked well maintained. I relieved Ian Donaldson who was really pleased to get off as he'd been on for nine months through the winter and it had been a bad year not only for storms but also for ice and icebergs. It was a good handover with no problems but Ian had only been gone ten minutes when I had the harbour police knocking on my door. The ship was taking fuel and we were breaking numerous regulations. With a bit of diplomacy and a few beers I got the fine reduced to 200 Deutsche marks. I then went and saw the chief engineer and tore a strip off him, which wasn't the best of starts. He actually didn't seem the least worried though.

I was the only European on board as the rest of the crew were all Indian. The only thing that bothered me was what sort of food would be served but when I went down for a meal I was pleasantly surprised as it was a pretty reasonable steak and chips with not a curry in sight.

We sailed the following day and had thick fog all the way down the North Sea and the Channel. I was quite impressed by the 1st and 2nd mates who performed really professionally. The 3rd mate was absolutely useless, though, so I had to stay on watch with him all the time. It was a quick call into Le Havre for 200 containers then off to Canada. I was pleased to find that the schedule was for 18 knots and we could actually do 21 though we used a tremendous amount of extra fuel to do this. The ship was also equipped with weather fax machines, which gave me a map every two hours showing the positions of storms and the direction and height of the swells. I always enjoyed interpreting the weather maps so this looked like my cup of tea. I made numerous adjustments to our course on the passage and managed to avoid the worst gales though it added a few miles to the trip.

As we got close to Newfoundland we passed lots of huge icebergs, which showed up well on the radar but my worry were the growlers, which didn't show on the radar, and could a lot of damage if we hit one. I was surprised when we got into the Gulf of St Lawrence by how much ice was around. The icebreakers were still working freeing ships that got stuck. I was lucky that there were two large ships ahead of me so we just slowed down and followed them and let them break the ice for us.

We got to Montreal twelve hours ahead of schedule without using any extra fuel so I was quite pleased with myself. We had three days in Montreal as the ship was completely discharged and then reloaded. It seemed to be mainly empty containers for the trip back but they filled quite a few of them with mustard and flax seed rather than have them empty. At least we were earning money on them.

We sailed from Montreal on the 1st April with still a fair amount of thick ice around. The coastguard lifted most of the buoys in the autumn when the ice arrived and they hadn't even started to replace them so it made navigation a bit more hazardous. There was quite a lot of thick ice in the Gulf of St Lawrence but I managed to find some open leads and we progressed pretty well. I decided to go over close to the Newfoundland coast hoping for thinner ice but late in the afternoon we came to a grinding halt in really thick ice. I managed to extricate us by backing and filling and just hoping the ice wouldn't damage the propeller every time we went astern.

We got going again and I was surprised to meet another container ship, the *OOCL Challenge*. She had sailed a day ahead of us and when we talked on the VHF radio we found she'd been stuck several times and was now coming back to try a much more southerly route. She was a fair bit bigger and more powerful than us so when she turned south I followed behind. It took us over a day to get into clear water and back up to full speed. The *OOCL Challenge* shot off at maximum speed to try and make up the lost time but we carried on at service speed as we hadn't actually lost that much time and the weather maps showed we should have a good trip if we went on a great circle route north of Scotland. About halfway across I had to change the plan and headed for the Channel as although the winds were moderate we were rolling around heavily in some big swells.

Just as we were passing south of Lands End we got a 'Mayday' message from a ship on fire about 30 miles south of us and Falmouth coastguard requested we proceed so we shot off at maximum speed. When we got there the ship was well on fire and a helicopter was lifting the crew off and landing them on another vessel. There wasn't much for us to do so after three hours we were released. This deviation had added a lot of extra time so we had to go at full speed to get to Hamburg on time. This was the fastest ship I'd ever been on and doing 21 knots we absolutely flew along but we were using about 30 tons of fuel a day extra so it was going to be expensive. Luckily we got favourable tides up the Channel and North Sea and I was able to slow down after eight hours and I still got to Hamburg two hours ahead of our slot.

It was a quick turnaround and four days later we were heading out across the Atlantic after our stops at Hamburg and Le Havre. The *Canmar Triumph* was operated by a company called Canadian Maritime, which used to be the famous Canadian Pacific Company. They were operating six ships on the route with two of us doing the Hamburg/Le Havre run and the other four calling at Rotterdam and Felixstowe. I was a bit disappointed not to be calling back into the UK every three weeks but then I found I was exempt from British income tax as long as I stayed away long enough so I didn't complain too much.

I decided to keep well south this time and it was a much better passage though we were slowed by the adverse effect of the Gulf Stream. I was happy to see how much the ice had melted when we got back to the Canadian side and to see that the coastguard had got most of the buoys back in position. Our problem this time was the extra volume of water coming down the river from the melting ice but we got to Montreal well ahead of schedule again.

Whilst in port I was pleased to meet up with Dennis Macleod, who I'd sailed with 20 years before. He'd got a job as port captain and seemed to be thriving on it. I went out for a couple of meals with him when we visited Montreal and it made a really pleasant change from trying to converse with my crew. Although they all spoke perfect English I could never find any common ground for conversation and found myself becoming something of a recluse. The agents in all the ports would to take pity on me and I would get taken out for a nice meal at least once in every port, which made up for it.

It was a quick turn round in Montreal and we were soon heading out again. The weather was warming up nicely and most of the ice had disappeared but I still kept well south of Newfoundland just in case. When we were in ice we filled the ballast tanks to keep the ship deeper in the water and hopefully avoid damage to the propeller and it also helped our momentum if we did get stuck in ice. It was obvious that we were clear of the ice as we passed Newfoundland so we started pumping out the ballast water and headed south towards the Gulf Stream.

It was nearly all out and we were charging along happily when the 2nd mate called me to the bridge as he'd received a 'Mayday' call on the VHF radio from a sinking ship close to the Newfoundland coast. The ship was in really thick pack ice about 50 miles north of us so I was sure there would be other ships closer that could help him but the Canadian coastguard called us and said we were the nearest and would we proceed. We hurriedly started refilling the ballast tanks and headed into the ice. It was not good as the visibility closed in and there were some largish icebergs in among the ice, which didn't show up well on radar.

It took us three hours to find him and we got there just in time. The ship was listing 40 degrees and going more by the minute. She was obviously in poor condition and the crew had launched a life boat but it had smashed when it landed on the ice. They then launched a life raft, which sat nicely on top of the ice. I couldn't get really close as every time I went ahead towards them the ice moved as well. I couldn't figure out how to get closer to them when one of their crew started walking across the ice towards us pulling a rope attached to the raft. When he got close we could see he was wearing only a t-shirt and shorts and was in bare feet! We put ladders over the side and just as they were going to board us a voice came over the radio asking what the situation was. It was a Canadian coastguard cutter who told us not to let them board unless there was danger to life. I was just trying to work out what this was about when the cutter loomed out of the fog astern of us. The survivors on the ice went into a panic and started throwing boxes and packets out of the life raft. I told our crew to haul up the ladders so they couldn't board which took some time for me to get across to them. The cutter then put some of its crew in survival suits on the ice and they took the survivors on board. They also picked up the life raft and various objects off the ice. It turned out the ship was Colombian and had

212

been dropping off drugs all the way up the coast and the coastguard had been watching them. At least I didn't end up taking eleven Colombian drug smugglers into Hamburg. I reckon that would have caused a few problems. The coastguard released us but it took us another five hours to get out of the ice and resume our passage at full speed. It seemed there was to be something every trip to try and make us fall behind schedule. Thankfully we had a good passage without any storms after that and we went north of Scotland, which saved a few miles.

It was the usual routine in Hamburg and Le Havre and soon we were heading back across the Atlantic. In the evenings I would walk round and round the main deck, weather permitting, for exercise. Three days out I was walking round when I met a strange bloke on deck. I was totally bemused. It turned out he was a Romanian stowaway who'd figured it was now safe to come out of hiding. Another two appeared later so I had to send all sorts of messages to the Canadian and French authorities and anyone else who may be interested. The company was not best pleased as large fines were levied on ships bringing stowaways to Canada. The company also took the view that I was solely to blame for not finding them before we sailed. I later found out that they were assisted by some of the crew who had hidden them in a paint locker and given them food.

The three stowaways proved to be a real pain. Several items went missing from the crew's cabins and they were the obvious suspects. They broke into the galley and cooked their own food in the middle of the night (though I can't say I blame them) and just generally wandered around the ship as though they owned it. I got fed up with this in the end and we found a cabin that could be locked with a toilet adjoining so I got them locked up in there for the last few days of the voyage. I got a message saying that this time in Montreal would be a very quick turnaround as there wasn't much cargo around and I came up with the idea of keeping them on board and returning them to Le Havre, which would save the company a lot of money in fines etc.

We berthed in Montreal on the 30th May and duly kept them locked in the cabin. The Canadian authorities obligingly provided an armed guard outside the door. All went well until we started unmooring when one of crew came running up to the bridge saying the stowaways were committing suicide. We tied up again and I went down to investigate and found one of them had cut his wrists with a broken bottle. We had to call an ambulance and then the other two threatened to do the same so I had to call the immigration and have them all removed so not only did it cost the company the fine but there were hospital costs and the ship was delayed for about eight hours while we completed all the paperwork. Not really the best of results and I was fully expecting a severe bollocking from the company but actually never heard anything at all.

So it was back off across the Atlantic again with me resolving to have 24 hour guards on the ship next time we were in Le Havre and sod the expense. The ice had all but gone now and the only problems were the numerous icebergs drifting south from the Arctic. I took the ship way south into the Gulf Stream for the passage back in the hope that the warm water would soon melt any bergs and we got the advantage of an extra knot of current.

The trips were becoming a bit monotonous now and the only advantage was that we all knew the run and what to expect and I knew the officials and agents in all the ports, which made the paperwork very easy. I had now been on board for three months and had signed up for a nine month contract so I wasn't looking forward to the next six months at all. I was totally sick of the food, which seemed to be deteriorating day by day and even the crew were complaining. I took to going ashore in Montreal to a local supermarket and stocking up with ready meals, which I heated up in a microwave and ate in my cabin so at least I was surviving. My social life was non-existent and the only people I seemed to have a conversation with were the 1st mate and his wife. My highlight was the two or three days in Montreal when I got a chance to go out with Dennis, the port captain, or the stevedores. The meals were always expensive but it was worth it for my sanity.

In mid July we were heading back towards Hamburg round the north of Scotland and it was a lovely summer day with a light southerly breeze blowing off the land. The smell of the heather was fantastic and I got really homesick and I even got to the stage of thinking I could easily swim ashore from here and sod the ship.

When we got to Hamburg I got a message that I had to phone our head office in Hong Kong, which didn't bode well. Due to the time difference I had to wait until eleven o'clock at night. I wandered ashore to the agent's office feeling somewhat apprehensive especially when I was transferred to one of the senior managers. He started off by congratulating me on doing a really good job and made no mention of the stowaways. He then said that the company was buying a new vessel, which would be running out of the UK regularly, and they would like me to take command of it. This would mean I'd only do one more trip on the *Canmar Triumph* and I would take two months leave before joining the new vessel in Rotterdam. It sounded too good to be true. Of course I agreed and he said he would arrange my relief next time back in Hamburg. He also said that as I had kept the *Canmar Triumph* on schedule there would be a bonus paid in Montreal next time. After the phone call I just about skipped back to the ship and couldn't even be bothered to bollock the 3rd mate who was half asleep in a chair instead of being on deck.

The next morning was a bit of a downer, though, as there was a telex from the manager saying he'd got the timing wrong and I'd have to do two more trips but it still meant I would only do five months on board.

The next two trips seemed to go really slowly and the food was even worse. The agent in Hamburg had given me some different types of sausage to try so one evening I took the nicest looking down to cook in the microwave. I was sitting waiting for them to cook when there was a bloody big bang and they blew up completely coating the inside of the microwave. I spent the next hour cleaning everything up and vowed to prick the next lot before I tried again.

We managed the next two trips without any stowaways though they were constantly wandering up and down the quay looking for an opportunity. Three nearly made it but they got on board before we started working cargo and were somewhat dismayed when a container was lifted off and exposed their hideaway. The local gendarmes arrested them but as we sailed I noticed they were back on the quay looking for a ride.

The weather in the Atlantic had improved as we moved through summer which was just as well as my weather fax machine packed in and I had to do with radio messages which detailed the positions of the weather systems. I generally managed to avoid the worst weather and was always ahead of schedule.

On the last trip when we got to Montreal I was invited ashore for a meal with the skipper of another Anglo Eastern ship that was tied up astern. It was the usual good do, paid for by the shippers, so we didn't stint ourselves. It started off at about one o'clock and we didn't get back to our respective ships until five both slightly the worse for wear. During the conversation it was mentioned that Anglo Eastern had bought a ship from the Maersk Line and it was due to come into service in November. I chirped up that I was going to command it and they all fell about laughing. This particular Maersk ship was renowned all over the world for breaking down. It had two gantries for self-discharging and loading called Munck Loaders and although the idea was good they were notoriously unreliable and when they broke down the ship would be sent out to anchor until they were repaired. On top of this the ports it was calling at were Jeddah, Mumbai (Bombay) and Mombasa.

If you ask any skipper which are their three least favourite ports I'm sure these would top the list. Mombasa has a terrible reputation for stowaways and the port of Jeddah won't allow entry if you have stowaways on board so they have to be taken to Suez and landed and then the ships can return to Jeddah adding at least three days to the voyage. In Mumbai there is always a constant stream of officials wanting to fine the ship for some infraction of the regulations, which has to be cancelled with cartons of cigarettes and bottles of whisky. Of course in Jeddah all the alcohol has to be locked up whilst in port and if there is any infringement the skipper is held responsible and can be arrested. This was starting to look like a disaster and I was out of the frying pan and into the fire. We sailed the following morning and the only thing that brightened me up was the agent coming down with an envelope full of $100 bills as my bonus.

I gave it some serious thought as we headed back. I nearly blotted my copybook too as I'd decided to sail out through the Belle Isle Strait north of Newfoundland on my last voyage as it was nearly clear of ice. As we were clearing the Strait we very nearly hit an iceberg that would have done some serious damage. I spent the next 24 hours on reduced speed with lookouts posted on both bridge wings but didn't see anything else to bother us. We were treated to several fantastic displays of the northern lights for the next few days.

I pondered the situation as we headed east. I could tell the company that I'd changed my mind, which would go down like a lead balloon, and I'd have to put up with another four months of Indian cuisine and days of talking to myself. I could take the leave and join as instructed but I couldn't honestly see me lasting more than a trip on that ship on that run. The last alternative was to pay off and take my leave and then not join the new ship but this would mean they wouldn't re-employ me and I definitely wouldn't get a reference for another job. The hardest part of all this was not being able to talk it through with anyone even though it was my decision. As we approached the north of Scotland a message came through that Alan Matthews would relieve me in Hamburg and I would stay on until Le Havre to show him the ropes. That took option one out of the equation.

We berthed in Hamburg in mid August and Alan joined on arrival. He'd been on containerships before and could see no advantage in me staying to Le Havre, which is a pain to get home from, so I left the following morning. I had a bit of an adventure at the airport when I was taken aside by airport security and asked what was in my suitcase. I had no idea what they were talking about but they had x-rayed the case and thought I was carrying hand grenades. It turned out that I'd bought some frozen lobster tails for a knock down price in the fish market in Montreal and these were in a polystyrene box in my case. Once all was revealed I was allowed to board the plane watched by some bemused police officers. It was a quick flight down to Schiphol and then over to Newcastle where Diane picked me up and took me home to Carlisle.

It was a nice time to be home but I had decisions to make

CHAPTER TWENTY ONE

Dredging again

m.v. Britannia Beaver
3rd January 1992 – 30th November 1994

At least it was a nice time of the year to be home but I was still agonising over what to do next. The dreaded phone call came sooner than expected and they wanted me to join the new vessel in two weeks time. I took a deep breath and told them that I'd decided I wouldn't join and explained my reasons, which didn't go down very well. The personnel manager at the other end of the phone just muttered something and hung up. So I wouldn't be getting another job there.

I was obviously a year older but obviously not wiser and unemployed again. I now started seriously thinking about working ashore but I spent days scouring the jobs ads and could see nothing that suited me. One job that caught my eye was skipper of the *Gondola*, which was being refurbished on Coniston Water by the National Trust. It had been a private yacht but was now being fitted out as a passenger craft taking tourists on trips round the lake. The only trouble was they wanted someone to put some venture capital into the project and be part of the business and at this time capital was the last thing I had. I managed to get signed on the dole, which helped a little bit, but they were absolutely no help at all when it came to finding a job. Another option was assistant manager at a water bottling plant that was just setting up a few miles away but I never even got an interview for that.

I was still perusing the Lloyd's List for anything suitable and a couple of marine related jobs came up in Workington but it would mean moving there and neither Diane nor I fancied that. Diane was now working full time so at least some money was coming in but I was working my way through the bonus quite quickly.

Early in November I was looking through Lloyd's List and there was a job for a skipper on a new aggregate dredger operating out of the Thames. I banged in an application and was surprised to be called down for interview. The company was an aggregate firm called Robert Brett's from Canterbury and they had decided to expand into marine aggregates so had just bought themselves a £12,000,000 state of the art dredger. It was a sister ship to the *Arco Axe* so I least I'd got some experience with that type of vessel. They had employed an ex skipper called Paul Philips from ARC Marine and were starting from scratch. I'd met Paul a couple of times whilst in ARC Marine and got on with him reasonably well. The interview took place on board the vessel, which was laid up in Chatham. The interview didn't go particularly well as Paul was hoping for one of his associates from ARC to join him and it was obvious that he didn't really want me. I was very surprised when I got a phone call saying I'd got the job and would start in the New Year. It meant I had another month off pay but at least I had a job again.

I joined the *Britannia Beaver* first thing in the New Year in Chatham. She had been bought brand new from the Appledore Shipbuilders in June and brought there to lie up and prepare for sea. Brett's had never owned a dredger before so this was a brand new venture and a very steep learning curve for all involved. They appointed a manager based in Gravesend to sell the aggregate and took on an engineer from ARC as an engineering superintendent. The ship was meant to run itself from crewing to storing and generally operating the vessel. It was a really exciting project and in theory should be perfect as we wouldn't have a head office making wrong (in our opinion) decisions. Paul Philips was the senior master and I was appointed relief master and we would alternate on a two week rota. When I joined there was only Paul on board with a 2nd engineer, Paul Deacon, and a cook employed on a daily basis to cater for us.

Paul Philips left after a couple of days and I was left to my own devices trying to figure out what stores we'd need. I set about organising my pilotage licences for the Thames and Medway and was really pleased when they renewed my old licence with the minimum of bother mainly because the number was 12345.

I had to figure out where the vessel was likely to trade and order all the relevant charts and pilotage books. There was also all the paint and tools to be ordered and I started to feel a bit overwhelmed especially when I saw the prices on the invoices. This all kept me fully occupied for the fortnight until Paul returned. His job this time was to employ and assemble the full crew. He had a lot of contacts from his time in ARC so he did a bit of poaching and recruited the majority from there. When I returned in two weeks he had a nucleus of senior officers so we were able to check out and test all the equipment. Over the next month the full team were assembled and at the end of February we sailed out for our first dredge.

Everything went really well though Paul kept asking various questions about bits of equipment and I had to blag my way through it as I'd never actually done a dredge myself on this type of vessel. Brett's had their own wharf on the Thames at Cliffe just downriver from Gravesend and this was to be our home port.

We had a really easy time of it as we then lay for two days before going for another cargo. Paul had picked two good cooks so the food was great and there was a really good atmosphere on board. Two days before I was due to go on leave I had to turn the boat round on the berth to enable discharge. I completely misjudged the tide and made a real cock of things. We ended up drifting down onto a sunken barge and putting a large dent in the hull. Thankfully I didn't damage the propeller, as that would have been very expensive. I left the ship feeling really down as that was the first time I'd ever damaged a ship in my career. It turned out that I'd damaged the bilge keel as well so the ship was sent up to the Tyne to drydock and sort things out. I rejoined her there after my leave. We sailed two days later down to the patch off Great Yarmouth. When we started to dredge we couldn't get the pump to start and after three hours trying we gave up and nipped into Harwich to get some assistance from shore electricians. It took them ten hours to sort it and then we went out again and managed to pick a decent stony cargo. I only did one more cargo on this rota so it was a very leisurely life.

As the year progressed so the work picked up and we went to more and more ports. We got regular cargoes for Dover so I got my pilot's licence for there and enjoyed nipping in and out between the ferries and hovercraft. We were also getting some cargoes for the Continent and became regular callers at Amsterdam, Antwerp, Dunkirk and Le Havre which made life much more interesting. The company also bought some new licences so we now dredged in the eastern entrance to the Solent and on a little area about ten miles off the north Kent coast known as Area 108. I always found this an odd patch as the bottom seemed to change very quickly. We had a sophisticated navigational system working off satellites, which gave our position within three metres, and we could record our track on a computer so, theoretically, we could return to exactly the same stop each time. There must have been a couple of really old wrecks down there as we often dredged up various bits of rigging and once a small anchor. Paul Philips sucked up an old military shell, which blew up as it went through the pump causing all sorts of damage.

When we discharged in Amsterdam they had a device on the jetty that removed magnetic material from the cargo and I always wandered over and see what sort of things we'd picked up. There was always spent ammunition from aircraft, bits of aero engines and sometimes instruments so there must have been a few dogfights overhead during the war. Dredging in the Solent always seemed to produce cannonballs but these rapidly deteriorated when they dried out which was a pity.

Our first cargo into Southampton was quite interesting. I was on board but Paul Philips decided he would return to oversee things as it could lead to a big contract. We dredged on Area 108 and he spent ages getting the stoniest cargo he could find. We went off down to Southampton but had to anchor in the Solent to wait for the berth. Paul was in charge and when he picked up the anchor he went hard a starboard and full ahead to get out of the way of a departing ship. To our amazement we promptly turned hard a port and very nearly got wiped out by the passing ship. There was quite a bit of abuse over the radio from the other vessel as it was pretty close. After a bit of backing and filling we came to the conclusion that there was something seriously wrong with our rudder and in the end had to call for tugs to take us into port. When we got alongside we found that the rudder had fallen off completely and in doing so had damaged the blades of our variable pitch propeller. We ended up stuck in drydock in Southampton for six weeks while everything was repaired.

I took the ship out from drydock and our first cargo was another one back to Southampton from Area 108. They specified another stony cargo and although I went back to the same runs I spent nearly twelve hours trying to get a similar cargo but it was a lot sandier and the receivers were not at all pleased. I was over the moon when Paul got the next cargo and his was even sandier than mine. It seems he'd made a rod for our backs by giving such a good first cargo.

My last cargo into Southampton was in December and it started off really well. The cargo was really noisy coming on board and I thought we were doing really well until I went and had a look at what was coming in and it wasn't stones making the noise but hundreds of oyster and mussel shells. I quickly moved to another run and was pleased to fill the remainder of the hold with a pretty good cargo. The receivers were pleased with the cargo until the shells appeared but accepted it in the end as the stone was mainly going to making roads and the shells would crush down nicely. As we sailed a huge log that was used as a fender on the quay broke adrift and got sucked into the propeller. Two of the blades were pretty badly damaged so it was back into drydock for repairs again. This time it was only for four days so we were soon out dredging again.

We laid the ship up in Chatham over the Christmas period and all went home for the week except for Ian, the chief engineer, who stayed to keep an eye on things. When we returned we had an extra week in Chatham renewing worn out sections of pipe and generally overhauling everything. We also got fitted with the latest in position finding equipment, which would make dredging quite a bit easier as we were able to record our runs and mark the good areas.

Once we'd sailed it all became routine with very little down time. I was beginning to find the dredging side of things a real bore just chugging up and down a line for five or six hours at a time. The ship handling side of things I absolutely loved especially working in tideways and into awkward berths. I started to look out for pilotage jobs but it would have meant relocating and we were really settled in Cumbria so eventually ruled that out. One option that came up was North Sea pilot which involved boarding large vessels off Folkestone or Brixham and piloting them round all their Continental ports but I needed quite a bit more experience and the work could be really demanding at times.

I was increasingly getting more and more fed up with Paul

Philips though. We were supposed to work as a team but he seemed to take great delight in changing everything that I did and insisting that I got his permission before altering anything. I rapidly found out that everything I did was quickly reported back to him so on every handover we had an argument about something or other. I also couldn't cope with the accounts as nothing ever seemed to add up and we were often thousands of pounds adrift. In the end I did a set of accounts for my time on board and submitted them at the end of each tour.

In June whilst out walking in the Lake District I damaged some cartilage in my right knee and ended up having an operation to sort it out. Paul insisted I take a complete trip off even though I was fit again the next day and it completely upset all the rotas. He used the time however to train up the two mates as skippers and it became obvious that he was trying to work me out of the job. One good thing that came out of it was he organised a radio course for me, which I took at Wray Castle on Windermere.

It was a ten day course and I drove down from home every day and thoroughly enjoyed myself though when I returned on board it was clear that at least one of the mates was capable of taking over.

By the time the end of the year came round again I was beginning to dread joining the ship and the inevitable arguments. I was also sure that if I ever made a mistake I would have been sacked so I had to be extra careful. Thankfully I never did any more damage to either the ship or any of the berths.

I had always taken a keen interest in the weather and weather forecasting so I was pleased when we got a visit from the port meteorological officer while we were in Gravesend and he suggested we became a weather reporting ship. This meant reporting the weather conditions at the ship every six hours and radioing them to the Met Office in Bracknell. They provided us with a full set of thermometers and a precision barometer. I found it really interesting and it often passed the time on a long dredge. When Paul came back from leave he banned everyone from taking records while he was on board as he said it distracted people from doing their duties. At least the equipment was left on board so we could send reports when I was there. I actually got an award from the Met Office for all my work and a present of a quality atlas which somewhat miffed Paul.

I rejoined the *Britannia Beaver* in January of 1994 after the

Christmas break and I was beginning to wonder how the year would pan out. I'd been with Bretts for two years now but I couldn't see it lasting much longer. We had a really busy start to the year and hardly got time to draw breath. They'd fitted a new impeller in the pump so I could do a dredge in less than five hours so I started to feel comfortable again. Paul Philips took a couple of trips off and one of the mates was promoted to do his rota so life became a lot more pleasant. There was also a rumour going round that Paul would be moving ashore to do a superintendent's job so I would be left to my own devices – life was looking good.

It was not to be, though, and every handover became something of a nightmare. As luck would have it my next door neighbour was a financial adviser and I asked him to have a look over my finances one week when I was home. Although I was only 53 he thought it was a really good time to retire and take out an annuity. I had always saved a bit extra into my retirement pot and he reckoned annuities were at an all time high and it was well worth thinking about. It certainly gave me a new slant on life, as I was sure I could find a nice little part time job to keep me occupied.

Things came to a head in October when Paul was relieving me. It was Diane and my 25th wedding anniversary on the 6th December and this would be right in the middle of my time on board so I was going to have to request some time off. The handover didn't start off at all well as we had a right slanging match about the accounts and it became obvious that there was a lot of money missing somewhere and I think he was convinced I had some of it. In the end I couldn't ask for the time off so I resigned and told him to stick his job. I was somewhat miffed when he brightened up, as obviously this is what he'd been wanting.

I travelled home and the next day got a phone call to say I would be paid up to the end of the year and I didn't need to do any more trips. It was very generous of the company and I accepted with alacrity. I had to drive down the following week to pick up all my gear and say goodbye to the rest of the crew. They were a really good bunch to sail with and I was quite sad when I drove home.

CHAPTER TWENTY TWO

National Trust

1995 – 1999

As soon as I got home I got my pension sorted out with Steve from next door. It was surprisingly good and I although it was going to be twelve years before I got my state pension I didn't really have to work. It rapidly became obvious that I would have to find a job or go stir crazy. After a few hiccups I applied for a part time job as shop assistant/recruiter for the National Trust. It was working at Acorn Bank Garden in the Eden Valley and was only a half hour drive away.

My main problems were that I knew virtually nothing about gardens apart from growing vegetables, I'd never worked in a shop or operated a till, and would also have to convince members of the public to join the National Trust. This was going to be interesting.

I got the job in January but didn't start work until mid March so to familiarise myself I volunteered to work in the garden for a couple of months. It was just as well – the garden is the largest herb garden in the north of England and I was lucky if I could identify a quarter of the herbs in the garden when I started. When I began work proper it was selling tickets and merchandise from the shop and trying to answer any queries. Luckily Chris, the gardener, was usually around to help me out. A big part of the job was recruiting people to join the National Trust and I discovered I had a bit of a flair for this though I can't say I enjoyed it.

It was really good working there on a fine busy day but real misery when it was raining and there were no visitors around. The shop was in an old dovecote and we had to keep both doors open so people knew we were open and it could get really cold in there.

I was only working three days a week so I wasn't overstretched. As the year progressed I got asked to fill in at other shops in the Lake District to cover holidays and sickness, which made life more interesting. I enjoyed working in the Keswick shop, down by Derwentwater, as it was always busy and the view from the door over the lake to Catbells was magnificent.

The job was only seasonal so we were all paid off in October and re-employed the following March.

I lasted five years of this gradually getting more and more disillusioned with the National Trust and the way it was run. Every week they seemed to employ a new manager for something or other and then the manager had to have a personal assistant and a secretary. To cover this expense they reduced the workers on the ground, which obviously meant they weren't looking after the land as well as they should. I didn't feel my heart was in it any more when I was trying to sell membership to something I didn't really believe in now, so I finished at the end of the 1999 season

But where to go next?

CHAPTER TWENTY THREE

Final fling – Ullswater Steamers

2000 – 2011

Over the winter I got myself involved with a voluntary community bus scheme called 'The Fellrunner' which served isolated villages in the Eden Valley and this took up a fair bit of my time but I felt I still needed something else so when an advert appeared in the local paper for crew to work on the Ullswater Steamers over the summer season I thought I'd give it a go. I went down for interview only expecting to get a job as a crewmember but ended up being employed as trainee skipper.

At this time the Steamers had two boats, the *Raven* and the *Lady of the Lake* which only worked during the summer months and over the winter a few staff were kept on to maintain and overhaul them but a new manager had just joined and he had grand ideas about running the boats all the year round. He had already upset most of the staff by changing the working conditions and a couple had resigned so I joined in the middle of this upheaval.

The first few weeks were spent preparing the boats for the season refitting the newly varnished woodwork and giving the boats a final coat of paint and spruce up. I found it odd to start with as everything was called in layman's terms. It was walls and floors instead of bulkheads and decks but I soon got the hang. The staff were from all walks of life who just wanted to work in a beautiful environment. There was a retired college lecturer, a bus driver, an ex lighthouse keeper, a postman plus a bunch of students who were taken on for the summer season.

One lunchtime I was sitting next to Roy Savage, one of the skippers, and as we chatted we realised that we had been in the same class at Carlisle Grammar School many years ago. We both wondered what the school would have thought about where a couple of its pupils had ended up.

The boats were built in the late 1800s originally as steamers but had converted to diesel in the mid 1900s. They were in good condition for their age but I couldn't believe how primitive they were. The steering consisted of a system of rods and chains connecting the wheel to the rudder. There were the controls for the two engines and that was it. The other thing that bothered me was that there were no watertight compartments in the boat so if it sprung a leak the whole boat would fill with water and sink very rapidly. The Board of Trade deemed it safe so who was I to argue?

Manoeuvring them was a nightmare as they had no draft and blew around on the water like a floating leaf. When they first arrived on the lake the crews were recruited from the local area and had no nautical experience at all. After a few disasters they developed a system that worked with the boats always approaching on the same line and shutting off the engines at a designated point. All the skippers had been trained to operate in this fashion and although I found it very constraining it seemed to work.

I initially started working full time but after two weeks decided that it was a bit much so negotiated a four day week, which was much better. The managers decided they needed someone to work full time so employed Dave Stanger, who already had experience with boats on Derwentwater, and put my training on hold. Actually it suited me, as I was quite happy crewing with no responsibility although my rope throwing when mooring required considerable improvement.

At the end of the season I was laid off which again suited me as I didn't fancy scraping and painting on the slipway in all weathers. When I restarted again in March I pointed out that my master's certificate required renewal at a minimal cost but they refused to pay for it so I let it lapse. It was a Class 1 Master's Foreign Going Certificate, which meant I could skipper almost anything anywhere but it wasn't good enough for Ullswater it seemed. In the end I had to take an exam for a boat master's certificate and undergo a survival training course, which all cost ten times more than renewing my original certificate but it was their money.

The following year in line with the new manager's policy for running throughout the year the company acquired another boat. It was a large wooden launch, which used to operate between the Channel Islands. It required considerable modification and I was seconded to work with Frank, the boat builder. I really enjoyed this work and though my carpentry skills are minimal I felt I contributed quite a bit towards the end result. The *Lady Dorothy* started in service after the normal season ended and just about paid its way especially on weekends. I was retained over the winter to help man her and also in the pier house selling tickets and making coffee.

I particularly remember one brilliant day on *Lady Dorothy* in January when there was thick snow everywhere but the clouds cleared and Roy Savage and I spent all day cruising up and down with no passengers. The fells all had a thick covering of snow and under a fantastic blue sky it was amazing.

I was finally allowed to drive when the new season opened in 2003. It was most enjoyable and I couldn't believe I was being able to cruise up and down one of England's most beautiful lakes and get paid for it. I loved the first run in the morning as there weren't many people around and the lake was at its most lovely.

The best part of the job, though, was the camaraderie of the crews and getting out and meeting different people. The down side was when there was a strong wind blowing. If it was blowing strongly from the north it made it extremely difficult to turn round at Glenridding at the south end of the lake and at Howtown, the midway point, the wind varied in direction enormously, which could make berthing there more than interesting. I managed to complete my time at the Steamers without doing any serious damage though I did clatter the piers a few times. Once when turning round off Glenridding one of the links in the chain steering jammed and I assumed, wrongly, that the rudder was hard over and to avoid being blown down onto a shingle spit went full ahead and completely misjudged it. We graunched our way over the spit making an awful noise and then shot into the deep water on the other side. Thankfully I'd only removed a bit of paint off the bottom and polished up the propeller blades but I made sure I stayed well away from the spit after that.

As the years progressed the Steamers acquired two more boats and expanded their services and became much more commercial. I much preferred the old way of working although it obviously wasn't as profitable. Two or three other crew were trained up to become skippers and I began to prefer working in the pier houses and selling tickets and chatting to visitors and giving them information about the area.

The winter of 2010 was a particularly bad one for winds and I began to worry about damaging the boats, so early the next year I gave my notice in and retired properly and was able to relax. I was now 70 so felt I'd done enough.

Looking back on my life I have to admit that the best times were when I was a cadet and junior officer as life was much easier going, though the work was definitely harder. I actually looked forward to going back to sea in those days and before I got married I preferred being away at sea to being on leave. I can't say I really enjoyed being master though I had a quite a few brilliant trips and sailed with some really good blokes. I don't think I'm the best at personnel relations so I found dealing with discipline hard at times but I think I managed to keep control and have a mostly happy ship, which was my aim. If asked I would say I'd probably do it all again but not in this day and age with all the paperwork and poorly trained crews.

As I mention in the preface the book was initially only for my family but hopefully it will bring back some memories for ex seafarers and entertain people who have never experienced a life at sea.

Printed in Great Britain
by Amazon